Dream
Interpretation
Ancient &
Modern

A list of Jung's works appears at the back of the volume.

C. G. JUNG

Dream Interpretation Ancient & Modern

Notes from the Seminar Given in 1936–1941

Reports by Seminar Members with Discussions of Dream Series

Edited by John Peck, Lorenz Jung, and Maria Meyer-Grass
Translated by Ernst Falzeder with the collaboration of Tony Woolfson

ⓟ PHILEMON SERIES

Published with the support of the Philemon Foundation
This book is part of the Philemon Series of the Philemon Foundation

PRINCETON UNIVERSITY PRESS
PRINCETON AND OXFORD

press.princeton.edu

Jacket art: Engraving by Paulus van der Doort, *Oratorium et laboratorium*, in
Heinrich Khunrath's *Amphitheatrum sapientia aeternae solius verae*. (1595)

Jacket design by Kathleen Lynch / Black Kat Design.

Library of Congress Cataloging-in-Publication Data

Jung, C. G. (Carl Gustav), 1875–1961.
[Kinderträume. English]
Dream interpretation ancient and modern : notes from the seminar given in 1936–
1941 : reports by seminar members with discussions of dream series / C. G. Jung ;
edited by John Peck, Lorenz Jung, and Maria Meyer-Grass ; translated by
Ernst Falzeder with the collaboration of Tony Woolfson.
pages cm. — (Philemon Foundation series)
"Published with the support of the Philemon Foundation."
Includes bibliographical references and index.
ISBN 978-0-691-15945-4 (hardcover : alk. paper)   1. Children's dreams—Congresses.   2. Children's dreams—Case studies—Congresses.   3. Dreams—Congresses.
4. Archetype (Psychology)—Congresses.   5. Psychoanalysis—Congresses.   6. Jung,
C. G. (Carl Gustav), 1875–1961—Congresses.   I. Jung, Lorenz, editor of compilation.   II. Meyer-Grass, Maria, editor of compilation.   III. Title.
BF1099.C55J8613 2014
154.6'3083—dc23
2013043632

British Library Cataloging-in-Publication Data is available

This book is published with the support of the Philemon Foundation and is part of
the Philemon Series of the Philemon Foundation. philemonfoundation.org.

This book has been composed in Goudy Oldstyle Std and Neutra Display.

Printed on acid-free paper. ∞

Printed in the United States of America

1 3 5 7 9 10 8 6 4 2

-·Contents·-

·· Note to the English Edition ··

Between 1936 and 1940, C. G. Jung presented a seminar on children's dreams and old works on dream interpretation at the Eidgenössische Technische Hochschule (Swiss Federal Institute of Technology) in Zurich. In 1987, these were published in German by Walter Verlag, edited by Lorenz Jung and Maria Meyer-Grass in a 680-page volume. For the English edition, it was decided to publish the work in two volumes, placing the seminars on children's dreams in one volume and the seminars on old works on dream interpretation in a second volume, to preserve thematic continuity. Footnotes made by the original participants, and by the editors of the German edition, are followed either by the contributor's initials or by (G). All other notes, including several original notes silently augmented, are by the translator and current editor. The translation and additional editorial work have been funded by the Philemon Foundation, a nonprofit organization dedicated to raising funds for the publication of C. G. Jung's unpublished works (www.phi lemonfoundation.org). The Board of the Philemon Foundation would like to thank its donors for their generous support, which has made this volume possible.

Those readers who have occasion to compare the two volumes of this seminar in the Princeton editions with the German text that serves as their basis will notice that the original single volume from Walter-Verlag / Patmos Verlag (Düsseldorf / Zurich, 2001) does not supply the same contents list for the dreams in the Cardano section found here (in both the Calendar Contents for both seminar volumes below—see xix—and in the section contents on p. 122 of this volume). In fact, the number and sequence of dreams is identical in both the German and English texts, but the contents list for that section in the German text omits five dreams: these correspond to the dreams numbered 4, 5, 6, 8, and 11 in the section contents (on p. 122).

Ernst Falzeder and John Peck

·- Acknowledgments -·

My thanks go to Ernst Falzeder, the translator of both volumes, and to Sonu Shamdasani, the Philemon Series General Editor, for their scrupulous and encouraging assistance. Ernst has provided the basis for the supplementary footnoting that both of us have carried out. I hasten to add that the longer, more speculative and expansive notes are mine, ventured when the occasion warranted that touch. Mr. Russell Peter Holmes shed light on an obscure reference in chapter 13 (by way of parallels to the dead abbess with a scorching hand), and Mr. David Oswald discussed several matters along the path that any editor of Jung's seminars must travel. An essay by Dr. David Tresan proved to be invaluable in helping me to round off a theme in the introduction; I wish to thank him here. My thanks also go to my editor at Princeton University Press, Fred Appel, his associate editor, Sarah David, and production editor Leslie Grundfest, for their aid and encouragement, and to both my able copyeditor, Dawn Hall, and my judicious indexer, Maria den Boer.

⊸· Preface ·⊷

The present edition is the first supplement to C. G. Jung's *Collected Works*, comprising the minutes of the four seminars on children's dreams, with additional explanatory editorial notes.

From 1933 onward, C. G. Jung gave lectures at the Eidgenössische Technische Hochschule (ETH) in Zurich, on individuation, on dreams, and on analytical psychology in general (see the Jung bibliography in the index volume of the *Collected Works*). In 1935, he was appointed titular professor of psychology at the department of *Freifächer* (elected subjects) (XII). In the following years, he gave various lectures and seminars at this university, including the four seminars on children's dreams, with discussions of selected literature on dreams, reprinted here. These discussions of fundamental questions concerning the human psyche are of extraordinary importance, not only because of their relevance to the history of science, but also for an understanding of the practical application of Jung's method of *amplification*. For this reason they represent a good introduction to analytical psychology—in which dream interpretation plays a central role—for readers who have so far concerned themselves only occasionally with psychological problems. Thus, C. G. Jung stated: "The purpose of this seminar is to practice on the basis of the material." This goal, the easily understandable language, and the apparent simplicity of the children's dreams particularly facilitate the reader's understanding.

The views on the psychology of the individual and on collective problems of our culture expressed in these seminars have so far been available only to a very limited number of persons. First, admission to the seminar classes depended on C. G. Jung's permission, in order to allow discussions in a relatively small group of people; and second, the subsequently compiled minutes were distributed only to the seminar participants. Thus, an embargo originally preceded each of the four seminar reports: "This seminar report is intended exclusively for the use of the participants of the seminar and the subscribers only. It must not be circulated, lent, or borrowed. No parts of it may be quoted or printed without the specific permission of Professor Jung." These restrictions were to ensure professional discretion. In addition, Jung had concerns about publishing certain contributions in their original form. As we will explain in the introduction, it was only much later that C. G. Jung allowed wider circulation of the seminars.

The completion of the present edition was only made possible by the work the original editors of the seminar proceedings devoted to recording and editing the notes. Without their commitment this valuable material would probably have been lost. We owe thanks to Hans H. Baumann, Kurt Binswanger, Marie-Louise von Franz, Liliane Frey, Aniela Jaffé, and Rivkah Kluger-Schärf. We are especially indebted to Marie-Louise von Franz and Elisabeth Rüf for their support and expert advice in the preparation of this edition, as well as to William McGuire for providing us with pertinent correspondence. We also thank the numerous contributing participants in the seminar, who have kindly given their permission for the reprint. Special thanks go to the psychology fund of the ETH and the Dr. Donald C. Cooper Funds for their financial support of the printing.[1]

In the spoken word recorded in this material, now accessible to a broader public, we are able to see C. G. Jung in a different light than in his written works, in which this side is not so apparent. Here, his human side, his humor, and his satirical vein come to fore as he takes a closer look at others and at himself. The—sometimes unguarded—irony with which he does this bears special witness to his lively and straightforward temperament. The reader is reminded again and again, in a pleasantly provocative manner, that the seminar's subject is not just a sterile theory, but the actual, lived reality of the child, and thus life as such. We all know this reality because its symbols affect each of us.

Fall 1986

Lorenz Jung
Maria Meyer-Grass

[1] [For the German edition only].

⁓ Introduction by the Original Editors ⁓

C. G. Jung did not find the time, in the midst of writing his immense body of work, to review the four seminar reports assembled here for their scientific correctness. He was convinced, however, that such editing would be necessary; he considered his own statements, as well as those of the participants of the seminars, to be, above all, oral contributions to the discussion, which would need to be elaborated more carefully and precisely when printed, in order to stand up to criticism. The most subjective factors may often influence the spoken word, and the inevitably subjective recording of the statements does not ensure that what is recorded is in fact always *exactly* what was originally meant. Despite these reservations, much later, toward the end of his life, he agreed to have the numerous seminars on various subjects published as an appendix to his *Gesammelte Werke* (GW). On 24 May 1956, he wrote to Gerhard Adler, a member of the Anglo-American editorial team of the *Collected Works*: "I completely agree to have the 'seminar notes'[1] published as an appendix to the complete edition of my works, and I ask you . . . to see to it that the necessary excisions, or corrections, of any possible factual mistakes be made. . . . If possible, however, the style should not be altered." On another occasion, he wished to have the following note printed at the beginning of the seminar notes:

> I am well aware of the fact that the text of these seminars contains a certain number of errors and other shortcomings, which would make corrections necessary. Unfortunately, I was not able to carry out this work myself. I therefore ask the reader to read these reports with the necessary critical eye, and to use them with caution. Apart from that, thanks to the representational art [of the chroniclers], they give a lively and faithful image of reality as it was at that time. (May 1954)

C. G. Jung may have been prompted to make these remarks by his wish to enable the reader to form an independent judgment, and at

---

[1] This expression in English in the original (trans.).

the same time to draw the reader's attention to the fact that some of the statements should not be generalized, but rather scrutinized with benevolent criticism.

Our present edition of the seminars on children's dreams is in accordance with C. G. Jung's wish to leave the texts as much as possible in their original straightforwardness. A completely verbatim report of the discussions, however, is neither possible, for the reasons mentioned earlier, nor was it aimed at; we rather tried to eliminate some of the obvious mistakes and misunderstandings in the records that were made after the fact. Whenever possible, the illustrations used at the time were used as the templates for those in this book.

In what follows we will briefly discuss the history of the four seminar reports. At the beginning of each of the meetings of the seminar, which lasted for about two academic (fifty-minute) hours, a dream interpretation or a book report was presented. These materials had been assigned to the participants by C. G. Jung at the beginning of the semester. Then the topic was amplified in a sometimes circuitous discussion. Some participants took down more or less accurate notes of the discussion, which were compiled at the end of the semester. In later years, the stenographic records by Rivkah Kluger-Schärf were of inestimable value for the editorial work. Even if the *exact* wording could not always be established, the style of the spoken word could be preserved to a very great extent.

We learn from the preface to the first recorded seminar, given in 1936/37, written and edited by Hans H. Baumann, Kurt Binswanger, Marie-Louise von Franz, Liliane Frey, and Rivkah Schärf, that the publication "was decided on by the collaborators only at the end of the semester, with Professor C. G. Jung's assent:" "It was made at the request of numerous friends of his psychology. The text is based, therefore, on notes in long- and shorthand, which were not meant to be used for a proper publication. Nevertheless, we think we have given, together with Professor Jung, a complete and faithful rendition of the commentaries." In 1935/36, before this class, the dream series of a boy had been discussed, which is reprinted in the appendix of the present edition, because there are repeated references to it in the following texts. Unfortunately, no further notes about those discussions are extant. We have also included a number of papers on the dream literature from antiquity up to modern times.[2] They provide an overview of the prevalent ideas on the topic of dreams in different epochs. We also include the discussion of a work that has still not been translated from Latin, *De Somniis* by Caspar Peucer.

The second seminar, given in 1938/39, was edited by Liliane Frey and Rivkah Schärf. That semester C. G. Jung presented a detailed introduction to the method of dream interpretation. We consider it to be so fundamental that we have placed it, disregarding chronology, at the beginning of the present volume. Although C. G. Jung repeatedly talked about dream interpretation at the beginnings of the subsequent seminars, no such introduction is extant from the first semester.

Liliane Frey and Aniela Jaffé edited the third seminar, given in 1939/40, on the basis of the notes of Rivkah Schärf. Here, as in the seminars of the other years, we added the missing papers of the participants whenever they were available.

The fourth and last report was written as late as 1975, and was privately printed by Rivkah Kluger-Schärf and Marie-Louise von Franz, in keeping with the original restrictions. In the foreword to their extraordinarily precise edition, the editors write:

> For a long time already, the undersigned have had the desire to publish this seminar, which contains, apart from the discussion and interpretation of children's dreams, the interpretation of dreams of the Renaissance scholar Girolamo Cardano, the visions of St. Perpetua, and the well-known dream of the 'Swinging Ax' of Dr. Hubbard. . . . To be able to present the texts by Cardanus and their interpretation with as much unity as possible, we had to sacrifice the chronological sequence of the seminar meetings. . . . A difficulty was presented by the papers of the participants of the seminar, some of which were no longer available. In these cases, the dreams on which the papers were based were replaced by short summaries or reconstructions with the help of the commentaries.

For reasons of unity and textual consistency, in the present edition we had to rearrange and make certain adaptations in the four original sets of seminar notes. Where changes in chronology were made, this is duly noted. All dates of the seminars, whenever extant, were added.

---

[2] All papers and discussions on the dream literature are collected in volume 2 of the English edition (see Note to the English Edition in this volume) (trans.).

All of the original footnotes were included; we have added notes of our own whenever this seemed useful for a better understanding. In these, the most important concepts of analytical psychology are briefly explained, although for a deeper understanding of the exact meaning of such terms we refer the reader to the numerous added cross-references to C. G. Jung's *Collected Works* (CW) or his memoirs, *Memories, Dreams, Reflections* (MDR). References to the volumes of CW are not by page numbers, but by the paragraph numbers of the passage in question. Whenever additional changes or omissions imposed themselves, they are indicated and explained at the place they were made, either by "ed." or by square brackets "[. . .]." For these corrections, and for many doubtful phrases, it was partly possible, in the interest of faithfulness to the original, to make use of the original notes of the seminar. For better recognizability, all dreams and longer quotations are italicized. An index has been added to facilitate work with this volume.

Without doubt, the four seminars on children's dreams are of great importance within the scope of Jung's complete works because they offer a rich introduction to the *practice* of Jungian dream interpretation. We find a particularly impressive application of the theory of the archetypes, because the personal context largely fades into the background in children's dreams, most of them remembered only in adulthood, and because archetypal images and situations come to the fore, owing to the child's greater proximity to the collective unconscious. In addition, the views expressed in the seminars are an important contribution, not only to the psychology of the individual, but also to the problems of modern society and to the questions of the basic religious needs of human beings. Finally, these records—snapshots, we might call them—are of interest for the history of science, because they bear witness to the development of important ideas and notions of Jung's analytical psychology.

⌐ Calendar Contents for the Full Seminar, Winter Term, 1936/37–Winter Term, 1940/41 ⌐

(coordinated with contents of the *Children's Dreams Seminar*)

-· Introduction ·-

PEDAGOGY AND PARTICIPANTS

In this seventh seminar series of Jung's to be published, more than in any other to date, a deliberate pedagogic intention structured his triple stranding of materials. That fact begins to account for the pragmatic sequestration of dreams recalled from childhood, in the portion of the seminar devoted to *Children's Dreams* already published (Princeton University Press / Philemon, 2008), from the assigned reports on the history of dream interpretation gathered here in a separate seminar volume, together with three extended series of visions and dreams selected by Jung for practical exercise. All of this material, devoted to both clinical and historical treatment, also spelled a turning point. Given in the classroom setting of the Federal Polytechnic, or ETH, from 1936 to 1941, it marked Jung's resumption of teaching (previously at the University of Zurich) after a long hiatus.

Its landmark character was not personal only. While Jung offered the course under university auspices, he restricted enrollment almost exclusively to practitioners of analysis (trained both medically and otherwise). His presentation of the subject—the dreams of children recalled in adulthood, coordinated with a survey of the literature on dream interpretation—also marked a first. Others, of course, had written on aspects of that long history, or had studied certain periods of cultural history in relation to dreams; for instance, Jung's younger French-Swiss compatriot Albert Béguin would publish his *L'âme romantique et le rêve: Essai sur le romantisme allemand et la poésie française* in 1937, during the second term of these seminars. Jung's course, however, on clinical material in tandem with his survey of dream interpretation—carefully selected but with no pretensions to supplying a history—was the first such to be offered by a major psychologist.

Beyond the pioneering aspect of these sessions, they nicely demonstrate another side of Jung's scope as a teacher—namely, his ability to suggest that the way in which medicine sees things shares a common basis with the imaginal way in which the heart sees them. His method in this respect remains suggestive, in the best sense (that is, carrying to fruition, or giving birth, just out of sight or over the border). Pedagogy implies method, often no more than method, whereas *paideia* for Greeks expressed a whole culture and encompassed any particular pedagogy. All of Jung's seminars demonstrate the culture-fostering way in which his mind worked. But this material provides a striking example of what might seem at casual glance to be simply a pedagogic trick— the inclusion of Eugène Marais's study of termites—but which in fact exemplifies Jung's way of seeing things, a germ of *paideia* as it were, an indivisibly medical-scientific and imaginal-psychological outlook. Jung included Marais's pioneering account, a pilot project in ethology, to ground the role of the sympathetic nervous system in preverbal, subcortical processes of communion and participation. Alongside a survey of dream interpretation, then, his plan for the seminar included this contemporary, far-out and deep-in foray into those levels of instinct, across phylum lines, which are bound to tease probing questions from us about behavior, and about the self-portrayals of instinct in both behavior and dreams. Ethnology needs the new ethology, because ethology redraws paths to psyche. Not simply a corrective to the millennial Western focus on a sensory, outward-directed, personalistic and environmental basis for a cerebro-spinal psyche, a focus that simply mirrors the world, Marais's little groundbreaking study, as Jung presents it, also directly insinuates an archetypal basis for the psyche (he included it at the end of the third of the four terms).

Therefore, in a seminar devoted simultaneously to both children's dreams and the development of dream interpretation, Marais's queen termite supplies Jung with a visible double for the invisible organizing factor in our own phylogenetic basement. The community around her is "almost . . . an archetype made real" (135), responding to signals that have to do with processes that both regulate life and also carry and transmit images, notably the royal symbols of the god-image in our systems of order. Jung's hint is that ethnology alone does not go deeply enough in regrounding a study of the soul. Such study must also pursue the traces of direct unconscious transmission and influence manifest in phylogenetic life processes, which directly inform any complete Western yoga of dream interpretation. As late as December 21, 1960, in Jung's reply to the analyst Albert Jung, he emphasized the role the sympathetic nervous system played in the drama of full engagement with divine influx, a totality far beyond conscious representation and not an exclusively spiritual matter. By the same token, however, biology could extend to Jung no more than powerfully suggestive analogies for the inheritance of archetypes, for instance (as I note below by way of Shamdasani's work). His pedagogic turn in 1936, then, while it limns the integrals his science offers to our culture, stood on sounder ground with ethnographic parallels than with biological ones. Potentially spanning the psychophysical spectrum from infrared to ultraviolet, nonetheless Jung's work at times must cast a pontoon bridge across waters where he would hope that a masonry span might stand one day. And such is the broad implication for us, if not for his seminar participants, of Marias's Thoreau-like inquest into the ways of the white ant.

A significant number of the participants, at least in this case, were MDs—as indicated by Jung's aside apropos Dr. John Hubbard's material:

So he is also a member of our trade, he is a doctor. That's no coincidence. He is a doctor because he has to deal with suffering humankind. He gets in touch with suffering people, and his whole life consists of experiences with sufferers, which establishes a very close relationship with them. That is why many old doctors quite naturally develop some philosophy and are known for having their own views. This has always been so, also in the Middle Ages. These dreams of Dr. Hubbard are the fruit—as we can feel—of a life marked by human experience; not only the dream of the king, but also the other dreams. (1916, 327–28)

However, we would do well to construe "doctor" in the broader sense, which includes the proven lay analyst. While recruitment for any of Jung's seminars was heterogeneous, the imprint of medical training marks some of them. In this seminar, those with backgrounds outside of medicine included Mss. von Franz, Schärf, and Carol Fisher Baumann, her second husband Hans H. Baumann, Liliane Frey, and several others. Among those en route to advanced degrees in humanities were

Liliane Frey (philosophy and psychology), Rivkah Schärf (Semitic languages and the history of religions), and Hans Baumann (German studies and architecture; Baumann did not become an analyst). Von Franz, who took her doctorate in classical philology at twenty-six in the 1941 Winter Term, when she reported on the visions of St. Perpetua, had chosen classics over her competing interests in medicine and mathematics, prompted by a dream as interpreted by Jung, around the time of her 1936 seminar report on the physician Caspar Peucer.[1] Drs. Bash, Heinrich Fierz, Jacobi, Kitzinger, Levy, Nothmann, Reichstein, Spitz, Steiner, Waller, Wespi, and perhaps Dr. Kurt Binswanger (one of the transcript editors) represent the medical quorum identified by Jung, numbering ten, perhaps eleven, of the twenty-nine attendees, or around one-third. Among the figures whose writings or dream material is reviewed, Girolamo Cardano was a prominent physician, as was Caspar Peucer, the humanist son-in-law of Melanchthon. The professional diviner Artemidorus, although no doctor, assiduously researched the nocturnal lives of persons of every age and class in his time, acquiring something of the physician's feeling for the vicissitudes most people confront. The English Dr. John Hubbard was of course Jung's near contemporary.

The span in this particular roster is best exemplified by Kenower Bash and Carol Fisher Baumann, the daughter of Yale economist Irving Fisher, who while raising her children in Zurich became an independent researcher, translator, and lecturer, working on Black Elk among other Native American themes, Far Eastern spirituality, and women's psychological experiences of childbirth.[2] Kenower Bash, who earned his MD degree toward the end of these seminars, became professor of psychiatry at Bern and a training analyst at the Zurich Jung Institute and was cited for one of his essays by physicist Ludwig Meitner in a letter to Wolfgang Pauli in 1958.[3] Between these two figures in the group

---

[1] Obituary articles by Chuck Schwartz and Dr. Alfred Ribi, respectively, cite medicine and mathematics as the disciplines that ceded place to philology: Emmanuel Kennedy-Xypolitas, ed., *The Fountain of the Love of Wisdom: An Homage to Marie-Louise von Franz* (Wilmette, IL: Chiron, 2006), 34, 18.

[2] See the detailed biographical sketch by Amy Bluhm in *Jung History* 1 (Winter 2005/6): 16–19.

[3] Kenower W. Bash (1913–1986), "Gestalt, Symbol, und Archetype," *Schweizerische Zeitschrift für Psychologie* V, 127–38. Cited by Meitner for its reference to "Feldforsche," addendum 2, letter

are those others, both women and men, whose therapeutic calling may or may not have held hands with their academic credentials. An apocryphal testimony from a crossover figure like Bash, the late Dr. Joseph Wheelwright, MD, preserves a glimpse of the atmosphere that probably informed inclusion in this informal guild. Only half self-mockingly he marveled, "Once I had seen what was involved with so-and-so in their work with the Mahatma, I ran to him like a puppy, my tail wagging, and said, 'Can I be like you when I grow up?' So after a bit of work Jung said, 'Wheelwright, you're the most disorganized young man I have ever seen. So why don't you just go off to St. Bart's in London, like so-and-so, and get an M.D., and then come back, and we'll see.'"[4]

One further reflection on medicine's role in dream interpretation is in order, if only because it drew Jung's comment in his memorial essay on Freud of October 1939, published during the last term of these seminars. In acknowledging Freud's demonic intensity as patient sleuth and unmasker of neurosis, Jung characterizes Freud's influential outlook as very much a doctor's, in an Enlightenment spirit, without philosophical coloring of any kind—yet as such, firmly in a long tradition of inquiry into the psyche, where "the really decisive discoveries have been made within the sphere of medicine" (Jung, CW 15, §60). *The Interpretation of Dreams*, "a fount of illumination for us young psychiatrists," at last rescued dreams from centuries of oblivion, restoring them to the status they enjoyed in ancient medicine, though in a different key (§65). Freud's attempt to tie his anatomy of neurosis to primitive psychology in *Totem and Taboo*, however, rendered an inadequate account of primitive mentality, and *The Future of an Illusion* only further showed the weakness of Freud's materialistic grounding in philosophy, along with "the fact that he had no understanding of what religion was about" (§67). In effect Freud reduced the spirit—"the adversary of the soul" in Ludwig Klages's adage—to mere psychological formula (§72). Therefore it was plain to Jung that it was up to himself and others to

---

3090 to Jaffé, in Karl von Meyenn, ed., *Wolfgang Pauli: Wissenschaftliches Briefwechsel mit Bohr, Einstein, Heisenberg u. a.* (*Sources in the History of Mathematics and Physical Sciences* 18) Band IV A, 1957 (Berlin/Heidelberg: Springer, 2005), 3091. A bequest from Bash, who worked extensively in Iran, established the Golestan (Persian for rose garden) Fellowship at the Netherlands Institute of Advanced Study.

[4] Oral comment to the author, 1989.

carry on the practice of dream interpretation, along with the survey of its history, through the doorway that Freud had opened but to which he had clung fast, all the while maintaining a foothold in medicine's premier contribution to psychology. The study of dreams, and likewise the history of their interpretation, henceforth would knowingly have to extend what had long been done with "the demonically vital" things at work in the psyche—namely, to "try the spirits whether they are of God" (I John 4:1), because only the spirit, and not intellect, can cast out the "spirits" (§73). In all of these remarks in his tribute to Freud, after acknowledging that medicine's plow broke the plains for crucial psychological husbandry, Jung then claims the adjacent cultural acreage—the venerable therapeutic systems of the religions most notably, and an alert philosophical outlook—as indispensable for the psychologist. Thus not only Jung's own Kenyan venture into ethnology animates his comments during these seminars, but also Marais's pioneering ethology of the white ant, with consequences for the analysis of dream processes and the theory of archetypes. For the latter theory, however, the consequence marked a partial theoretical dead end, which plays a role in the next section.

Τό δρᾶμα; or, the Play's the Thing

Throughout the sessions devoted to this material, as also to the dreams of children remembered as adults, one unstated parallel does in fact hold between medical practice and the action or plot template in Jung's approach to dream interpretation. It remained unstated for some of the same reasons that it stays unremarked today. The Aristotelian template for action in the *Poetics*, applied by Jung to dreams, was part of a consistently developed analogy between medical practice and tragedy, one that students of both literature and psychology have mostly forgotten. The old analogy was even more specific, and proportional: the plot, or *praxis*, which Aristotle called the *psyche* of drama, was to the play's development as a disease was to the course it ran (with the play's turning point or *peripeteia* proportional to the *krisis* or change point in illness). What makes *Poetics* such an unusual treatise is its pointed Hippocratic construction, limb by limb, with tragedy seen as treatment, and the Hippocratic goal of homeostasis or self-regulation—in line with Jung's view of the dream's dynamic function—fully instated with respect to mental balance.[5] The final loosening or untying, the *lysis*, also draws on disease terminology. As I will argue later, because this analogy remained implicit for both Jung and his seminar participants, it is up to us to fill out the picture that marries the unfolding of suffering and release, or illness and easing, with the actions of staged dramas and dream dynamics—the diagnostic picture, to be exact.

As for the tone of questioning Jung pursued in this material, it stands somewhat apart from that in his other seminars. Although the participants usually remain unidentified in the exchanges, it seems likely that everyone felt the occasional force of Jung's colloquy. More than in his other seminars, Jung drew out certain phases of questioning almost in the Socratic manner. The transcripts of these sessions are peppered with deliberately leading questions, salted tartly with gentle barbs and rebukes. While the same spirit animates brief patches of discussion in the other seminars, nowhere else is it quite as teacherly as here. Of course, the university context to which Jung had returned largely accounts for this tone. And the matter treated by Jung with pedagogic insistence is his repeated exposition, in the sessions on children's dreams, of the dramatic template for typical dream processes. More about this emphasis follows in the next section.

Noting the main themes Jung pressed home in these seminars on both children's dreams and the history of dream interpretation, I am mindful of Dr. Joseph Henderson's title, *Thresholds of Initiation*, and its implications for dealing with both aspects of the world, outside and in. That is, Jung several times puts his finger on the influence of conflicts set loose in the greater world upon the individual psyche, not only in mature doctors like Hubbard but also in other people. This topic emerges only gradually as a master theme, yet it sets up a mirror relation between parallel influences: the fateful and overarching patterns

---

[5] These and other aspects of the comparison, in the context of Aristotle's strong family background and initial training in medicine, are developed by Elizabeth Craik in "Tragedy as Treatment: Medical Analogies in Aristotle's *Poetics*," in *Dionysalexandros: Essays on Aeschylus and His Fellow Tragedians*, ed. Douglas Cairns and Vayos Liapis (Swansea: Classical Press of Wales, 2007), chap. 17, 283–99.

of conflicts on the loose collectively, and the thrust of potential individuation in dreams recalled from childhood. The intentional but also neutral, just-so processes unfolding within are mirrored by history's just-so paradigm shifts and clashing outbursts, equally directional and unconscious. One outcome of these discussions is to sharpen the focus on these two strands of fate. One of them unbraids itself proleptically from the fibers of birth. The other blows in from the storm outside, as tribal fascinations that routinely gobble up energy and solicit identification in times of major transition or open outbreak. They, too, like certain shapes taken by individuation, may represent new content and prove to be irresistible to those who are ready to turn the page. As for initiation, however, it seems that the saving trick in both cases, with either the big-world shindy or the single destiny, is to come through standing on both feet—no longer one-sided and incomplete—and relatively free of gluey adherence to either the archetypes of the inner swarm or to identifications with mass culture, the nation-state, the clan or club or klatch, the energy sinks of ambition or consumption, and now the dispersed holocaust of ecocide. As discussions of the assigned reports on dream interpretation proceed, mixed with practical work on shorter and longer series of dreams, Jung demonstrates how these two reaches of draw, both outward and inward into mystical participation or identification, compose reciprocating images, the macrocosmic and microcosmic defaults either side of a sword bridge. That bridge defines both regions by razoring between them into an ample relationship with the psyche.

At first one might not expect such paired themes to rise from this material. Yet their coemergence is not really surprising. The same mix percolates through both the *Visions Seminars* of 1930–34 and the seminars on Nietzsche's *Zarathustra*, which ran nearly concurrently with the ones on children's dreams (*SNZ* 1934–39, and *CDS* 1936–41). The rise of the European and Russian dictatorships impinged on the participants with the heaviness of the *entre deux guerres*, which Jung addresses when returning here to the dreams he had discussed at Sennen Cove, Land's End, in Cornwall during his first, unrecorded seminar in 1920, the dreams of Dr. John Hubbard. On the table for everyone again lay the palpable mirroring of crisis-heavy collective themes by responses from the individual psyche. The last two terms, from winter

1939 through the first months of 1941, ran coevally with the inaugural phase of World War II.

With the publication of Jung's *Red Book* (1913–28) in 2009, one can now appreciate how much this reciprocal clash of violent collective outbreak with the strong upsurge of autonomous inner dramas defined Jung's personal experiment. Therefore what gradually emerged as reciprocal themes in the *Children's Dreams Seminars* had been holding Jung's attention consistently for more than two decades. The preceding and concurrent seminars, on Christiana Morgan's prolific outpouring of active imagination, and on Nietzsche "the prophet" in *Also sprach Zarathustra*, had followed the seminar in 1928–30 on the study of practical dream analysis, the practice on which this present material dwells in two complementary ways. By interspersing dreams from childhood, as recalled by adults, with ad hoc chapters in a history of dream interpretation from Artemidorus through Girolamo Cardano and more recent figures, Jung was extending roughly parallel lines through both the single lifespan's inner theater and the drama of Western history. This micro-macro parallelism, though not consistently evoked, remained ready, like loose stone, to rumble with what Shakespeare called "the fell points of mighty opposites." Throughout Jung's syllabus, the chief material witnesses are marked by their extraordinary receptivity to this harmonic. As a seasoned veteran and student of such receptivity himself, Jung had become a reclamation architect in such parallel halls of shattered and leaning mirrors, weaving the relevant images, from both the mass and the single person, into a loose design.

One may paraphrase his seminar's roughly related motifs as follows (for both the dreams from childhood and the survey of dream interpretation), in radial rather than linear order, several of which the rest of this introduction will take up:

- Divination and control, over against anticipation (the prospective function of dreaming) and wisdom;
- Conflict issuing into either stasis or a resolution that changes things;
- An action template for how most symbolic processes regularly unfold;

- The nuclear and radial character of order in symbolic processes, which fosters concentric amplification rather than causal reduction to root figures;
- Likewise, the occasionally atemporal or out-of-sequence arrival of turning points in extended symbolic processes, in which symbolic thinking-by-doing sometimes anticipates itself;
- Time as such, or living qua living, constituting a fifth psychic function; and "coming into being" (I, 27) as Jung's prelude to the current phase of emergence theory;[6]
- The longue durée of collective symbolic progressions, meshing with the single lifespan, in Jung's "ethno-psychological method";
- Fate, collective or singular, alongside individuation; and
- Heuristics, or the attitude of continuously hypothetical discovery, sustaining learning over against explanation.

---

[6] A bit of commentary is called for at this point. Joseph Cambray's recent *Synchronicity: Nature and Psyche in an Interconnected Universe* (College Station: Texas A&M University Press, 2009), and his "The Place of the 17th Century in Jung's Encounter with China" (on Leibniz and supervenience), *Journal of Analytical Psychology* 50, no. 2 (2005), study Jung's work as "an implicit haven" for the holism that preceded modern emergentist thinking. For further introduction, one may also consult John Haule, *Jung in the 21st Century: Evolution and Archetype* (vol. 1) and *Synchronicity and Science* (vol. 2) (London: Routledge, 2011).

For a full account of Jung's role vis-à-vis contemporary emergence and complexity theories of pattern and order, see especially David Tresan, MD, "Jungian Metapsychology and Neurobiological Theory," *Journal of Analytical Psychology* 41, no. 3 (1996): 399–436, where he distinguishes three phases for the doctrine of emergence—first, the perennial phase of religion, art, and holistic philosophy; second, the vitalist reaction against evolution construed as blind chance, which "led ineluctably to the notion of a supraordinate intelligence, a God-concept," therefore banished from modern science; and third, the novel strand present since around 1975, likewise assuming "an ordering principle extraneous to ego . . . [though one that] does not flow directly from a supraordinate being but rather from the way matter automatically sorts itself out under certain circumstances." This recent strand of theory supposes "a limited organizing principle that does not fall into the extreme of holism or, consequently, of that wholesale downward causation which is akin to vitalist doctrines and difficult to defend scientifically. The newly discerned self-organizing principles are data driven, definable in mathematical terms, and objectively verifiable." Jung's thinking after 1928, with the borderline concepts of Self and individuation, "seemed to gravitate to the holistic position." However, "in breaking with the vitalistic tradition, he subtly and persistently turned to and retained an epistemologically open and ontologically non-committal stance appropriate for psychology but incompatible with religion" (409). Since archetypal knowledge shines light both on what precedes it and on what follows, and since the third kind of emergence theory had not constellated during Jung's time, he could not perceive it, and his farthest-reaching ideas could anticipate it only "in less formed ways" (428).

This commentary continues in note 22 below.

Western modes of divination have developed in a broadly historical manner, passing from sheer strip mining for the purposes of utility—grubby resource extraction in Artemidorus and others, for the routine purposes of control, prudent navigation, or even aggrandizement, and "the mastery of time" ("time my possession," boasted the great physician, astrologer, and mathematician Girolamo Cardano)—to the more discerning engagement with an inner natural process that neither tells us what to do nor considerately respects our human limits, but nonetheless deepens a capacity for response. In avoiding identity with inflation from without or within, one can begin to survive immersion in overwhelming affects while rotating the function wheel so as to retain insight into conflicting forces met either within or out in the open. Thus divination may slowly become mature investigation with tools acquired through immersion: insight, endurance, and courage. Therefore time, during the course of these sessions, passes from being a resource to be forklifted for profit, health, or life insurance, to what Jung in the sessions on children's dreams provisionally calls an impersonal function, implicitly to be set alongside the other four functions in his typology. "My view on this is that time is a psychological function, identical with living as such. Such a view cannot be proved but is extremely valuable heuristically" (Children's Dreams, 100–102). Thus Cardano's passion as astrologer and dream analyst, which was to submit the flow of one's life to a lucid form of subjection, much as the city of Los Angeles has channeled the river that bears its name through miles of concrete, in retrospect expansively anticipates today's patiently hypothetical attitude—heuristic in both senses, both discovering and also showing features of something unintentional yet still directed, and still largely unknown.

That heuristic attitude in large measure determines the psychology that one practices—and "practice on the basis of the material" is the ethos at work here (see Children's Dreams, 28). No matter how illuminating, one's method will lapse into a dogmatic posture if it pursues, as some modern psychologies have done, causal connections. Rather than designating a causal perspective, early on Jung calls his attitude toward learning, and also teaching, "conditional" (Children's Dreams, 4). Especially with children's dreams, in which personal material yields pride of place to "the storeroom of the human mind," Jung's "ethno-psychological method" is the most consistently instructive attitude, leading one to keep solutions experimental, provisional, and "unsatisfactory." Such dreams remembered in adulthood lend themselves to this experiment with particular aptness, teaching the Theseus-like groper in the labyrinth to finger several threads at once: enlargement rather than reduction of motifs (amplification rather than *reductio in primam figuram*); concentric rather than linear investigation and grasp, with nuclear-and-radial rather than simply sequential manifestations; dealings with collective rather than individual images; and an easing-up on the attempt to understand in the interests of rendering a configuration more thoroughly "visible" (*Children's Dreams*, 26).

The findings delivered by this procedure can be startling. For instance, in the longest part of these sessions, devoted to eleven dreams spanning thirty-seven years of Jerome Cardan's life, Jung identifies the *peripeteia*, or process turning point in the entire series, as a dream that comes *before* that process actually starts to go downhill—a fact the reader may not notice until scrutinizing the dating of the dreams and the sequencing of their discussion (see the two charts in the first footnote to chapter 13 below). It is noteworthy that by this point in the proceedings Jung does not mention this wrinkle—or at least the transcript does not record him doing so. We are justified, then, in assuming that by the time Jung takes up Cardano—the centerpiece of his demonstration—he has trusted his charges to have grasped his "conditional" method for following the radial and concentric probes among acausal movements of the psyche, which nonetheless seem to follow the apparently linear course of time. That is, by then he has assumed that his charges have absorbed his teaching aims for the whole seminar. One can have sympathy for those in the group who may have been slower to drink deeply from those springs. One wonders, for instance, how many of them noticed that the teaching sequence for Cardano's dreams twice departs from the calendar sequence, for reasons that Jung passes over in silence (see the second chart, first footnote, chapter 13).

Explanation cannot be one's aim either in the course of such inquiry or in the teaching of it. Instead, a walk around the mountain deposited by nature, like the circumambulation of Mount Tamalpais by the Miwok Indians of California, slowly discloses both the object and one's relations to it. One uses both feet, both eyes, and both cerebral hemispheres, practices retention and endurance, but *commands* nothing. Even the climb *up* such a living and dynamic storehouse of phenomena is not vertically *up* but rather, as tribal usage has it, along Jung's radial and concentric lines, *into* the mountain.

In Jung's handling, through the channels of historical and cross-cultural divination (Western astrology and the Chinese *I Ching*) as well as the quantum phenomena of how symbolic processes appear to "run"—notably in a dream or fantasy's process template or "unfolding of actions" (*Children's Dreams*, 161) or in mythological processes that feature development ("the transitus of the gods," ibid.)—patient study slowly discloses the look, if not a complete theoretical account, of how temporal unfolding dovetails with configured meaning. The outcome of such study-in-practice anticipates today's upsurge of research, in several scientific domains, of theories devoted to *pattern emergence*, in a *field* either living or inorganic. But that outcome, "the coming into being, and the fundamental meaning, of dreams" (*Children's Dreams*, 27), follows only from "many experiences" or trials in the pedestrian but spacious Mount Tamalpais lab. Just *how* actions unfold, in the purposive but nonhortatory unconscious, remains a question that emergence theory still walks around, notwithstanding the rapid growth in its lexicon of terms (see footnote 12 below). In this respect, the combined sessions on children's dreams and the survey of dream interpretation, though dwindling in the rear-view mirror of the decades, fix upon something that will challenge emergence theorists (cf. footnotes 6 and 22) to articulate more finely and fundamentally—namely, the persistently hypothetical grasp of such *coming into being* in unconscious mental life in view of the rough-and-ready philosophical process terms that Jung brought to these matters both then and later, through the 1940s and 1950s (notably in "Theoretical Reflections on the Nature of the Psychical" [1946, 1954]).

From the later 1930s through his work on the synchronicity hypothesis in partial collaboration with Wolfgang Pauli, the reach of Jung's speculation grows in depth and differentiation, while his fidelity to the "pure happening," or *reinen Geschehens*, of psychic process[7] sustains his

---

[7] See the first pages of my "*Etwas geschah*: Orphaned Event and Its Adoptions," *Spring* 84 (Fall 2010), for relevant passages in Jung's work on pure psychic process-event or happening.

earlier outlook on the wisdom of provisional grasp. These seminars from the end of the *entre deux guerres* erect scaffolding around such coming into being, as discussed below, which consist of Aristotelian planking (made smooth by Hans Driesch's "psychoid" Darwinian plane) supported by Kantian framing members, the first brought in by plain paraphrase and the second chosen for their respectful stand toward the unknowable quid inside the mountain. The sections of Aristotle's *Poetics* devoted to the structure of action rendered symbolically—not in some schoolboy's summary of the phases in a drama, plotting its praxis, but rather that same outline heuristically mated with inscrutable developmental cues in the unconscious—supplied Jung with his terms. They sound like a teacher's terms, but they also serve an investigator up against final limits: not *explanation* from causes and grounds, but *heuristics* elucidating the still somewhat inscrutable infinitives *dran* and *poien*, to act and to configure. Such is the ground on which Jung lightly landed and nimbly moved.

This Aristotelian summary would have first come to Jung, of course, during his *Gymnasium* years. He usually invokes that summary without attribution, since anyone would recognize it as Aristotle's, as Mr. Baumann does here in summarizing plot, or *Handlung*, in his report on Delage's theory of dreams. However, that way of applying the action template also alludes to its genuine anonymity or natural basis—a view I take to be implicit in Jung's practice. If so, that thread in Aristotle's poetics suits the weave of his biology and natural history; he read it accurately not only from Sophocles and Aristophanes but also *de natura*, from the way things go. The nugget for Jung in this action template is the pressure or drift in psychic energy, the apparent purposiveness in life processes, which is akin to the finalistic perspective invoked by him for certain dreams, but which typically remains a bane in modern science, and certainly is baneful to theorists of unconscious processes when those processes are tied to the least shred of traditional teleology. Because Aristotelian categories have long been deployed in regimental fashion in theology, aesthetics, and metaphysics, Jung preferred to paraphrase this nugget in non-Aristotelian terms; as he told Ximena de Angulo in 1952, "To Schopenhauer I owe the dynamic view of the psyche; the 'Will' is the libido back of everything." Ms. de Angulo went on to quiz him, asking if individuation "was what made a tree grow into a tree, if it was not the same thing as the Aristotelian entelechy. . . . He hesitated, and I had to say it again another way, but then he said it was the same thing."[8]

Jung's hesitation cues us here; he neither excludes nor embraces the teleological term, but reframes it. Readers of the Collected Works can follow Jung's adjustment of entelechy to his "phylogeny of mind," or to his frequent characterizations of both "shaping limit" and "boundary concept"—thereby seeing, in the process of doing so, how biology and comparative zoology, the theory of knowledge, and a multilayered grasp already nudge the inherited action template up against an envelope.

Marilyn Nagy proposes that Eduard von Hartmann's invocation of pervasive directionality in natural processes gave Jung a means of consolidating earlier hints, notably Schopenhauer's, with support from Hans Driesch's philosophical biology, in framing the individuation process.[9] Sonu Shamdasani's chapters on Jung's development of dream interpretation offer the most nuanced and informed perspective on what I have sketched here. The following itemizes only the most salient parts of a remarkable cascade. From 1912 on, the dream for Jung was itself both nature and the royal road to cultural history; it expressed both Haeckel's biogenetic law of recapitulation (of phylum history in the individual) and the functionally self-personifying representation that, with support from Havelock Ellis, he called "dramatizing." (Although the "strong" variety of Haeckel's hypothesis has been set aside, its main lines persist.) All of this pointed to symbol formation as the master

[8] "Comments on a Doctoral Thesis" (1952), in C. G. Jung Speaking: Interviews and Encounters, ed. William McGuire and R.F.C. Hull (Princeton, NJ: Princeton University Press, 1977), 207, 211. The Aristotelian entelechy—or soul, which carries within itself its own purpose or aim (wrt/ to Jung, see footnote 12 of this introduction, below, and then Bächtold's report on Macrobius, below)—also played a considerable role in Goethe's construal of the individual developmental process, with pertinence to Jung's process of individuation. See Paul Bishop, Reading Goethe at Midlife: Ancient Wisdom, German Classicism, and Jung (New Orleans: Spring Journal Books, 2011), 151, 172, 182, 192–93.

[9] Marilyn Nagy, in Philosophical Issues in the Thought of C. G. Jung (Albany: State University of New York Press, 1991), 234; see footnote 10 below for his later citations from Driesch. Another secondary source for the Aristotelian template, taking up teleology and medicine along with the classic themes of recognition, catharsis, etc., is Zwei Abhandlungen über die Aristotelische Theorie des Dramas (Two Essays on Aristotle's Theory of Drama) (1880), which reprints the earlier controversial Grundzüge der verlorenen Abhandlung des Aristoteles über Wirkung der Tragödie (Fundamenals of Aristotle's Lost Treatise on Tragic Action) (1858), by the rabbi and classical philologist Jakob Bernays, student of Ritschl and associate of Mommsen. It was drawn on by Nietzsche in his study of Greek tragedy, and later by Freud.

trope of psychic process, whose function was adaptive in evolution, developing latent powers through fictive-creative rehearsals; teleology described this function within a polypsychic, compensatory, nonego frame in line partly with Freud's causal mode, but more broadly with the biologist Karl Groos's play theory, Théodore Flournoy's antisuicidal automatisms, the inferior personalities theatricalized by mediums, Gerhard Adler's prescient function, and Alphonse Maeder's teleological function. Alongside all this ferment, comparative embryology by way of Ernst Haeckel early had lent to Jung a biogenetic basis for reading in individual psychic terms the encoding and retelling—redramatizing in the customized, on-call ways noted above—of repertoires from our entire species development, naturally and culturally. The above findings by Jung and his colleagues orchestrated Haeckel's master principle in ways that Jung summarized as "functional or autosymbolic phenomena." In the vanguard of this procession, in 1885, had marched the German neo-Kantian thinker Carl du Prel, emphasizing both the healing function and the dramatic form of dreams, in the last respect amplifying a note struck already by Samuel Taylor Coleridge and Georg Lichtenberg. Du Prel called the dream "a completely accentuated drama."[10]

Jung's comments on the prospective functions not only of dreaming but also of regression, from *Symbols of the Transformation of Libido* (CW 5, 1912) through the *New York Lectures on Psychoanalysis* (at Fordham University,[11] also 1912) and the first general essay on dreams (1916), sketch a scientific regrounding for the dynamics of anticipation, or purposive arrangement, in certain unconscious processes. Freud's own observations on regression compel one to shift the etiological fulcrum he placed under childhood experiences to a place directly beneath the present moment during neurosis (*New York Lectures*, §377), a shift that lends regression itself a prospective slant, for regression already anticipates, however gropingly, "new ways of adapting"(§406). In

---

[10] Sonu Shamdasani, *Jung and the Making of Modern Psychology: The Dream of a Science* (Cambridge: Cambridge University Press, 2003), 124–25, 138–43, 183–84. For the early and decisive impact du Prel made on Jung in this respect, see also Shamdasani's *C. G. Jung: A Biography in Books* (New York: Norton, 2012), 29–30.

[11] These have been reissued separately: see Sonu Shamdasani, ed. and introduction, *Jung contra Freud: The 1912 New York Lectures on the Theory of Psychoanalysis*, Philemon/Bollingen (Princeton, NJ: Princeton University Press, 2012). This introduction lends further context to what I outline here as a scientific regrounding of only one theme in Jung's work from 1911 to 1916.

his paragraphs on teleology and regression, Jung cites his own *Symbols of the Transformation of Libido*: the "prophetic dream" is only the rare, special case of "certain very fine subliminal combinations that point forward. . . . Dreams are very often anticipations of future alterations of consciousness" (*Symbols*, §78n18). The same "combinations" are named in the *New York Lectures* ("The Prospective Function of Dreams," §453), where "the teleological significance of dreams," as demonstrated by Alphonse Maeder, is precisely what Freud had neglected in favor of historical determinants (§452). Four years later in 1916, in the paper on "General Aspects of Dream Psychology," Jung compactly links the compensatory function of dreams during neurosis with their quasi-teleological tendency. In a regression, "the—under normal conditions—merely compensatory function of the unconscious becomes a guiding, prospective function [einer *führenden, prospektiven Funktion*]" (CW 8 §495, where Maeder's work is cited again).

Jung therefore integrated his view of this orienteering function in certain dreams at the climax of a broad inquiry constructed along that line by many hands, and at the point where his own psychology was soon to diverge from a more historically determined one. While the lever may have been those barely perceptible subliminal elements entering into hazy combinations, what they moved was an entire psychology. One might say that a prospective function was the tongue depressor with which Jung looked down the throat of a historically determined dynamic psychiatry, and made it cough. This fact is worth underlining in our day, when philosophical biology has banned teleological readings of life processes, and when our literary theorists by and large have convinced themselves that narrative action and authorial agency, those worthy buckets, have turned into sieves. Worth all the more, because, when it came to Jung's assessment of dream actions, he parked his present-tense, future-anticipating reading of things on the same Aristotelian action template that then-recent biology and psychology, spanning Driesch and du Prel, had invoked in one way or another. Which, then, is hardly out of keeping: far from being an old saw in a caricatured finalistic carpentry, that action template is one more patterned energy as inscrutable as the compensatory aim-taking function of the psyche itself.

To paraphrase the tension sprung into Aristotle's action template by this astonishing theoretical surge in the first decades of the twentieth century, one can say that *plot*, that threadbare term in English for action, or *praxis* in Greek, *naturally* unfolds from the nonego, to frame, resolve, and memoriously invest psychic adaptations to conflict and challenge with backing and input from our remotest ancestors. Literature is its flower; this prior matter supplies the taproot. While Kant equipped Jung with a bulkhead against unwarranted assumptions about what can be known, Haeckel had built him a bridge across which Schopenhauer's push toward an expanded libido theory could join Jung's fine tolerance, underwritten by the research chorus named above, for the inscrutable knowingness apparently at work in unintentional natural processes—a headless teleology.[12]

Both the seminar on children's dreams per se and this volume on a select history of dream interpretation compose one long demonstration. Uniting them both, and many of their shared conceptual motifs, is the strategic tension sustained by Jung around the description of process

---

[12] The basement thrust of purpose in organic development, while headless, is still not entirely mindless. As Nagy demonstrates later in her book, Driesch—Ernst Haeckel's student at Jena, and a double-threat hitter who turned to philosophical biology after 1911—postulated a nonmaterial ordering entity (deriving from Aristotle's *entelechy*; see footnote 8 above) that constructs an organism's actuality (compare Aristotle's *energeia*), "a mind-like movement which seeks form," and which is "neither energy nor force, nor causality nor substance, nor soul, nor God . . ." in Driesch's terms "an extensive manifoldness" that is "psychoid . . . that is, a something which though not a 'psyche' can only be described in terms analogous to those of psychology" (cf. Hans Driesch, *The Science and Philosophy of the Organism* [London: A. and C. Black, 1908], 2: 82). Jung cites Driesch in comparable passages in his later paper of 1946, six years after the seminars on children's dreams, "Theoretical Reflections on the Nature of the Psychical," CW 8, §368—"'the elemental agent discovered in action,' the 'entelechy of real acting,'" where he also cites Eugen Bleuler's adaptations of Driesch's terms.

For Jung's summary of his early internal debate over the presence or absence of purposive direction in the unconscious, see his review in the 1925 seminar on how he veered both toward and away from the purposive position, which for him began with Schopenhauer's teleological adoption of a "creative efficiency" and blind "direction in the creating will," to which Jung added von Hartmann's element of mind in the unconscious. He finally extended purposive direction from the unconscious-with-mind to the universe, making a sidelong empirical approach to that vexed metaphysical question by way of the fact that mind in the unconscious preserves a deep inventory, "millions of years old . . . [and therefore in keeping with] some main current in the universe" (Sonu Shamdasani, ed., *Introduction to Jungian Psychology: Notes of the Seminar Given in 1925* [Princeton, NJ: Princeton University Press, 2012], 4–5, 12; 1989 edition edited by William McGuire).

Adolf Portmann, reviewing the neovitalist thinking in Eugen Bleuler's biology and the later Darwinism that influenced Jung, nicely observes that "Jung's writing often emphasizes the importance of the function as that which develops its own structures" ("Recollections of Jung's Biology Professor," *Spring* [1976]: 151).

See footnote 16 below for a concluding perspective on Jung's finalistic viewpoint, and footnote 22 for its ties, or not, to emergence theory today.

purposiveness. Kant manifestly raftered Jung's epistemological ceiling, but Aristotle no less manifestly lent footers to his process theory. His choice of the Aristotelian hologram for represented action, a selection that constituted no mere fallback position or crypto-Aristotelian move, marks the compass-foot pivot for his swings through arcs of nonlinear process, as far as the accounting that we might plausibly give of them. What a startling recovery of means, initially from the Stagirite: to Kant and Schopenhauer, by way of du Prel, Haeckel, Maeder, Groos, Flournoy, Ellis, and perhaps Driesch . . . *and* by way of both the entelechy and mimetic-action template.

It is particularly startling when one goes on to recover Aristotle's bivalent grasp of what makes a represented action whole. The causality within that whole is refracted, or rendered quantum in character, by one's position. *Archê* and *teleutê*, beginning and end, depend entirely on the *meson*, or middle, which is defined as the point from which causality appears either as necessity (looking back toward a beginning) or as still open to determination (toward some end). And that is not the only doubleness in view: the actor experiences this double perspective on caused and causing, necessity and freedom, as being distinct from the spectator's perspective in which the whole show unfolds fatefully. From within the action, chance remains active until the perceived end, but seen from outside, the action appears to be necessary. So, the agonistic and theatric, or existential and theoretical modes, together frame *mimesis*, to which Aristotle adds that in tragedy the two perspectives collapse in upon each other. The spectator is brought on stage; the knower or theorist of the necessary is made to feel the moral challenge of indeterminacy or freedom.[13]

It is only two steps from this double perspective built into dramatic *praxis* by Aristotle[14] to quantum physics and Jung's psychology in the 1930s. The first step comes by way of Werner Heisenberg's parallel introduction

---

[13] See the detailed analysis in Michael Davis, *Aristotle's Poetics: The Poetry of Philosophy* (Lanham, MD: Rowman and Littlefield, 1992), chap. 7, 49ff. In an unspecified way, Stephen Halliwell sketches a "dual-aspect mimeticism" in the *Poetics*; "Aristotelian Mimesis Reevaluated," in *Aristotle: Critical Assessments*, ed. Lloyd Gerson, vol. 4, *Politics, Rhetoric, Aesthetics* (London: Routledge, 1999), 328. For a complementary focus on literary aspects, see Leon Golden and O. B. Hardison Jr., *Aristotle's Poetics: A Translation and Commentary for Students of Literature* (Englewood Cliffs, NJ: Prentice-Hall, 1968).

[14] At least to my knowledge, one cannot derive this bivalent assessment of Aristotelian *mimesis*, and the corresponding poetics of the action template, from von Franz, Hillman, or other writers who relate themselves to Jung's work.

of the theorist into the drama of subatomic process (rather than staged action), and then by way of Jung's related propositions that (a) dream dramas are staged in compensatory relation to the waking standpoint. Jung phrases this matter in the first volume of these seminars by saying that "the dream leads us into an action, into an [instinctual] experience, that no longer corresponds to conscious experience" (*Children's Dreams*, 162). Jung also marks the fact that (b) the 2 percent relegated to individuality, the margin of conscious participation in development, manifests *because* the ego is thrust into the perceived field of enactment as an agent.

The fated *and* the freely determined: both of these perspectives compose tendency or meaning in a whole action or *praxis*—and it is this quantum view, or particle/wave, determined/determining bivalence, that rounds out the view of an as-if causality (the as-if factor will be treated below) as at once determined and actively determining, although it must be perceived alternately as one or the other. This same double view attends Jung's take on the turning point in a dream action in Aristotle's terms—the *peripeteia* or peripety. For awareness expands at that point, within the actor, to include what a spectator can take in more comprehensively. And whether or not the dream ego "gets it" during the dream, that actor meets up with his waking counterpart soon enough, to have a little seminar. What they say to each other—their integral—is what the work on dreams comes to, but also is exactly what *mimesis* serves. Only this serially doubled perspective, then, lends sufficient amplitude to descriptions of purposiveness in psychic processes. Without its quantum reach, the very sense of one's terms will both flatten and refract; *causality* and *aim*, with their warranted synonyms and modifiers, will retire into the bunkers of armed camps.

Aim turns out to be the more ductile term of art. The purposive thrust of a drama, for Aristotle its *telos* or aim, pushing through the change point to a homeostatic clearing of both ignorance and suffering, suits down to the ground Jung's sense of the neutral but directional thrust of a dream series. Those "mousetraps" for libido called complexes obstruct the general aim of development, the telos of the individual life process: that much is emphatic for Jung, in the sessions devoted to children's dreams. Some of his most vigorous teaching in *Children's Dreams* (417ff., on the five-year-old girl's dream of the devil, her father, and the shaft in the garden) shows how easily we misread the dynamic aim, the *als-ob* or as-if directedness, at work in early phases of growth. The two essays from the World War I decade later revised several times, into the early 1940s—"The Structure of the Unconscious" and "The Relations between the Ego and the Unconscious"—both follow the transformative *"drame intérieur"*[15] of the unconscious psyche. The layers of revision and rethinking in volume 7 of the *Collected Works* preserve the bedrock formulations brought by Jung to the main task with respect to aimed natural processes—namely, teasing apart the senses of *Zweck* or aim in philosophy, biology, and the psyche. As we have heard Jung say above, dream processes have no goal or no teleology in the philosophical sense, but rather, in *compensating* the conscious situation and therefore *not* working toward some preexistent end, they choreograph or "group together elements" in ways that one *must* see "from the standpoint of finality" ("sondern fordert auch eine finale Betrachtungswiese . . . zur Konstellation gebracht werde").[16] The must-factor here has to do with persistent enactment, a primary *drama* perpetually staged by nature and functioning prospectively with respect to development. Without telling us in so many words—either in these sessions, the *Children's Dreams* sessions, or elsewhere—Jung advances the working hypothesis that Aristotle's template for dramatic action and nature's templates for psychic symbolic processes are one and the same.

Current emergentist thinking in the sciences stands to refresh Jung's provisional observations in this focal area, however resistant that thinking may remain to Jung's reading of the great opposition between nature and spirit. The language of vitalism in nineteenth-century biology and philosophy of science yields first, with earlier Jung, to his as-if final standpoint or perspective, and to process structures serving prospective, finalistic functions; then still later, after Jung and Pauli's collaboration, that language yields to terms for the psychoid realm and synchronicity. With Sonu Shamdasani's sections on the phylogeny

---

[15] Jung's phrase in his preface to the second edition of "Relations" (1935), CW 7, 123.

[16] See the long footnote 19 to §501, CW 7 (note 6 in the German edition). While one cannot "deduce the pre-existent fixation of a final end" from these constellations, "it would be weak-minded to sacrifice the point of view of finality. All one can say is that things happen *as if* there were a fixed final aim." About that "all one can say," especially pertinent is Shamdasani's review of the missed opportunity, in analytical psychology since Jung, to work toward a biological grounding for archetypes; see footnote 18 below.

of mind in *Jung and the Making of Modern Psychology: The Dream of a Science* for background nourishment, one can make out a track that roughly parallels the one taken in biology. Jung's finalistic view of the dream, as his path to a comparative or phylogenetic psychology, already had built upon his sense, as early as 1909, that "a phylogenetic basis was necessary if the theory of neurosis was to be placed on an evolutionary and developmental level. . . . The study of mythology and history are to psychology what the study of phylogenesis and comparative anatomy are to biology."[17] A dream action, then, in memorious and compensatory terms, parallels in small the large-scale adaptive development in life forms. If one comes around to that viewpoint, should it then surprise us that folktales antedate myths, and dream actions anticipate Aristotle's template for drama? At the same time, however, as Jung wrote to biologist Adolf Portmann, he "was no longer at home in modern biology," which soon came to include Konrad Lorenz and Nikolaas Tinbergen's ethological work on instinct. Michael Fordham, mindful that Portmann's attempt, in view of the inadequacy of the biogenetic law to bridge psychology and biology, had failed to prompt a reworking of analytical psychology's archetypal hypothesis in biological terms, realized that an insufficient basis in heredity could not be papered over by Jung's assumption that archetypes, like instincts, were inherited.[18] And there the bridge to biology has remained broken. In the material of the session devoted to Marais's pioneer observations of termites, while Jung does not throw up his hands entirely, his analogy between psychic levels across phylum lines stays *provisionally* paideutic: "We have to assume that *the life forms are contained in the sympathetic nervous systems in the form of images*, so to speak" (101 below). His lively cross-species probe into collective human bonding and social organization by way of behavior in colonies of the white ant was, as he knew, a net thrown around an absent quarry. "After all, the word 'instinct' doesn't explain anything" (102 below).

Although Jung leaves us to draw the inference about his working hypothesis on the action template, he remains modest in his supposi-

---

[17] Shamdasani, *Jung and the Making of Modern Psychology*, 214.

[18] Ibid., 266–67: "The implication was that the inheritance of archetypes was established by analogy rather than by proof. With the exception of his own work, Fordham's reformulation made no further headway in analytical psychology than Portmann's."

tions about how symbolic processes run or unfold.[19] That respectful but fizzy menu compels us to acknowledge, during today's springtime of emergence theory in physics, biology, and psychology,[20] just how lively the unknowns remain across the several disciplinary venues. Which is also to say that such rear-guard areas for the scientist still hold some of the goods on "the coming into being, and the fundamental meaning, of dreams." The study of largely collective dreams—typically those from early childhood—not only demands amplification or concentric walk-about tours, but also stalls on the stumbling block of as-if purposive symbolic enactment. Jung does not suggest, either here or later, that his revamped template for unfolding action is merely the way in which things happen to happen. Rather, he implies that all historical and literary expansions of serial meaning—all narratives whether staged or imagined—build upon this triadic process-quotient of aimed psychoid nature, framed developmentally as (a) an emergent situation, (b) its conflictual enrichment, and then (c) either a visionary halt before the shape of that conflict or a resolution that in some way alters the original situation. Rather than repeating the truism that a myth or a Greek drama enacts a typical complex, one goes on to admit that both the complex and the staged drama, inner and outer lives alike, radiate from psychoid comings-into-being. As I noted earlier, Jung leaves largely unstated in this material, and elsewhere, the consistent analogies stamped into his borrowed action template, between the medical alleviation of suffering and dream psychodynamics. This is either deliberate soft-pedaling on his part, or an oversight, which, taken either way, stands as one of the least remarked but still most remarkable features of his approach to dream interpretation.

"The unfolding of actions" at this foundational level turns waking life into one long series of walkouts from an uninterrupted theatrical production. Therefore its symbolic processes, more than we can know, enact us. These seminars dance around the causal/acausal webs of meaning that Jung's final work on the synchronicity hypothesis specifies more finely. In Greek, an unfolding, imaged-forth action is the *drama*,

[19] In Greek, *drama* is both an act and an unfolding action on stage; *dramema* and *dromema* are running, the race that is run, or the racecourse.

[20] For comprehensive and current surveys by analysts of some of these matters, see Cambray, *Synchronicity*.

"the thing done" or performed; never a fully conscious affair, "symbolic thinking is thinking by doing" (*Children's Dreams*, 161), and so the action template lifted from Aristotle stands in for the whole of psychic phenomenology, the dramatic self-staging that graphs "emergence" in two ways (to use the term nontechnically, as Luigi Aurigemma did in his essays on Jung's practice[21]): either homeostatic compensations of the conscious standpoint and attitude (dreams) or abruptly drastic whole-body irruptions (visions). Forget those broad facts, and we resemble the gentleman who mislays his lady's name.

Still, linking Jung's work to the theories of emergence now in train among the sciences remains a delicate matter. The lady's future offspring may be anticipated, but their features cannot be foreseen—an Aristotelian nose and a Jungian earlobe may appear, but meanwhile it is prudent to let ancestors be ancestors.[22] As for that ancestry, it has taken a long time for this writer to understand that Jung's scientific modesty toward a template for essential psychic manifestation and self-representation recommends that we would do well to rely on *Empfindung*, or inner sensing, to go on looking as closely and for as long as possible at *Geschehens* (sheer happening). That is, he leaves the Aristotelian process-tablecloth on the emergence table for symbol and libido, along with utensils from nineteenth-century German biology and philosophy, as a tribute to how well a primary hypothesis can still serve when placed in that position.

[21] Luigi Aurigemma, *Jungian Perspectives*, trans. Craig Stephenson (1989; Scranton, PA: University of Scranton Press, 2008).

[22] Continuing from footnote 6 above, on the matter of Jung vis-à-vis emergence theory, Dr. Tresan's précis serves well. In his view, both Jung's Aristotelian template for dream actions and his keen lookout for the purposiveness at work in fateful children's dreams, emerging prior to the stage where a normal ego coheres, evoke teleology but also linger in the anterooms of current emergentist thinking. Theoretically speaking, Jung has fashioned one of the most tantalizing of transitional objects: an already/not-yet intuition of how the Aristotelian entelechy, with its aimed tendency or seed potency, needs to be deployed but also must be held, with even mightier process templates, on a short leash. Jung's reformulation of psychic energy already lends a necessary precondition to emergence, and the finalistic perspective undergoes strong ventilation by the long-gestated hypothesis of synchronicity. Also, his view of symbol formation, while baptized mathematically as the "transcendent function" in 1916, in today's terms can stand in for "the factor that catalyses emergent activity" (Tresan, "Jungian Metapsychology and Neurobiological Theory," 412), and Jung's umbrella term "synthetic method" a few years later can join these terms in heralding emergentist thinking (ibid.).

Fate, Freedom, Anticipation

Around the understanding that we are acted on or done unto by the objective psyche—or how we are dreamed, as he puts it in these sessions —Jung weaves a tapestry of reflections, in the combined sessions of these seminars, on the psychic anticipations of a life-span's destiny or line of fate.

In one potent example of anticipation—strictly dynamic but momentous—from the discussions of dreams, he notes the fateful aspect of the number three, which typically, either through repeated trials or rote repetition, "makes something *effective*" (*Children's Dreams*, 3 and 115), and thereby leads to the solution of the drama, or links one to a demonic factor. "What is most important happens *afterward*: a destiny is established. We can also formulate the idea this way: *the number three triggers the number four*, causes something that should establish the wholeness of the person" (ibid.). The calendar itself institutes three four-month partitions, astrology's trigons (*Children's Dreams*, 99). The same pivotal development can be seen here in this material, in the third of Perpetua's visions, where she is cleansed of the doubt that would have held her back from martyrdom (her unbaptized brother is cured of "cancer of the face, that is, of vision")—thereby opening a path to the fourth vision's gladiator trainer, with Perpetua's realization that "there is no way back." This third vision locks in the development, merging Perpetua's individual movement into the late second century's "transition . . . from deep darkness into a first dawning," both dimensions now sealed fatefully: "Once we know, we cannot *not* know" (below, 112). That third phase dramatically—quite literally so, as the *drama* or thing done—does unto her what she also at last chooses to do.

The movement into three, establishing effectiveness, of course (running or *dramema*), is also tragic drama's movement through its change point, usually with dawning awareness, into resolution. By way of this analogy, of drama to dream action powered by prime-number drivers, a dreamer gains the unity of that development—four as the unity of three—which commits the dreamer to knowing what he cannot unknow; thereafter, like it or not, small-d destiny is with the dreamer on that particular score. In this matter of how dream action builds, one can reap the final harvest of Jung's view by turning to his final reflection on "the necessary statement" vis-à-vis prime numbers in *Memories, Dreams, Reflections*, then going back to his essay on "The Phenomenon of Spirit in Fairytales," which amplifies the progression from three to four, and finally turning to related themes in Marie-Louise von Franz's *Number and Time*, which grows directly out of Jung's late reflections on natural numbers.[23] This is worth tracking if only because it unifies Jung's work around the force that impels realization, a force that can drop from sight when interpreters grow restive with the structural path to meaning in psychic processes.[24]

The bugaboo of teleology in current discussions of emergence, particularly in biology, from philosophers as notable as Marjorie Greene to the present, has run aground on a sandbar that Jung avoided when navigating the shoals of purpose or aim. Is destiny a matter of being enacted rather than acting, and therefore having little or nothing to say about fated factors? Well, no problem, but *only if* one manages gracefully to grant these gods their portion while at the same time reminding oneself that the 2 percent allotted to our individuality, our relative freedom,

[23] See chapter 11, "On Life after Death," in Jung, *Memories, Dreams, Reflections*, recorded and ed. Aniela Jaffé, trans. Richard and Clara Winston (New York: Pantheon, 1963), 310–11; Jung, "The Phenomenology of Spirit in Fairytales" (1945, 1948), CW 9.i, the supplement, §s 436–55; and Marie-Louise von Franz, *Number and Time: Reflections Leading toward a Unification of Depth Psychology and Physics*, trans. Andrea Dykes (Evanston, IL: Northwestern University Press, 1974), 109 ("Threefold rhythms are most probably connected with processes in space and time or with their realization in consciousness"), and 43–44 (dream actions tend to lay out three "phases of transformation" [Manfred Porkert: since 1975 the Munich sinologist and specialist in Chinese medicine], quite often with demonstrable ties to synchronicity, thereby reinstating psychophysical parallelism).

[24] David Miller, for one, lodges this complaint against von Franz, and implicitly against Jung in his 1948 essay, in "Fairy Tale or Myth?" *Spring* (1976): 158. Von Franz would have one come at folktales "set to perceive development (plot) and structure (form) as being the sole factors in determining narrative meaning." That is, von Franz and Jung contend that these are *primary* factors because of the plane on which they operate, where what they do leaves room for nothing else— and therefore leaves them as the *sole* agents, whereas there are other planes. However, a doctor, who wants to isolate praxis, *krisis*-peripety, and diagnostic summary does not at first mix those primaries with other, very interesting things. We are back to the action template's pragmatics or usefulness; the literary man does well to stand by the old analogy between medicine and poetics, or illness and tragedy, which discerns and retains a grip on all these matters.

James Hillman's emphasis on the necessity of the psychic image (not to be jockeyed so as to permit escape) by extension shakes hands with Jung's "cannot *not* know" factor in the fourth or unity-stage of three. Compare Hillman's "Responses" (to David Griffin), in *Archetypal Process: Self and Divine in Whitehead, Jung, and Hillman*, ed. David Ray Griffin (Evanston, IL: Northwestern University Press, 1989), 255–58.

is also acknowledged by *drama* or "the thing enacted." In other words, the predisposed drama demonstrably and repeatedly shows itself bearing witness to that 2 percent, in the bivalent quantum way spelled out above, much as the mandala shows us not only the psyche peering into its own psychic background but also peering at us. The processes that chug along without our having any say-so cyclically address our ability to engage in the whole drama; thus the dream series becomes our best window onto their waves of approach and withdrawal. In volume two here, that long-wave version of the process, which rises through several phases of approach to a classic turning point or *peripateia* and then disintegrates, Jung demonstrates at length from Cardano's dreams selected across a span of thirty-seven years.

In that respect, Jung's selection of childhood dreams recalled in adulthood, which are shown to anticipate long-term developments, provoke a particular reflection when set alongside the great Cardano's assiduously recorded dreams. While we have no such inaugural dream for Cardano, a polymath who developed his own variety of algebra, we do watch him, through Jung's heuristics, approaching the opportunity to grasp the nettle and then failing to do so. This illustrious achiever's missed appointment with an unrealized quotient of his destiny plants a sad flag where ordinary folk sometimes manage to heed the prompting—that is, they manage to collaborate with the kind of development demonstrably sketched by nature in the originating dreams of many children. Like death, what life lets one see from the psychological final viewpoint is democratic; psychic realization is correspondingly aristocratic, but not through some kind of guarantee.

In all of Jung's recorded seminars, there is nothing quite like his treatment of Cardano's selected dreams, showing "a circular [natural] process that proceeds on its own . . . [and] seems (with some reservation) to be a genuine series" (below, 195). This treatment, the centerpiece of these sessions, illustrates our topic here—namely, the demonstration of offstage prospective tendencies that complement or even contradict the ego's aims. The great physician and polymath Cardanus, Girolamo Cardano, Jerome Cardan, approaches "a deep caesura in life . . . when a fundamental change should occur but does not" (190–91), one that involves the dead, the future, and also "a problem of the age" (the lack of a philosophical attitude toward growth, below, 193), all leading to an outcome not apparent to the biographers: "So Cardanus really went to the dogs" (below, 194). Which is not to say, however, that Cardano was not rescued by the occasional anticipatory dream from a looming hazard: Jung closes the Cardano sequence with one such brief dream, in which the ominous snake is most likely not an awakened Kundalini but rather his clients the ruthless Borromei.

In the eleventh or next-to-last dream selected, the dream that most impressed Cardano, we are shown how ego ambition whips unconscious resources, as a mule, into its own service—"the whole of the unconscious is used for a purpose"—and so veils potential libido as a whole. In fact, an earlier dream also had featured a mule, where Jung had remarked its indication "that the unconscious will eventually give him a kick. But he will certainly make an easy profit without having to work hard," because the kick also implies fertilization (154). Therefore the unconscious later reflects itself back to Cardano as his mule once more while also confronting him, in a Milano that turns to Naples but is also named "Whip," with libido that otherwise would have guided or led him differently (211–212). The dream compensatorily puts on show those aspects of libido that, other than being mounted and ridden, have been swept aside or subjugated. And what was thus exploited is primary, "because we would expect order in consciousness and disorder in the unconscious, whereas it's exactly the other way around" (167). One might say that the natural, circular unconscious process typically shows us an image-circle, or *mandalam*, whose as-if purposiveness contrasts with the *ambit* or circle of our ambition. Our attitude toward the tendency of a given dream process accordingly proves to be fateful.

However, Jung shows that the process *has already indicated* that Cardano missed this appointment with part of his destiny, by dealing with the dream of the black sun out of chronology; whereas it falls fifth in calendar terms, Jung advances it to ninth place in his own sequencing. In the lived cycle, the drama's turning point thus anticipates matters that Jung has it illuminate in retrospect. (Using the introductory chart below, and rearranging the teaching-sequence numbers according to the corresponding calendar dates, the chronology as it was lived runs as follows: 1, 2, 4, 5, 6, 9, 10, 7, n.d.[8], 3, 11, n.d.[12] [where underlined 9 is the peripeteia or turning point].) Jung's teaching sequence therefore moves this chronologically prior 9, the black sun dream, three places further along, so as to have it cast light—the enantiodromic swing to black light, the unconscious *as such*—onto the two preceding dreams (7 and 8 in the teaching sequence). Of those, Jung has moved Alexander's lion combat, which fell four years after the peripety, into line with the brief wolf-slaying dream set at the papal court, where Cardano is shown capable of killing off his ambition directly. By following this pair—the repositioned lion combat and undated wolf slaying—with the chronologically prior turning point of eclipsed consciousness, Jung displays the peripety *as if* it grew out of Cardano's tyranny, which prevented him from living up to the potential shown in the other two dreams. The *anticipation* of a development is thus made to *backlight* it as well. Jung's teaching trick—slyly we are presented with the backlighting first, sans explanation—builds in delayed recognition or *heureka!*, demonstrating that nature has more than one way of writing like Dickens. Jung thereby pays his seminar participants the compliment of being curious enough to con the dating, of inferring his reason for changing the placement of the drama's turning point in the queue, and of perceiving nature's elegance in giving advance notice of the fateful blackout of conscious potential if Cardano lets ambition ride his psychosoma-mule. Jung refracts the process template through a time prism so as to alert us, from more than one angle, to an achronic ratio of fate to freedom. That is, in the untangling of determined tensions, room remains for recognition and response, biology's equivalent of the *kairos* moment, a ripeness beckoning to adequacy and courage.

Remaining inscrutable, that dynamic ratio of course resists speculative summaries. Nonetheless, if four psychic functions orient us and if time is likewise "a psychological function," then nature not only issues commands but also, when we manage to intervene (a very recent possibility, as Jung remarks in this survey of dreaming), dramatizes "living as such" through disclosing a line more fundamental than our purposes. (If you mean to die for this, Perpetua, then we shall collaborate with you from the ground up, but we shall not push you.) This fifth function also hints at a goal other than our cherished objectives. (If you wish to make a killing with your gifts, Signore Professore Dottore Cardano, go right ahead, but finally we shall ironize your greatness.) In Jung's phrase, life dreams *us* rather than letting us dream *it*, working as a master *function*, finally *heuristic* or theatrical, like the old oracles spelling out cues to effectuality and realization but explaining nothing. Jung's way of teaching, in this respect, shadows a developmental power that, although it engages freedom with destiny, declines to do more than hang out, sans explanations, along the tension arc of heuristics.

In the light of these themes, the selective survey of dream interpretation Jung assigned tellingly invests the Romantic era, and Kant's philosophy of the inscrutable *noumenon* at work behind phenomena, with a caveat Jung spelled out during the session devoted to Lersch's history of the dream in Romanticism. Reading from Dr. Charlotte Spitz's paper, to the effect that a generally Romantic view respected "an ultimate 'ungraspable' behind everything . . . Reality . . . cannot be seized,'" he reminds the group that Kant was read in his own time with a specifically helium lift in feeling, which construed appearances as emanating from something unknowable, as illusions possessing reality. Jung then cites Goethe's invocation of refraction in *Faust II*: "We have life only in its flung-off colors" (below, 80). The teaching moment at this juncture, which takes up a whole generation's expansive feeling for the reading of Kant, sweetly leaves the seminar participants to reflect on certain changes of collective epistemic mood over the long haul. For it is only a few steps from this Romantic reception of Kant, by way of Paul Carus and Eduard von Hartmann, to Schopenhauer's Aristotle and Driesch, where the same *noumenon*, now in Jung's backyard, throws off refractions, this time, of the scrupulous awe incited by the veiled directedness of individuation. This brief stretch of Jung's discussion nicely illustrates how his way of teaching insinuated leaps from the assigned texts, and from responses by participants, to a nearly palpable but ever-elusive process relationship.

All of Jung's seminars transmit the sense, in their meandering cross-disciplinary expositional colloquies, of being as freehand as Max Beckmann's ink drawings for Goethe's *Faust II* while also being capable of resolving momentarily into the solidity of a panel by Piero della Francesca. Yet his seminars remain poised among opposing alternatives, quantum-exploratory *and* pragmatically judicious, as in the Mozartean second coda to the Cardano section in this seminar, where it's No Go the Kundalini and Yes to saving one's hide as an MD. Jung's Beckmann-Piero palette constantly resolves into Thomas Eakins's portrait of surgeon Samuel Gross, demonstrating with scalpel in his clinic.

In conclusion, the parallel major theme in these sessions, which it shares with the urgent reflections on contemporary events in both the *Zarathustra* and *Visions* seminars, I shall sketch in a few brushstrokes only. Outbreaks of conflict in history, and paradigm shifts in the psychic depths, are both topical throughout these discussions because they are suffered—that is, because they keenly affect individuals' chances for adequately reading their own barometers and working out their destinies. Perpetua, like both Tertullian and Justin Martyr, was engulfed by the condensation of a new spiritual direction then ripening in the Roman ecumene. When it came time collectively to reassimilate pagan antiquity into a waning Christian culture in the Renaissance, the polymath Cardano mirrored the implosive-explosive tension between recuperation and novel reach in his precise, impressive, but also overweening ambitions. Finally, such impact on the single person from outside stands as close as the Great War, Europe's first round of suicide. There Dr. John Hubbard exemplifies the impact Jung had studied closely and deeply in his own case, when precognitive dreams of that war precipitated the initial plunge into his protracted work on *Liber Novus* or the *Red Book*. Had Jung known more about Hubbard in the late 1930s, this brother doctor might have struck him as a weaker reed. Nonetheless, Hubbard's material, the subject of Jung's first seminar on dream material coming directly after the Great War, returns here on the eve of World War II as the contemporary example of a heuristically lucid dialogue between outer conflict and inner grappling, and of being dreamed by conflict while dreaming it.

Jung's surveys in this vein have a direct bearing on the matter of unintentional aim in the psychic process. That bearing comes from the steely point of the fate stylus, which writes large in shared life but jots its sharp miniscule within us. Its nib inscribes on both scales, inviting us to audition for roles in a big shindy, but also simply pressing down hard from wars and the rumors of wars, revolutions and pogroms, financial earthquakes, propaganda floods, and climate-forcings. Jung's way of seeing things does not parallel Kafka's great tale "The Penal Colony," which enacts a major cultural shift around a primitive, bodily, ritual enactment of just such inscription. Instead, with his eye on the semiobscure, semirevelatory hints from psychic process about the line of fate anticipated in children's dreams, or on the responsive tremors in the dreams of Perpetua and Dr. John Hubbard, Jung takes life's pulse. For life remains unrealized if merely imposed by *Heimarmene* or the stars, but becomes effectual through the 2 percent factor when that touches fate's wiry line. *Eureka*, something there! Heuristics, or something to take careful note of, again and again.

A. Older Literature on Dream Interpretation

CHAPTER 1

Macrobius: *Commentarius ex Cicerone in Somnium Scipionis*[1]

Paper by W. Bächtold

Mr. Bächtold: Macrobius lived around AD 400. He was a Neoplatonist in Rome who wrote in support of pagan antiquity. Besides his commentary on Cicero's *Somnium Scipionis*, to be discussed here, his works are the *Saturnalia* and contributions to grammar.

The text of Scipio's dream in Cicero's *De re publica* is extant only in the work of Macrobius, and has been reconstructed from that source. The dreamer is Scipio Africanus Junior (*Africanus Minor*). He lived from 185 to 129 BC, dying at fifty-six (= eight times seven years, which will be important later on). By adoption he became the grandson of Scipio (*Africanus Maior*). In 146 he conquered Carthage, and in 133 Numantia. He was killed in 129 BC.

Scipio visited Africa together with his invited friend Masinissa. They discussed Scipio Senior (*Africanus Maior*), who had defeated Hannibal. The following night he dreamed:

> [Abbreviated summary] Africanus Maior—his spiritual father—appears to him and prophesies that he, the son, would destroy Carthage in two years. At first he would be sent to various countries as a legate, then become consul, and finally dictator and restorer of the state. He would

---

[1] Ambrosius Aurelius Theodosius Macrobius, *In Somnium Scipionis.* As in *Macrobe, Varron et Pomponius Méla* (Latin and French), trans. D. Nisard, ed. M. Nisard (1850; Paris: Dubochet, Le Chevalier, and Garnier, 1883) (G).

For an English translation since the 1930s, see William Harris Stahl, trans. and introduction, *Commentary on the Dream of Scipio by Macrobius* (1952; New York: Columbia University Press, 1990).

achieve pre-eminence, provided that his relatives did not kill him be-
forehand. Then he is told that those who had distinguished themselves
by their virtues [virtutes] would live on after death. At that point young
Scipio professes his wish to die. His father warns him that he is not allowed to do, for that would arrogate a right reserved to the gods. His
father then reveals heaven with its nine spheres, and then the earth,
divided into several zones. Finally, his father reveals to him the immortality and divinity of the soul, declaring, "deum te esse scitare."[2]

This dream was recorded by Cicero, and Macrobius wrote a long commentary on it. Chapters 1 and 2 of his contribution contain the introduction and philosophical disputations; in the third chapter he presents a classification of dreams into five categories:

1. *somnium:*   dreams proper

2. *visio:*   vision (*la vision*)

3. *oraculum:*   oracle (*l'oracle*)

4. *insomnium:* (*le rêve*) [dream image, insomnia]

5. *visum:*   phantasm, phantasmagoria (*le spectre*) [dream vision, ap-
                 parition]

According to Macrobius, the last two categories are not worthy of
explanation, because they contain nothing divine (*divinatio*): in the *insomnium* we experience the same as in waking daily life, the same hard-
ships and labors. These dreams are about our love, our enemies, about
food, money, or prestige, in the sense that sometimes we win them,
sometimes we lose them. The *insomnium* is gone with the night, lacks
meaning and significance, and in no way can we profit from it. The
visum appears when we are neither asleep nor awake, but still in a semi-

[2] The Latin text is inexact, for *deum te igitur scito esse* (Know therefore that you are god [or, (a)
god (within)]). See Cicero, *De Re Publica* bk.VI.26, and cf. below, 11. In his edition of Cicero's
text, James Zetzel (Cambridge: Cambridge University Press, 1995, 250) says, "Cicero's emphatic
statement of the distinction between mortal body and immortal soul, and of the identification of
the person with the soul rather than the body (or the combined soul and body) is Platonic (cf.
especially *Phaedrus* 115c–e and *Laws* 12.959ab.)." Cicero restates his point, referring to this part
of *On the Republic*, in his *Tusculan Disputations* I.xxii.53: "But if the soul turns out not to know
the nature of the soul itself, tell me, please, will it ever know that it exists, not even know that it
moves? This is the basis of Plato's argument expounded by Socrates in the *Phaedrus* (A. E. Douglas, ed. and trans. [Warminster: Aris and Phillips, 1985]).

conscious state. Fantasy figures appear that cannot be found in nature. They dance around us, sometimes instilling joy, sometimes sadness. People believe that stomachache in sleep is caused by these creatures. So these two kinds of dreams cannot help us read the future.

This case is different with the other three kinds. The *oracle* presents itself as follows: an honorable, important person appears (father, mother, priest, deity) and enlightens us about what we ought or ought not to do, what is or is not going to happen. The *vision* is a look into the future. We dream of something that will happen shortly afterward, for instance, of a friend who will visit us. The *dream proper* (*somnium*) invariably expresses itself, according to Macrobius, figuratively (symbolically), and in such a confusing way that we have to interpret it. This dream proper is divided into five subcategories:

a. *proprium*: about the dreamer himself, in an active or passive role

b. *alienum*: about another person

c. *commune*: the common experience of a group in the dream

d. *publicum*: about a community: city, square, theater, etc.

e. *generale*: the universe (heaven, stars, earth) speaks to the dreamer to tell him something new.

In Scipio's dream, we can find the first three categories and all five subcategories: (1.) the oracle (his grandfather Africanus explains the future to him); (2.) the vision (he sees the place where he will live after his death); (3.) the dream (without interpretation it is impossible to understand what he has been told). The five subcategories can be found as follows in the dream: (a) proprium (he, Scipio, is led to the higher regions); (b) alienum (he sees other souls in the realm of the dead; (c) commune (what he sees also relates to him, because after his death he will have the same experience); (d) publicum (dealing with Rome's victory over Carthage); (e) generale (he sees movements in the heavens and hears the music of the spheres).

How is it that Scipio has such a "great dream," being still a simple soldier at that moment? The general view was that such dreams were dreamed only by the "*magistratus et rector rei publicae*."[3] The answer to

---

[3] Latin: the leader and ruler of the community or state.

this question therefore would be: because Scipio is *initiated* into the secrets of nature, excels in manly bravery and virtues (*virtutes*), and distinguishes himself by worldly wisdom.

Virgil speaks of the two gates of the underworld, through which dreams come, one made of ivory, the other of horn. According to Virgil, *true* dreams come from the gate of horn alone. Porphyry[4] explains this as follows: "Truth hides; however, the soul can sometimes see it when the body has gone to sleep and gives the soul more freedom. The rays of the deity reach our eye only in a refracted way, as if the light were shining through horn."

In the fourth chapter of the book, on the goal and intent of the dream, Macrobius tells us that deserving souls return to heaven and enjoy eternal blessedness, which is worth more than any worldly fame.

And now, unbelievable as it may be to our eyes, Macrobius begins interpreting the dream in exactly the same way that we do in our seminar. He examines one part of the dream after the other, looking for parallels in mythology. In particular he draws on *Orphic*, *Pythagorean*, and *Platonic* teachings.

I would like to treat this method in greater detail, as we must follow the same procedure in the interpretation of a dream. As we know, dreams often express themselves in symbolic language, give no more than allusions, or are incomplete. Ideas appear, or better, images, which at first have no meaning for us at all. We have to enrich these images, infuse them with meaning, give them content. Of course this should not be done arbitrarily, but according to a very specific method. We have to enrich the dream with ideas, submit it to comparison. Hence we could speak of an amplifying and comparative method.

An analogy exists in comparative anatomy. An animal's organ seems unintelligible from a purely morphological point of view, but as soon as we view it with the help of comparative anatomy, that organ is seen in context and is full of meaning. We draw on several ancillary sciences, such as embryology, paleontology, etc. In a similar way, we also use ancillary arts, such as the mythologies of all peoples and countries, sagas and folktales, religions, and history. In these fields we are looking for parallels to a given motif. And we find them; further connections and explanations often emerge, accounting for why something is one way or the other.

[4] Porphyry (ca. 232–ca. 304), Greek Neoplatonist.

Perhaps it was even easier for Macrobius than for us. As a man of antiquity, for him mythological concepts were much more alive. He drew on the whole body of Pythagorean, Orphic, and Platonic teachings and cosmology for his commentary, proceeding quite comprehensively, so that here it is impossible to give an account of everything. I must limit myself to the most interesting points.

Macrobius selects various dream passages that deserve special attention. He begins with the phrase in which Scipio Africanus Maior says to the younger man, verbatim:

> For when your age will have completed eight times seven recurring rotations of the sun, and when these two numbers, each of which—although for different reasons—is considered to be full, will have completed, according to the natural rotation, that number of life years imposed on you, then the attention of the whole country will be directed toward you and your name, ... etc. .... if you escape the treacherous hands of your relatives (chapter 5).

Then follows a discussion of numbers in general, and of seven and eight in particular. When man lets his thoughts gradually rise from objects in nature toward divine phenomena, numbers are an intermediary stage between the actual phenomena and the divine. For bodies can change, due to their molecular composition, but numbers are quasi-eternal values, beyond becoming and passing away. Macrobius speaks of the *plenitudo*, the "fullness" of numbers. His train of thought is as follows: we have a body that has a certain number of areas and lines, and although the body is something material, in relation to it areas and lines are immaterial. This is even truer for numbers in relation to lines.

Professor Jung: We can see how precisely Macrobius is proceeding here, and one will either marvel at it or be bored stiff. But let us not forget that the book was written 1,500 years ago. Concepts then were not yet as precise as they are today; still, concepts had to be conceived, mostly in a very long-winded way. This is simply an aside about the interesting way in which human thinking has developed.

Mr. Bächtold: Among the numbers, the *number eight* is particularly *plenus*.[5] It is composed of $4 + 4 = 2 + 2 + 2 + 2$. In addition, the eight has an extraordinary relation to heavenly harmony. Moreover, eight is composed of the prime number 7 and the monad 1. So we are dealing

---

[5] Latin: full, completed, strong, resonant, perfect.

with the Pythagorean number system here. Macrobius also says that for Pythagoreans eight is the symbol of *aequitas*, that is, equity, balance, etc.

Chapter 6 offers similar speculations about the number seven: 4 + 3 = 7; 4 x 7 = 28. Humans have seven organs, etc.

In chapter 7 Macrobius discusses a significant afterthought: "if you escape the treacherous hands of your relatives." In his opinion this is curious: why does the speaker not know for sure if it will happen or not? Disturbing prophecies are always ambiguous, but they contain correlations that can lead to the path of truth, if the interpretation is made wisely and perceptively. The dream alludes to what may happen, not what will. We can escape such a fate if we are prudent, but to accomplish it we need our mind and skill as antagonists in the effort. One can appease the gods by sacrifices, for instance.

We see from this passage that Macrobius interprets it in exactly the same way that we would. The dream shows *possibilities*; it is ambiguous with regard to the future. When we deal with dream interpretation, we will incline toward fatalism. Human freedom no longer seems to exist, because everything is predetermined anyway. But the dream is ambiguous and ambivalent with regard to the future. It shows possibilities, and we just might succeed in averting a threatening fate and "placate the gods" by intense devotion or conscious working through.

Let me remind you of the mountain climber's dreams that Professor Jung once related. The dreamer made light of them and then indeed fell to his death.[6] So we see that a dream can also warn us.

Furthermore, chapter 10 holds a certain interest. Scipio asks in the dream if his father and the dead in general are still living. Macrobius outlines the whole ancient view of the underworld and continued existence after death, in particular Platonic ideas: the body is the grave of the soul (Plato). I will give only a short sketch of the Platonic doctrine of the soul. Before birth the soul is a sphere,[7] that is, it is still a unity because opposites do not yet exist. (We also find a parallel in the Chinese sphere.)

---

[6] Such a dream is told in C. G. Jung, CW 16, para. 323.
[7] Cf. *Children's Dreams Seminar*, 38n16.

Then this sphere proceeds to birth, to incarnation. It then loses its spherical shape, that is, its unity. The soul wanders on the Milky Way from heaven to earth. The Milky Way intersects the astrological zodiac in Cancer and Capricorn, the two gates of the sun. The first gate, Cancer, is the gate of man, while the second gate, Capricorn, is the gate of the gods. Through the first gate souls descend to earth, through the second they return. Macrobius says about the Milky Way that milk is an infant's first food. According to Pythagoras it is the first step of descent, the first impulse toward earthly embodiment. As the sphere descends, the *monad* becomes a *dyad*. It enters into the world, the body, the forest, into *hyle* (substance, matter).[8] According to Plato, it gets "drunk." In this drunken state the soul flows further downward and receives specific characteristics from each planet.

Planets	Specific characteristics
Saturn	reason, logic
Jupiter	energy
Mars	passion
Sun	feeling and phantasy
Venus	wishes and desires
Mercury	capability of expression
Moon	procreativeness

These ideas are taken over by Macrobius and formulated with the help of the corresponding dream text of Scipio (cf. figure):

The first of these circles is the celestial circle (zodiac, fixed stars), which encompasses all the others, itself being the highest god. The eternal, rotating orbits of the stars are attached to it. Below are the seven circles (planetary orbits), which move backwards, in a direction opposite to the rotation of the heaven.

[8] *Hyle*, Greek for wood or forest, was Aristotle's term for matter or substance, as opposed to *eidos* (form).

(Then follows a list of the planets, starting with the farthest out: Saturn, Jupiter, Mars, Sun, Venus, Mercury, Moon.) All that is underneath this is mortal and transient, except for souls, the gods' gift to humankind. Everything above the moon is eternal. For earth's globe is immobile and the lowest of all. All matter is drawn toward it by its gravitational force.

The dream of Scipio tells the following about the soul:

> For humans were created on condition of their being the guardians of the globe, which you see in the middle of this temple, and which is called earth. Man has been given a soul from those eternal fires that you call the heavenly bodies and stars. They are round and spherical, animated by divine spirits. They complete their circles, paths of marvelous velocity.

Macrobius remarks that Cicero uses the word *animus*[9] in both the correct and incorrect senses, because *animus* is mind and reason (*mens*), and no one doubts that it is more divine than the *anima*.[10] Animus, however, often means anima. On the one hand, we have a *mind*, *animus*, originating in those eternal fires we share with heaven and the stars; on the other hand, we have a *spirit*, *anima*, imprisoned in the body, cut off from the divine *mens*.

At the end of this discussion Macrobius summarizes the concept of the *soul* in different philosophers:

Plato calls it   "that which moves itself"
Xenocrates   "the self-moving number"
Aristotle   "*entelechy*," i.e., something carrying its purpose (its goal) within itself
Pythagoras and Philolaus   "harmony"
Posidonius   "idea"
Asclepiades   "concurrent exercitation of the five senses"
Hippocrates   "subtle pneuma that is distributed throughout the whole body"
Heraclides Ponticus   "light"
Heraclitus   "spark of the stellar essence"[11]

---

[9] Latin: mind, intellect, soul, feelings, heart, spirit, courage, character, pride, air.

[10] Latin: wind, breathing, soul, life, heart. One should also note in this connection that Cicero's usage of *mens* may adopt a shift already made, in later Platonism, from *psyche* for soul to *mens*: see Zetzel, *De Re Publica*, by Cicero, 250.

[11] *Scintilla stellaris essentiae*.

Zeno	"condensed spirit in the body" (a spirit concentrated in the body)
Democritus	"spirit between the atoms, so mobile that it penetrates every body"
Critolaus	"originating in the quintessence"
Hipparchus	"fire"
Anaximenes	"air"
Empedocles and Critias	"blood"
Parmenides	"originating in earth and fire"
Epicurus	"a kind of mixture of fire, air, and spirit."

For all these philosophers, the soul is immaterial and immortal.

There follow further discussions based on the dream, about astrology, stars and fixed stars, the sun and its various names, and finally the harmony of the spheres and music.

Scipio contemplates suicide in the dream, because life would be only the "death of the soul," but this is denied to him, because only the gods may free us from the earth. If we leave this life by suicide, we will not be purified, and our souls will float around the earth.

In the twelfth chapter of Book II, Scipio writes that he has heard a dream full of wisdom. First he is told the hour in which he will die through treachery. Thus he learns to despise transient life. To encourage him after this frightening message, he is shown that he will live after death as a wise and good citizen. When he wants to commit suicide, his natural father Paulus appears and prevents him. Thus his soul is temperate in hope and fear, but capable of divine contemplation.

Then Macrobius's discourse reaches its climax, leading to the end of the treatise, where Scipio is told, *"Deum te esse citare,"*[12] that is, the soul is not only immortal but also a god. This is revealed to him only after he has discovered what is frail and mortal, having no part in divinity.

In summary, we can say that three important points are touched upon in Macrobius's treatise:

(1) The concept of different kinds of dreams and their meaning: this ancient classification continued through the Middle Ages, and even today our view is still really no different. As we know, the Middle Ages took over the whole philosophy and natural science of antiquity. But

---

[12] As noted above, on 4, Cicero's text correctly reads, *"deum te igitur scito esse"* (know therefore that you are god).

while ancient scientific texts were subjected to a certain experimental verification at the beginning of modernity, "dream science" not only made no progress but also was even neglected and forgotten. In my view, it is now the task of our time to subject this neglected field to a thorough examination, because the neglected unconscious exercises a poisoning, destructive effect, with catastrophic effects on today's politics and economy.

(2) The method of dream interpretation in antiquity: today we use essentially the same method, as I have shown. Now, however, even more material is at our disposal, in that we have found customs and religions in non-European countries that are extraordinarily old or primitive, that is, primordial.

(3) The dream as an initiation: for ancient man the dream is a *religious* experience, a preparation for death, the great finale of life.

Professor Jung: From the paper we have seen very clearly that antiquity interpreted dreams in exactly the same way as we do. As far as the strange metaphysics is concerned, which Macrobius brings up in connection with dreams, one can add that even though the soul as a spherical object is alien to us, we still dream of it in that way. It's a well-known archaic idea. I'd like to give you an example. I treated a woman from America who stayed in Europe for some time. Midway through a series of interconnected dreams, suddenly a strange, short, and impressive dream appeared:[13]

The dreamer is alone in a house. Evening falls, and it occurs to her that she now must close the shutters and windows. She slowly starts to feel creepy. She locks everything. Then she remembers that a back door is still open, which she still must lock. She goes to that door and tries to lock it, but then discovers that the door has no lock and cannot be secured. The dreamer is stupefied, her fear mounts, and she thinks about ways of locking the door nevertheless. It gets darker and darker, and suddenly the door flies open, and something black and round shoots into her stomach. She wakes up with a scream.

I told her that this had to be something telepathic, and that she should memorize the exact date and write down the dream. It was a house she

[13] This dream is also discussed in vol. 1, chap. 1.

had last visited twenty years ago. One of her aunts lived there, whom she had never seen since. She was completely cut off from her, and had heard nothing from her. She didn't even know if that aunt were still alive. Three weeks later she received a letter from a niece, saying that the aunt had died that very day. This is the telepathic effect, which always takes the form of a "visitation," meaning, "it announced itself." This *visitatio*[14] is often represented by a spherical psychic effect. This is an *ancient* idea, which she definitely had not learned in school, and so was new to her.

Platonic concepts were also developed out of experiences like the one in this dream. And Plato already encountered a theory according to which the soul was spherical in shape. There must have been a whole *corpus* of esoteric theories that taught transmigration. Transmigration is an original theory, rising out of immemorial darkness, from times that were stamped, as it were, by such experiences, a period that also harbored the experiences of medicine men or priests. Our knowledge eventually developed out of just such experiences.[15] These experiences are authoritative for us, too, as a description of certain facts and as psychological case histories. So it is to our advantage if we are able to resort to such ideas.

[14] Latin: visit, visitation.

[15] Jung's extension of intellectual history into the immemorial is Macrobian, and therefore would have been demeaned by modern scholars until quite recently. Lynn Thorndike, for instance, describes Macrobius's esteem for the universally comprehensive character of Virgil and Cicero's texts as "extremist." For like Philo, he writes, Macrobius attributed to their single writings, notably Cicero's treatment of Scipio's dream, the ability to supply universal knowledge, indeed that it "was a work second to none and contained the entire substance of philosophy" (*The Place of Magic in the Intellectual History of Europe* [New York: Columbia University Press, 1905], 106).

·· CHAPTER 2 ··

Artemidorus: *Five Books on the Art of Dream Interpretation*

Paper by Grete Adler

Ms. Adler: My paper is based on the monograph of Monsieur Edmond Le Blant[1] on Artemidorus of Daldis and his work in five books,[2] one of the main sources for the treatment of dreams in antiquity and also for ancient superstition. As a philologist in the spirit of the nineteenth century, Le Blant had only minimal interest in, and even less understanding of, the dream as a research topic, and his study gives but an inadequate picture of Artemidorus.

On the maternal side, he was descended from Daldis in Lydia[3] and was initiated into the mysteries of Apollo Daldianus. He lived during the second century AD and wrote, "upon Apollo's appeal," as he says,

[1] Edmond Le Blant, *Artémidore* (Paris: Editions Klincksieck, 1899) (G).

[2] "Artemidorus of Daldis . . . has furnished us with the most complete and careful elaboration of dream-interpretation as it existed in the Graeco-Roman world" (Sigmund Freud, *The Interpretation of Dreams*, trans. A. A. Brill [New York: Random House, 1950], 10n2).

"Born in Ephesus, one of the intellectual centers of Asia Minor, Artemidorus lived during the Antonine Age of the second century C.E. . . . One of the distinctive features of the work produced by the savants of the era [including Philostratus, Galen, Ptolemy, and Pausanias] was its encyclopaedic quality. . . . His fieldwork, his delineation of the types of dreams, his attention to the relevance of context to oneiric meaning, and his methodology for the 'translation' of dream image to experiential situation: all these bear the mark of the systematizing intellectual curiosity of his age. . . . In Lane Fox's pithy description, 'his conversation and notes embraced all classes, a well-to-do woman in Italy who dreamed she was riding an elephant, members of the upper classes in the Greek cities, orators, Roman knights, a tax collector, convicts and criminals, the poor, the sick and the slaves,' as well as numerous athletes, rhetors, and sophists" (Patricia Cox Miller, *Dreams in Late Antiquity: Studies in the Imagination of a Culture* [Princeton, NJ: Princeton University Press, 1974], 77–78).

[3] An ancient kingdom of Asia Minor (Anatolia), known to Homer as Mæonia.

five books on the art of dream interpretation that to a large extent have been preserved. (His books on other branches of the art of divination have been lost, however.) The fourth volume contains a polemic on dream interpretation, that is, rejoinders to skeptics; the fifth volume collects prophetic dreams that have come true. His son likewise became a dream interpreter and also lived in Daldis.

In Le Blant's view, Artemidorus is merely a scientific compiler and a source for ancient customs and curiosities, a pantheon of ancient cults.

Professor Jung: Artemidorus is more of a practitioner, but naturally a learned man as well and not just a compiler. He himself worked on about three thousand dreams.

Ms. Adler: Gods as dream motifs were at the center of his interest. Also of importance were the circus, the theater, illnesses, mortal danger and death, seafaring, the dream of the slave's escape, and so on. These motifs are of pivotal importance, and more or less intelligible to us if we take into account the special position of ancient man toward such phenomena in his life. We must see them at first in the way a peasant dreams of cattle, or an Arab of a camel. What makes ancient dream language so alien and inaccessible to me, however, are those hundreds of little motifs from the most intimate everyday occurrences in antiquity: motifs referring to customs, quoted verses, details of cults, proverbial sayings, and so on. These confront us in much the same way that automobiles, streetcars, postage stamps, electric bells, or household appliances would confront a Roman or Greek looking at our dreams. Our reading of Artemidorus is complicated by the intimacy of ancient dream language. We'd have to have an extremely good knowledge of history and myth to follow clearly the ancient dream drama. In the dreams quoted by Artemidorus, gods, temples, and cults abound, just as they did in the domestic and public life of antiquity. Le Blant writes, "In the age of Artemidorus, the dominant idea seems to have been reverential awe toward the gods. In fact, the greatest part of the *Oneirocritica,*[4] on their temples and statues, is about them."

A dream sequence about offering a sacrifice, for instance, could carry a positive meaning, as could the adorning of temples or statues, the making of music before the gods, and so on. But just as easily the same

---

[4] Greek: dream interpretation. Oneiros is the Greek god of dreams (G).

sequence could indicate something bad; sacrifices could be a sign that the person offering them is guilty of offending the god. As for the god's cult image, it led exactly the life of an ancient king. When someone in a dream washed or anointed the god, that act signified making amends for having offended the deity. It was equally frightening for a dream to show that a god had vacated its dwelling. This was equivalent to an enemy having abducted the local god after inflicting a defeat. It was also a bad omen in a dream if the gods offered sacrifices to each other, because that meant that they had not received enough sacrifices from human beings. Only if the gods appeared *exactly* according to the cult regime, with all the proper emblems and paraphernalia, was it a good omen. "If the immortals were seen to appear differently than how one could have expected, without their attributes and faculties, that was an ominous sign: Pan without his rural clothing, dressed according to Roman fashion, Asclepius[5] enthroned as a judge, Hecate with only one head" (Le Blant). I don't know why it was so frightening for the deity not to act exactly according to tradition and cult in the dream. Might it be the primitive's fear of the unusual, of a new and unknown situation?

Professor Jung: A deviation from ritual instills anxiety. Each deity expresses a certain vital psychological fact. Each modification also means a modification of the *psychological* material, and thus danger or conflict, a conflict with precisely the god who expresses that fact. If the god in the dream has changed, then the dreamer is about to deviate from the benevolent and upright principle and will thus incur the wrath of the gods. He is "a blasphemer," so to speak.

Ms. Adler: Also, when two hostile deities appeared in the same dream, that was seen as negative, probably because ancient man was afraid of being crushed by the dichotomy of two such mighty principles. An equally negative omen in dreams was an appearance by any of the Egyptian and Near Eastern gods, although they had found a home in Rome and Greece and were officially recognized.

Professor Jung: One must take into account the actual mindset of antiquity in the second century. It was characterized by an artificially superimposed Isis cult, and Eastern syncretism. The Romans no longer

[5] Greek god of healing.

had an understanding of their own cults, and they were drawn to the most alien deities. For Artemidorus, when these cults appeared in a dream they were dangerous, because those powers undermined ancient cultural identity.

Ms. Adler: Further important motifs to be listed are: the circus, the theater, athletic contests, gladiators, athletes, actors, and flautists. Le Blant writes: "When we read this work, theatrical and circus performances—apart from the fear of gods—seem to have preoccupied people the most. The Olympic and Nemean Games[6] are mentioned on every page, as well as the combats between wild animals and gladiators of all kinds: *retiarii*,[7] *hoplomachi*,[8] *dimachairi*,[9] athletes, acrobats, pugilists,[10] actors, mimes, flautists. Certain dream interpretations in it promise them victories, crowns, and cenotaphs."

Professor Jung: This is the particular dream language of antiquity. Dreams of primitives, on the other hand, speak a very different language. For instance, they dream of a lizard that does strange things, or of dangers and phenomena that are completely alien to us.

As a rule, only meaningful dreams were recorded in antiquity, because only they were important. Nobody paid attention to ordinary dreams. There are also different *dream styles*; certain dreams, for instance, can be dreamed only in America. They have a specific local color.

Ms. Adler: Executions and sensational trials seem to have appeared frequently in dreams. These motifs, indicating guilt, moral problems, and fear of punishment, may still represent some part of the psychology of ancient man, but already lead to problems and symbols with which we are familiar from Christian culture. There is the cross, but still only with the negative connotation it had in antiquity. "The image of crucified men haunted their minds. Like them, one had to bear one's cross, that is, die. Whoever in their dream carried Pluto, Cerberus, or any other demon of the underworld on his shoulders also had to die. The

---

[6] The Nemean Games were one of the four Panhellenic Games of Ancient Greece and were held at Nemea every two years. Like the Olympic Games, they were held in honor of Zeus.

[7] The *retiarius* (net-man) was a gladiator who wore no armor and used a net and a trident.

[8] The *hoplomachus* was a particularly well-armed gladiator, equipped with a thrusting spear and a short sword or dagger.

[9] The *dimachairus* was a gladiator who fought with two swords, one in each hand.

[10] Fistfighters.

same fate awaited a malefactor who dreamed that he danced with wide-spread arms or flew away in the air" (Le Blant).[11]

So much for the motifs in ancient dreams. I shall mention certain other less frequent motifs in a short discussion of the methodology of ancient dream interpretation. Then as today, one seems to have used the association method in order to interpret a dream. However, we will look in vain for any indication that Artemidorus used a dreamer's *personal* association material to unravel the dream. For ancient man, the *individual* problem seems to have been much less central than for Christians and average people today. The numerous myths of gods and heroes were always at hand as association material. Serapis,[12] for example, is identified with Pluto,[13] because his name also consists of seven letters. The sight of Bacchus in a child's dream was a bad omen.

Professor Jung: Dionysus[14] is seen as dangerous in a dream, because his cult liberates the instincts. In the Villa dei Misteri[15] there are representations of orgiastic cults. Young goats are torn apart by the Maenads[16] with their teeth. Raw flesh was devoured in the orgies, an expression of the renewed liberation of the animal nature of man. The Dionysus cult is vegetation and fertility magic; it gave the feeling of being born again.

Ms. *Adler:* In addition, and as already mentioned above, all kinds of other data from collective mental life were used as association material, for instance from sayings, from famous or then fashionable literary productions, and so on.

Although we find no individual association materials and only few individual problems, Artemidorus's art of dream interpretation all the more took into account the dreamer's *concrete* life situation; for example,

[11] Cf. the analogous contemporary dream in C. G. Jung, CW 16, paras. 323ff. (G).

[12] Egyptian god of fertility.

[13] The Roman name for Hades, the Greek god of the underworld.

[14] The Thracian god of wine, also known as Bacchus in both Greek and Roman mythology. He is viewed as the promoter of civilization, a lawgiver, and lover of peace, as well as the patron deity of both agriculture and theater.

[15] The frescoes in the Villa dei Misteri in Pompeii (cf. A. Maiuri, *La Villa dei Misteri*). In 1957, Jung's pupil Linda Fierz-David wrote a psychological study of these frescoes; see *Women's Dionysian Initiation: The Villa of Mysteries in Pompeii*, trans. Gladys Phelan (Dallas: Spring, 1988). Reprinted with additional chapters by Nor Hall, in *Dreaming in Red: The Women's Dionysian Initiation Chamber in Pompeii* (Putnam, CT: Spring, 2005).

[16] The female devotees of Dionysus, also called Bacchae or Bacchantes. Inspired by him to ecstatic frenzy, they accompany him in his wanderings and as his priestesses carry out his orgiastic rites. In their wild frenzy they tear animals apart and devour raw flesh.

if someone was married or just about to get married, or his social rank. The same dream meant something completely different if a sick or a healthy person dreamed it. The ill Plutarch, for instance, dreamed that Mercury showed him the way to heaven. He died a few days later. A good example of free association is the following. "For someone who was about to go on a sea voyage, a dream that he was to be crucified was a favorable sign. The cross seemed to be able to avert the danger, because it is made of wood, just like the ship, and because the mast represents a cross. For nonseafaring persons, however, the cross had a completely different, mostly negative, meaning, as already mentioned above. A dream of being transformed from a man into a woman was extremely unfavorable. For slaves and courtesans, however, it meant the opposite, the liberation from their miserable situation" (Le Blant).

Professor Jung: We also find *medical* dreams in Artemidorus, which later were used by doctors for making diagnoses. "Right leg turned to stone" means paralysis, "house burned" means deadly fever. For ancient man, the gods had a completely direct influence. Fate, morality, and thinking depended upon them. There was no room, therefore, for personal psychology. This mentality prevailed until the seventeenth or eighteenth centuries. At the beginning of the seventeenth century, psychic activity was seen as nothing but perceptual sensation. There was no activity of the soul per se, for everything was due to the influence of the "upper heaven," *instillatio* or instilling, that is, the dripping of heavenly water. When it hits the brain it causes what we call "sensation." Therefore nothing was left for the individual. "I do not see, but light appears to me through God's grace."

Also, in antiquity one did not say, "I fell in love," for that was brought about by the gods, by Eros. One was whipped by a demon. Not I, but "the god within me." I am *entheos*.[17] Psychic causality did not exist within man, but was a projection. Simpler people still show this psychology today. It was only Christianity that transferred the eternal existence of the gods into man himself. That was the origin of human self-awareness. When we read the texts of saints, we are amazed by this strange objectivity, and we ask: what has become of the individual? While these expressions are human, we cannot make out the actual

[17] Greek: enthused by god.

individual person in them. The reality of the person is missing. It was only in the eighteenth century that such world projection abated.

Ms. Adler: There is another deficiency, which is even more important and remarkable than the lack of personal association material and the relative unimportance of personal problems. The extraordinarily rich collection of dreams by Artemidorus gives us the impression that dreams were always interpreted only with regard to their *concrete* prophetic potential, and that there was no desire to reach an understanding of their *symbolic* meaning. Artemidorus makes all kinds of prophecies: illness and death, shipwreck, a lover or husband's infidelity, and divorces. But in each case it seems to refer to an actual life situation.

Professor Jung: One reason for the lack of symbolic meaning is Artemidorus's selection of dream material. We must not expect him to have any philosophical considerations. His dreams are taken from everyday life. The dreams in this collection come from the regular clientele, the people who daily come to the consulting room of the general practitioner or the clinical psychologist. They are, nearly without exception, "minor dreams." The "great dreams" of those who had individual religious problems, however, are missing in Artemidorus's collection. In antiquity, the dreams that needed to be interpreted symbolically emerged in a strictly separated environment behind temple walls. When someone wanted to be initiated into the Isis cult, he often had to wait for years until he had the right "initiation dream." Such dreams were not made public, but remained shrouded, just as the whole process was, in deepest silence.

Ms. Adler: In antiquity the scintillating dual and multiple meanings characteristic of dream symbols already attracted the greatest attention. This posed a great problem to dream interpreters, and many people were skeptical about it. In his book Artemidorus fought for the cause of dream interpretation; he wrote one volume expressly to counter the skeptics.

The gods of the underworld, for example, chiefly indicated mortal danger, although Pluto did not always carry such an ominous meaning; his virtue was being able to rescue from great doom those who had confidence in him beyond any reasonable hope. Asclepius had a positive meaning; if, however, he unfortunately approached the dreamer or even entered his house, that was a sign of severe illness, because then he was needed. The appearance of the Dioscuri[18] was an omen for storms at sea, or trials, or land battles, but equally well they could be rescuers from extreme danger, just like Pluto. Even Fortuna[19] gave rise to hope for good fortune if she appeared at rest and richly adorned, whereas her volatile aspect prevailed when she promenaded in the streets.

To dream of dying meant many different things. For some it indicated someone's bereavement or the imminent end. For others it was the prediction of their cure, of becoming famous, of a happy marriage, or the purchase of property. Slaves could entertain hopes of liberation, because death meant liberation. Two further examples: Serapis was called on by a man who had to undergo a difficult operation, and told him that the iron would free him from his suffering. The iron did indeed free him, but by bringing about his death. Perhaps, says Artemidorus, the unfortunate man had failed to take into account that he asked advice from a god of the underworld. The other was an ill man who dreamed of entering the temple of Jupiter and asking if he were destined for recovery and life. Jupiter lowered his head in response, which the patient took as an affirmative sign. Although he died, Jupiter had not deceived him; in lowering his head toward the earth, he announced to the supplicant that his funeral was imminent. Artemidorus expressly states, "The gods could not lie to the Romans, if the latter deciphered the meaning of their answers." This problem is not entirely unknown to us: it is not the ambiguity of dream symbolism that sets an obstacle for understanding the dream, but usually the interpreter's lack of understanding.

Notwithstanding his scant comprehension of dreams, Le Blant acknowledges the immense role that dream life and with it the preoccupation with dream interpretation have played in the history of ideas both during and since antiquity.

[18] The Dioscuri were Castor and Polydeuces (or Pollux), the twin sons of Leda and Zeus and the brothers of Helen of Troy. Because Zeus came to Leda in the form of a swan, they are sometimes presented as having been born from an egg. Pollux was a formidable boxer, and Castor was a great horseman. Together they were the "Heavenly Twins," often associated with the constellation Gemini.

[19] In Roman mythology, Fortuna personified luck, hopefully good luck, but she could be represented veiled and blind, as modern depictions of Justice are, and came to represent the capriciousness of life.

--· CHAPTER 3 ·--

Synesius of Cyrene: *Treatise on Dream Visions*

Paper by Rivkah Schärf

Ms. Schärf: Synesius[1] was born around AD 370 in Cyrene. He was a Neoplatonist and pursued his higher studies in Alexandria and Athens. For three years he was an envoy in Constantinople. At the beginning of the fifth century he converted to Christianity, and in 411 was elected bishop of Ptolemais. He died around AD 415.

Among other books, he wrote the following philosophical treatises: *Egyptian Tales* and *On Divine Providence*. Starting from the Egyptian myth of the brothers Typhon and Osiris, who fight the battle between good and evil, he developed Neoplatonic ideas about the combat between light and darkness in the cosmos and in the human soul. A later work is *Calvitii Encomium* (*In Praise of Baldness*),[2] a "sophistic pleasantry" according to Grützmacher and Volkmann, who wrote monographs on Synesius.

---

[1] For more information on Synesius, see the *Catholic Encyclopedia* (including online) and A. J. Bregman, *Synesius of Cyrene, Philosopher-Bishop* (Berkeley: University of California Press, 1982). Patricia Cox Miller writes that Synesius was more positive than Tertullian about "the connection between dreams and imagination. In his hands, the self as an abstract concept springs to life in a shimmering world of reflected images, where dreaming brings the soul into contact with a process of imagining that does not dissolve or obscure the real but rather gives it edge and focus (Migne, *Patroligia Greca* 66, 1281–320). For Synesius, the entire cosmos is a heterogeneous unity of 'signs that appear [*sēemainei*] through all things.' With the cosmos thus completely metaphorized, dreaming functions as a semiotic code, or, perhaps better, as a therapy of the sign that allows the dreamer to negotiate experience with more confidence and also with a more reflective temper" (Miller, *Dreams in Late Antiquity*, 70). See also below, 124, 156, where Cardano's commentary on Synesius's dream book is cited (the *Synesiorum somniorum*).

[2] Of which complaint he himself suffered.

A further work, *Dion*, represents a defense of philosophy against various contemporary attacks. Philosophy would free the soul of sensual passion and elevate it to the good by means of reason. Aristotle, Plato, and Dio of Prusa served as models for him; the latter gave the work its name.

In the same year as *Dion* he wrote his *Treatise on Dreams.*[3] He writes that whereas his book *Dion* was provoked by popular revulsion, his book on dreams was prompted by God. To his teacher, Hypatia of Alexandria, he wrote, "The whole treatise was worked out in one night, or rather during the rest of the same night in which I had the dream vision that prompted me to write. In some passages, two or three times, I became someone else, so to speak, listening to myself. And now, every time I read the work, I get a very strange feeling, and a divine voice resounds in me, as the poet says (Grützmacher)."

According to Synesius, dreams are of a *prophetic* nature. They hint at what will happen in reality. They are wise but by no means clear. It is part of their wisdom, however, that they are *unclear*, "because hidden from man the gods lead their lives." Knowledge as such is with God, being strong enough by its nature to be knowledge; man can achieve it only with an effort. The gift of prophecy, therefore, is the highest property of man. The wise man is related to God, "because he tries to be near Him with knowledge, and with struggles for knowledge, which constitutes the divine being."

According to Synesius, the possibility of prophecy is rooted in the harmony of the cosmos. In this one being, the cosmos, everything is closely related to everything else. Everything has a specific meaning, without exception. In the unity of the cosmos all parts stand in relation to each other. Whoever understands these cosmic relations is wise. He evokes one by means of another and uses what is at hand as a pledge for what is far away. Not all of these parts are in harmony; some go together well, while others fight each other, although the discordance is dissolved in the harmony of the whole. Synesius uses the simile of the lyre. In the world as in the lyre, opposites produce unity and harmony. Parts of the same sensibility can act upon each other. According to

---

[3] Synesius, *De Somniis*, in *Iamblichus, de Mysteriis Aegyptiorum. . .* etc., trans. Marsilio Ficino. For the later edition of this text, see *De insomniis* (*Peri enupnion logos*) in Migne, *Patroligia Greca* 66, 1281–320, and for a recent translation with critical commentary, see *Synésios de Cyrène IV: Opuscules I*, trans. Noël Aujoulat (Paris: Les Belles Lettres, 2004).

Synesius, all magical arts are based on this fact, too, as are all initiations and prophecies. Wise men can understand various correlations among parts of the cosmos. Some read the future from the stars, others from entrails, still others from cries, locations, or flights of birds. According to Synesius, dream prophecy is at the highest level among all these possibilities, because it originates in man himself, coming from within and representing the special property of each soul. Just as the spirit contains images of what exists in reality, the soul contains images of what will come to be, because the same relation exists between spirit and soul as between what is and what will be. Although the soul contains all images of what will come to be, it transmits only those congenial to the soul, mirroring them in fantasy, by which man perceives them. Just as the activity of spirit is perceived by man only when communicated by the guiding force of the whole organism, and anything not communicated by this force is lost to him, so do we not receive any perceptions of the soul's content before images reach fantasy.

Synesius says of fantasy that it seems to be a kind of life at a lower level, and a special variety of nature, because it also makes use of the senses. We see colors, we hear sounds and have the most distinct sensations of being touched, all while our bodily organs are completely inactive. This kind of sensory perception, Synesius says, is perhaps even more sacred, because during it we are sometimes in contact with the gods, who warn, prophesy, and in one way or another are concerned for us. It would not at all be inconceivable that someone went to bed as a complete layman, met the muses in a dream and conversed with them, and arose as an accomplished poet—not to mention the many cases in which evil attacks were disclosed, or sleep had made an illness go away as if it were a doctor. Fantasy can even open up this path to the most complete view of things for a soul that has never desired it, or never gave the task a thought. This transcendence of nature, and the equation of the unknowing with those capable of insight, are probably, all things considered, the most mysterious. Synesius refers to a pronouncement of the oracle: "Some are given knowledge of light by him through teachers; others are given his power during sleep."

Thus, of all possibilities of foretelling the future, the greatest "dignity of life" inheres in fantasy. Conceited seers, who used all kinds of arts to predict the future, disregarded dreams because they were accessible to everyone. Synesius countered that precisely the greatest goods could be found in the most common sphere. Of all visible things, for example, nothing would be more divine than the sun, yet nothing more common. God can be seen most basically with the help of fantasy, which is the sense of the senses, the most general sense organ. It is also the primary body of the soul. But it lives covertly and exercises its rule over the creature as if from a fortress. Compared to the animal-like perception in sense organs, fantasy is a more divine perception, linked to the soul. Nor is it less reliable than sense perception. The eye, too, does not show everything as it is in reality. Depending on the distance, something appears smaller or bigger; in water objects appear larger, and a paddle seems broken. Equally, for a weak-sighted eye objects become blurred and vague. So someone who suffers from a sick spirit of fantasy should not expect to have sharp and clear impressions. As for what kind of illness makes the spirit of fantasy turn dull and blunt, and how it is cleansed, purified, and restored to its normal condition, the answers must be sought in hermetic philosophy, which purifies one through initiation and makes him the dwelling place of God.

For someone who keeps the spirit of fantasy clean by leading a natural life, this spirit will be at his disposal continuously, because it hears the soul's stirrings and intentions. In contrast to the worldly shell, which even stands in opposition to the soul's nobler stirrings, its attitude toward them is not indifferent. The spirit of fantasy is the best, most basic instrument of the soul. If the soul becomes good, it will also become more refined and spiritualized; if it worsens, it will become blunted and mundane. This spirit lies (and here I quote from the translation) "like a contested border area between reason and unreason, between the physical and the nonphysical, touching on both. In it, the divine meets with its opposite, and, therefore, its nature is hard to grasp philosophically. It borrows and combines its own parts from both extremes, so that things otherwise far removed from each other now appear within *one* nature."

The area covered by fantasy is quite extensive. It even reaches down to creatures that do not yet possess reason. There it does not act as the instrument of a divine soul, but itself controls subordinate forces and actually represents reason in that creature; it thinks and acts quite appropriately on its own. Most things in human beings happen through it alone or in connection with other forces. Nor do we conceive thoughts without fantasy, except when someone momentarily is taken with an immaterial idea.

In addition, all kinds of *demons* live through fantasy, because in their whole nature they are imaginary and made of what will come to pass. Synesius, however, seems to attribute a metaphysical quality to them after all, because in the following, quoting from an oracle, he speaks of the underworld realm where shadow images belong. "Do not incline downward to the dark world; there is a deceptive abyss down there, and black, filthy Hades that lacks reason and breeds shadow images." Either God or demons and shadow images can prevail in the soul, or in fantasy, because the latter is engaged in a fight between above and below. Above, it is "dry and hot." Synesius quotes Heraclitus: "Dry is the wise soul."[4] It is able to attain the heights; otherwise it becomes moist and heavy, and sinks, due to its weight, into the earth's caves, into the underworld, the home of moist spirits. There life is cruel and full of anguish. It is possible, however, to ascend gradually again, purified by hardship and a changed life, because from birth onward the soul consists of *two lives* and thus walks on a *dual path*. Sometimes it concerns itself with the lesser way, sometimes the better. It comes from the upper spheres as part of the primary soul and descends with the help of fantasy into the bodily world. Until it returns to its original place, it must cohabit with its other component, matter. It can happen, however, that it is no longer able to ascend; this is the case when it merges with the depth, with evil. For the shadow image, it is appropriate to dwell in the depths, but not for the divine part of the soul. The worst case happens, therefore, when both fuse into a unity, and evil as such is no longer noticed. This is the situation of those who no longer aspire to rise at all. For someone who is still troubled by his situation will think of escape. The most important part of purification, therefore, is already achieved by will. Where the will is missing, any purifying initiation will be ineffectual. The necessary meaning of suffering lies in the fact that it cleanses the soul of ignorant joy with the help of pain. And wrongly so-called accidents, says Synesius, are to a great extent responsible for extracting the soul from matter. Exceptional strokes of luck are to be seen as traps

---

[4] "A dry soul is wisest and best" (fragment 118, Stobaeus, Anth. III, 5, 8).

set by masters of the soul's depths. Much strength is needed for the fight against matter, because matter has something bewitching about it, and enslaves the soul through its beauty. As an example Synesius quotes Heracles, who succeeds, with his thirst for freedom, in passing through his labors and in leading his spirit to where it can no longer be reached by nature's hand. But if the leap falls short, the effort to free oneself of matter still takes place within its sphere of influence; one is drawn downward again and will have to fight even harder struggles. Nonetheless, even if a fight is already going on between dark and light, good and evil, these opposites will not remain separated and irreconcilable forever. It seems, Synesius says, that the soul not only leads nature back again to the spheres where it originated, but that it also brings back up, together with the better part, what it had pulled down into material nature in its descent from the realm of fire and air. The complying lesser part can be in the light and partake of it. It is assigned a place in heaven, so to speak; then the pure body of the soul will probably live together with impure matter, but by mastering it.

The two most extreme fates of the soul are utmost brightness, on the one hand, when the soul reascends into the spheres after its fall and reunites with its origin, resulting in the highest bliss, and darkness on the other hand, when the soul sinks into matter. In between are many half-bright and half-dark places in the cosmos where the soul can remain. In its original purity it is the vessel of truth; if it has sunk into the depths, its spirit will be dark, vague, and deceptive. If it occupies a medium state, it will err in part and in part possess truth. The human soul's condition can be determined as follows: whoever has a pure and particular fantasy spirit, which records faithful images of things in both waking and dreaming states, may rest assured of being in good spiritual condition.

Synesius believes, however, that the soul can also be educated to that end. Philosophy can show how one could take care that spiritual life did not succumb to a fallacy. The best education would have one act in accordance with systematic knowledge, proceed in harmony with clear principles, and thus forestall the efforts of evil spirits. The powers conspiring against the spirit are best overcome by a judicious scheme of life.

After these remarks on the nature and fate of the soul, and on fantasy as its instrument, Synesius returns to the specific discussion of the gift of prophecy. To the extent that the soul practices piety in the described manner, purifying fantasy and approaching truth, it will receive the capacity to prophesy. Synesius points out that many sages led an ascetic life. It is only from this higher vantage point that prophecy is possible. Being on a higher level, it can perceive the corporeal as something lower. This would not be possible if it were united with the lesser part. Tranquil and undisturbed, it is thus able to transmit images of the future to the corporeal. This is precisely the "descent without descending," as the better part takes care of the lesser without being bound to it.

Synesius then indulges in long discussions of the advantages of dream prophecies over other kinds that require costly and time-consuming ceremonies and are accessible only to a few. The *dream*, however, is given to the poorest as well as the richest. And because this kind of prophecy is omnipresent, it is also the one *most similar to God*.

The benefit of dream prophecy lies, according to Synesius, in strengthening the hopes that play a salutary role in man's nature. Dream prophecy makes it possible to enjoy the beautiful in advance and to prevent the bad. This should not be mistaken, however, for the deceptive hopes that we nourish while *awake* and arouse within ourselves. The promise of dreams is a pledge of divine will.

Synesius then reports the services that dream interpretation has already rendered him personally. In philosophy, it helped by teaching him; during sleep it can fully elucidate much of what is unintelligible in the waking state, or at least facilitate its understanding. It has helped him complete his books, given him ideas, substituted better expressions for weaker ones, and removed stylistic infelicities. It has even given him helpful cues for hunting, for example, predicted a good day for the chase, which indeed happened. During his years as an envoy, his dream interpretations thwarted assaults by spirit-conjuring sorcerers, helped him carry out his diplomatic duties, and told him how to comport himself toward the king. Dream prophecy is a benevolent spirit at everyone's disposal, helping in one's daily work. Such wisdom is available to the soul that is at peace and not inundated by ordinary impressions that fill it with hosts of mishmash. It will present the images it harbors to those who turn their gaze inward.

It also transmits what emanates from God. It is connected to the god of this world, because both their natures have the same origin. Dream visions of this kind are completely, or almost completely, clear and explicit, so that they need not be interpreted. They occur, however, only to those who live virtuously.

Dreams in their great majority are enigmatic and must be interpreted. For Synesius, as we have seen, whether or not dreams are clear or unclear depends on the divine substance's degree of purity in the soul, on its metaphysical quality, as it were. In addition, the vagueness of dreams also stems from objects, in his view: everything that was and will be emanates images that phantasy picks up mirror-fashion. As these images are vague and cannot be recognized by any object, they roam around erratically without finding a stable location. As soon as they encounter the soul's life-spirits, however, which although image-like themselves are firmly placed in nature, they get attached to them and come to rest as if they had found their home. Clear images are sent out by the past, because its transition into life has already taken place; the clearest and most vivid ones are sent out by present reality, while indistinct ones are sent by the future. The latter radiate from inchoate beings, enigmatic formations sprouting from hidden seeds. It is quite an art, therefore, to interpret future developments.

Synesius does not offer a general *technique* of dream interpretation. He refers exclusively to *individual* experience. Just as a sailor can tell from experience that he will make port at a certain city after sailing around a certain rock, or that an army's appearance indicates the imminent arrival of its commander, deductions concerning future events can be drawn from dreams, because same goes before same and similar precedes similar. If someone has already seen a dream vision but has not remembered what it predicts for him, he is like a poor helmsman. For one would be able to predict a storm even when the air is utterly calm, if one knows that a halo around the moon calls for a certain kind of attention. Aristotle's statement—that apperception leads to memory, memory to experience, and experience to art—also holds true for dream interpretation. Dream books that collect such observations, however, are of little or no use, because the spirit of fantasy is highly differentiated by nature, pertaining to different spheres. Each creature possesses its own nature, because during its descent into matter the soul has lost, in varying degrees, its original nature. Just as muddy or disturbed water cannot reflect an object the same way as clear or still water, one cannot expect the same cause to have the same effect in all beings. Those who believe they can postulate universal rules of dream interpretation have not studied the nature of spirit. As a rule, they try to establish only the particular nature of their own spirit. Synesius adds, however, that he does not want to deny the existence of certain similarities.

In view of the fact that everyone depends on their own experience, Synesius recommends keeping not only *diaries* but also *nocturneries* in order to have memoirs of *both* states in our lives.

At the end of his treatise he discusses the usefulness of dream records as exercises in style, because capturing the fantasy realm in words is both particularly difficult and fruitful.

Let me briefly summarize Synesius on dreams as anticipations of *things that will happen* in actual life. He accounts for them as congruent and harmonious interactions among the parts of cosmic unity.

They reflect the future in fantasy, which is the instrument of the soul. Their clarity depends on the soul's purity, and so on fantasy's as well. On the one hand, this purity is *fate*, on the other the product of *conscious efforts*. The clearest dreams are had, therefore, by those who live in accord with divine reason. Synesius offers no method of dream interpretation, however. Since souls can assume any number of stages between above and below, each one is different. Dreams cannot be interpreted schematically, but only on the basis of each *individual's* experience.

Professor Jung: Synesius is the first to describe an *intermediate layer* of the soul. He interprets the notion of the soul psychologically, as a *spiritus phantasticus*. This fantasy spirit is a human *organ of knowledge*, an ideational function. It is identical with the psychic unconscious that sends us ideas. On the one hand, the unconscious is highly differentiated, while on the other hand it reaches down into the bodily sphere. The disturbances in neuroses are caused by fantasy. Physical illness is psychic illness in neuroses. If we do not grasp the nature of certain discomforts, we'll get bodily symptoms, for instance abdominal pain. *Primitive medicine* operates with *fantasy*, which somehow gets the "job" done. Fantasy offers suggestions about the unconscious that reach down into the body. A correct attitude often helps to forestall physical illness.

When I was in England, a patient with severe psychic conflicts came to me for treatment. After three weeks he told me that his psoriasis, which had resisted any medical therapy and which he hadn't ever referred to in analysis, had also disappeared, "although I hadn't done anything!"

The main idea of Synesius is that the dream has an *anticipatory* character. Dreams bring in new attitudes. They anticipate events and changes. The unconscious takes care of what reason is unable to provide for.

Synesius believes that prophetic dreams depend on the purity of the soul. The notion of a combat between light and darkness is of PersianManichaean origin. The unconscious cannot be judged without reference to the contemporary Weltanschauung. The unconscious always operates within a certain atmosphere. The existing general psychology must be accepted as a given fact. *Our* spiritual world is rooted in the spirit of the Middle Ages. Everything we read or think is infused with this spirit. Scholasticism was the great teacher of our time, in particular for the natural sciences. The Romans, for example, knew all the physical laws necessary for building a steam engine, but only scholasticism honed thinking sufficiently to bring those laws into practical application in eighteenth-century engineering. Strictness in educating the mind is medieval. In this respect Aquinas is the father of the natural sciences. The idea of the soul's purity in Synesius is probably a concession to the zeitgeist. In the case of children's dreams, for the young dreamer this concession to the zeitgeist is not yet significant.

CHAPTER 4

Caspar Peucer, *De Somniis*

Paper by Marie-Louise von Franz

Ms. *von Franz*: Caspar Peucer was born in Bolzano in 1525.[1] He spent the first half of his life as a professor in Wittenberg and as the personal physician to the elector, August of Saxony.[2] Being a humanist and the son-in-law of Philipp Melanchthon,[3] he took part in the "Last Supper controversy."[4] After Melanchthon's death he was even viewed as the standard-bearer of Lutheran orthodoxy. He was arrested in 1574 during the religious wars; upon his release in 1586, he went to the Duchy of Anhalt as the prince's personal physician. He died in Dessau in 1602.

His main works are: *Tractatus historicus de Melanchtonis sententia de controversia coenae Domini* (Amberg, 1596), *Elementa doctrinae de circulis coelestibus et primo motu* (ibid., 1551), and *Commentarius de praecipuis divinationum generibus* (Wittenberg, 1553). Our text *De somniis* is a chapter in the latter. In addition, he edited part of Melanchthon's *Chronikon Carionis* (1562–65).

---

[1] The following biographical data are taken from the *Encyclopaedia Italiana* (G).

[2] Seven electors among the many German dukes selected the Holy Roman Emperor. After Luther, religion divided them, diluting the emperor's influence prior to the outbreak of the Thirty Years' War in 1618.

[3] Philipp Melanchthon, also Schwarzert (1497–1560), German Protestant theologian and humanist writer, and associate of Martin Luther, who strongly influenced the development of Protestant theology (G).

[4] This controversy concerned the nature of the communion species (host): was it the "real presence" of Christ, and what did the individual, especially the nonbeliever, receive when taking communion? This debate flared up between two emerging camps within the Reformation: Luther and the German Reformers, and Zwingli and the Swiss Reformers.

Drawing on ancient dream theory, in particular on Macrobius, Peucer distinguishes *two* kinds of dreams in his work *De somniis*, caused by two different *causae efficientes*:[5]

1. Physical, material causes of dreams, that is, anything externally perceived by the senses and imprinted in the brain through the sense organs, the so-called *spiritus animales*.[6] These are called *procatarctic*[7] causes.

2. Spiritual causes of dreams. These are immaterial, without qualities that would affect the senses, and are called *prohegomenic* causes, that is, causes that lead toward the future. These have been inherent within our bodies "from the primeval beginning," or have been "gathered from elsewhere" by an individually differing *constitutio nativa*.[8] Some of these—the temperaments—are quite general in nature, originating in certain affections of the brain and of other parts of the body. Others are innate, different in each individual, and stem from a specific mixture of the seeds and the quality of heaven. In addition, certain acquired dispositions act as causes for dreams, which often displace the soul from its natural *habitus* and deflect it *para physin*.[9] As will become evident, their effect derives from the metaphysical sphere: God, Satan, angels, or demons.

According to these two basic factors, there are also two different kinds of dreams:

I. The *phantasmata*. They are caused by material causes. Nature produces them out of itself, as a result of external or internal stimuli, with the help of physical organs and the *spiritūs* of the brain. *Phantasmata* are, therefore, imaginings and ideas *without* any metaphysical background. Nevertheless, they can be full of indications for the future.

Professor Jung: Due to the belief in a secret correspondence between nature and soul, or macrocosm and microcosm, it was customary in antiquity, in uncertain situations, to put the question to something independent of man, for instance, animal entrails. It was up to the interpreter's

---

[5] Latin: effective causes.
[6] Latin: animal or bodily spirits.
[7] Latin and medical: beginning, predisposing, exciting, initial.
[8] Latin: innate constitution, natural creation.
[9] Greek: against nature.

art to explain the constellation. We are doing the same thing today with dreams. However, we are scarcely aware anymore that when we interpret dreams we place ourselves in direct connection with what happens in nature.

Ms. von Franz: Dreams caused by nature, however, can also be "completely without premonition or any specific intention." Either they simply repeat something from the present or the past, or are even completely meaningless, caused only by bodily affections, such as the dreams of inebriated, irate, feverish, or epileptic persons.

> II. The second kind of dreams, stemming from spiritual causes, are *visions* and *dream oracles*. They originate in God, the demons (namely, the angels and the apostate spirits), and Satan. In the first place, these are the dreams of the Holy Fathers and the prophets; these dreams are natural and have been sent by God. On the other hand are the dreams sent by the devil, dreams given by Satan to the pagans "in a state of doubt and anxious concern," after they had made godless vows and offered sacrifices to idols. These are *incubation dreams*, which Peucer discusses in the chapter on "De oraculis" in the fourth tractate. But the devil offered his dreams to pagans even without such preparations. Here also belong, according to Peucer, the dreams of the Enthusiasts[10] and Manichaeans.[11] Sometimes these devilish dreams do have meaning, but more often they deceive us, for instance, when (female) poisoners dream of ascending to heaven and seeing angels, or being in luxurious palaces, enjoying the embrace of love, etc. Thus, devilish dreams are nearly always ambiguous; if they are true on occasion, that is only to reinforce superstition.

Dreams can take the following *forms:* Firstly, "those given in apperception" (*teorematika*) represent future events directly as they will occur. Secondly, "allegorical ones" (*allegorika*) *figuratively* hint at the future in figures and riddles and, when coming from God, require interpretation. This latter kind, however, is a very special gracious gift from the Holy Spirit.

[10] From Greek *entheos*, enthused with God.
[11] Contrast the fire ascension in Mani as alluded to by Jung in *Children's Dreams*, 101, where it is compared to the Mysteries and Christ's transfiguration and ascension.

According to the objects interpreted, Peucer classifies dreams as Macrobius does, in five *categories*: those referring to the dreamer (*idia*), those referring to someone else (*allotria*), those referring to the dreamer *as well as* someone else (*koina*), public dreams (*demosia*), and cosmic dreams (*kosmika*). Peucer gives examples of these classifications with the help of Scripture and ancient dream collections.

Significantly, most of the rest of the treatise is devoted to defining and discussing terms for *physical causes*, primarily in the spirit of the peripatetic[12] school of medicine.

The *somnia physica*[13] are produced by the brain, in which diurnal excitation persists and is discharged at night. Day residues that "have remained attached to the sense organs" are repeated and circulated, while certain affectations in the inner organs—excess liquids, etc.— transmit certain stimuli to the brain through the nerves, often leading to monstrous dreams. Peucer describes brain structure as follows. Two forces are active in the brain, in the first place forces like those peculiar to the liver or heart, which function continuously without *ratio* or freedom of will, and fail to respond to suggestion or command. They provide conservation and renewal and, above all, nutriment to the brain. After nutrition has been "elaborated" by body heat, it is fed to the brain through *venulae*,[14] passing through the nasal and pharyngeal cavities and the "pores" of the skull. There is a certain "alogical" movement of the brain, producing dilations and contractions, by which the *spiritūs animales* are created out of the *spiritūs vitales*,[15] in that the latter are elaborated with the involvement of air, boiled, and then sort of ignited and illuminated "by a certain gleaming incidence of light or flash of lightning."

The second form of brain movement occurs through "guiding and rational" forces (in possession of *ratio*) that are subject to reason and will. The brain produces these after free mental decision and then suppresses them again. This happens quite independently, without involving other parts of the body. The *spiritūs animales*, on which the spirit

---

[12] I.e., referring to Aristotle and his disciples.
[13] Latin: physical dreams.
[14] Latin and medical: the smallest veins.
[15] Latin: vital or life-giving spirits.

"exerts its form-giving power," are active in this process, too. This mental activity takes places on three levels, that is, on the levels of fantasy (imagination, inner perception), of the actual act of thinking, and of the capacity for recollection (memory).

The act of sensory perception is brought about by the brain, which diffuses the *spiritūs animales* into individual organs, which in turn bring back what has been "pressed in from the outside." Thus, they become interpreters for the mind of what happens outside the brain. The nerves insert the *species*[16] of the external objects into the alveoli and frontal cavities of the brain, where a "structuring and form-giving rational activity weaves, in a well-regulated procedure, a long and wonderful thread or a fabric of thoughts."

The brain, as such, is a soft and liquid mass or *krasis*, that is, a mixture of primary qualities, which gives it a special *temperies*.[17] The brain's specific and intrinsic conditions lead to particular actions, for instance, confused, stupid, and slack ones in the case of idiots, who have a poor *temperies*.

There follow, in Peucer's *De somnia*, *phrenological*[18] studies of different shapes of the skull in general, and of the seat of individual functions. As Peucer goes on to say, however, many doctors reject the theory of the *spiritūs animales* and prefer to speak of a "middle substance" that originates in the brain and spreads out on all sides—similar to the core of a tree—and which is "altered," substantially changed, by the qualities of objects, and then is transmitted to the brain by the *sympatheia spiritualis*.[19] Plato holds still another view; in the *Theaetetus* he speaks of seal impressions and preformed images, but the problem of what is primary still remains. As Peucer puts it, the whole problem is "*obscurissima.*"[20]

[16] Here used in its scholastic meaning, perhaps best translated as "images." It is difficult to render the complete epistemological background of these terms (M.-L. v. F.).

[17] *Krasis* and *temperies* are terms from the Stoa, according to which each matter is composed of a particular mixture of "primary qualities," resulting in a particular *temperies* (roughly, tension or warmth), and giving it the potential to perform certain functions (M.-L. v. F.).

[18] Phrenology (from the Greek φρην, mind, and λογος, study), a theory that claims to be able to determine character and personality traits as well as criminality on the basis of the shape of the head. Very popular in the nineteenth century, it was developed by the German physician Franz Joseph Gall circa 1800.

[19] The *sympatheia spiritualis* is a kind of "being connected in spiritual involvement" of all things in the cosmos, by means of a mysterious, ubiquitous "middle substance" (M.-L. v. F.).

[20] Latin: most obscure.

In addition to all this, there are the inner *affectūs* in the body: "they change external objects and our ideas about them."

Professor Jung: Primitives think that the world is created by thinking, by consciousness. We think the world is there first, and then our consciousness. *Our* thinking goes from the outside to the inside.

Ms. von Franz: Consciously induced body movements after a sensory perception also follow, like mental activities, a *potentia dominatrix* (in this context something like "a potential for an act that is predominant in this case"), by which the *spiritūs* are spilled, so to speak, *explosively* from the brain into parts of the body. There are three "appetitions," namely, directed will, affective impulse, and instinctual desire.

In each *act of will* the following process occurs: *phantasmata* of the things one desires are generated in the brain. Then they are revealed to the spirit, which in turn submits them to the free will that makes the actual decision. The *spiritūs* are particularly pure; then a kind of lightning is produced, by which they are suddenly spilled into all the interconnected cavities of the brain. It is only by this mysterious force, this "irradiation"—that is, impacts from radiation—that heavy human limbs can be moved.

The three levels of *spiritual* activity occupy three different parts of the brain: (1) The *phantasia*, working in the frontal cavities of the brain, picks up the aforementioned *species* of external objects provided by the sense organs, and distinguishes and classifies them. (2) *Thinking* sorts and divides them, or "reasons," and "weaves more into them by logical conclusions," until it advances as far as first principles by the synthetic method. Or else thinking proceeds in the opposite direction, using the analytical method by starting from first principles, which are implanted into spirit by nature. (3) Finally, *memory* records and preserves everything. It puts the *species* into a posterior cavity, which is shared by the cerebellum and the spinal cord.

Despite the great role played by the brain in spiritual functions, it is spirit, the *lux nobilior*,[21] that is essential. Spirit is to be thought of as an immaterial light. In "sketching traces," the brain produces a preform of thoughts, making a dark outline of them; the spirit, however, illuminates, connects, and completes them. Although it cannot compose the

---

[21] Latin: the nobler light.

species without the brain and only illuminates them, it is nevertheless the decisive factor.

Professor Jung: Where does that notion of the *mens* (reason, spirit) as a light come from? *Mens* equals *lux* equals *lumen aeternum*[22]? This notion was derived by Peucer from Marsilius Ficinus,[23] who himself had originally taken it from the *Hermeticum*.[24] Actually, it is interesting how many ideas from the *Corpus Hermeticum* found their way into the philosophy of the Renaissance.

Ms. von Franz: Peucer puts forward the following views on the composition of dreams in the brain. The brain is desiccated by daytime exertions, and its movements flag. A need for nourishment and fertilization arises. Warm vapors from the whole body rise in the veins and arteries. Meanwhile, the solar heat absorbed during the day has boiled down the *spiritūs vitales*, so that they ascend with the vapors. They are precipitated by the cooler night air and moisten the root nerves. The regeneration of the *spiritūs vitales* also brings about that of the *spiritūs animales*. If somehow rougher vapors rise, however, they will confuse and daze the brain and produce *phantasmata*, whose development is particularly stimulated by those *species* that are strengthened by frequent thinking, as well as by residues of things heard or seen during the day. The same regulating force that is active during the day also operates at night, only less powerfully. If, in one way or another, there exists a prophetic potency in the brain, whether naturally inherent or caused by a special constellation of the stars, this "premonition of nature" will, as it were, cooperate and form the *phantasmata*, which correspond to this inner premonition, with the help of precisely that force that regulates the acts of the brain from the stars.

Professor Jung: Where do these prophetic dreams come from? The idea was that spiritual events do not take place *in ourselves*, but *in the stars*. Psychological concepts descended to us from the stars. Our unconscious thinks in the same way. It was only with the beginning of the natural sciences that new thinking began.

[22] Latin: eternal light.

[23] Marsilio Ficino (1433–1499), Neoplatonic philosopher, humanist, and alchemist at the Medici court, translator of Plato and the *Corpus Hermeticum*, Christian priest, and founder of the Florentine Academy. Also an astrologer and codifier of medical lore.

[24] Hermes Trismegistos, *Corpus Hermeticum* (G).

Ms. von Franz: Dreams stemming from inner secretions could be me-dicinally used for diagnostic purposes: the bilious, for instance, dream of conflagrations, of yellow colors, or of flying; melancholics of black smoke, nocturnal odysseys, or ghosts. Clear dreams can be produced only by a well-tempered brain.

As shown above, dreams of the future *also* stem from natural causes, al-though more distant, antecedent ones arise precisely from that prophetic capacity inherent in the stars. Often added to this is a natural, special disposition in the individual to recognize omens, a *sensus occultus*, which is inborn by a particular "in-fluence"[25] of heaven, and which arranges the dreams as images pointing toward the future. In any case, even these dreams still belong to the sphere of natural dreams.

Not originating in nature, however, are those other dreams inspired by God in the saints and prophets, according to Peucer. Pagan incuba-tion dreams and dreams of other fanatics come from the *devil*. These aim at disclosing new revelations that result in murder and idolatry. Furthermore, any furor or prophetic mania also comes from the devil; they are nothing but an *afflatus diaboli*.[26]

From all this, the correct attitude toward dreams becomes evident: only divine dreams are to be believed, they are beyond discussion. We can recognize them by the norm of the revealed word, because "the law of God is unalterable" (Jeremiah 36). Also sanctioned by God are *me-dicinal* interpretations, which lead to a knowledge of the temperaments and the *humores* (Galen).[27] In any other case dream interpretation is not allowed (Deuteronomy 18:10–12[28]). Although sometimes it may

---

[25] Original: *Ein-Fluß*, literally "in-flow," a play on the word *Einfluß* = influence.

[26] Latin: flatulence of the devil.

[27] Latin: humidity. The four humors (yellow bile, black bile, phlegm, blood) were four fluids that were thought to permeate the body and influence its health. The concept was developed by ancient Greek thinkers around 400 BC and was directly linked with another popular theory of the four elements (Empedocles). Paired qualities were associated with each humor and its season. "Humoralism," or the doctrine of the Four Temperaments, retained its popularity as a medical theory for centuries, largely through the influence of the writings of Galen, and was decisively displaced only in 1858 by Rudolf Virchow's theories of cellular pathology. Claudius Galenus of Pergamum (AD 131–201), better known as Galen, was an ancient Greek physician whose views dominated European medicine for more than a thousand years.

[28] "There shall not be found among you any one that maketh his son or his daughter to pass through the fire, or that useth divination, or an observer of times, or an enchanter, or a witch. Or a charmer, or a consulter with familiar spirits, or a wizard, or a necromancer. For all that do these things are an abomination unto the Lord" (KJV).

lead to the truth, more often than not it leads to falsehood. "Often they reveal more of the interpreter's mind than having an objective concordance with nature." As it is, all kinds of things are speculated about the future. Most such dreams are ambiguous, many even completely wrong. Dreams inspired by the devil are to be despised in any case.

Peucer then gives an example of such a devilish dream with *alchemical* symbolism:

> A certain Epitheles of Messina dreams that "he would find a taxus [yew] and a myrtle in a place called Ithona, and if he dug up the earth beneath them, he would find an old woman, locked up in a brazen room and nearly dead already." When day came, he actually did as he was told and found a brazen urn. He opened it and found very fine strips of white lead in it; they were in the form of a book, and the sacrificial rites of great gods were written upon them.

Peucer comments: "It is precisely this re-establishment of sacrificial rites that the devil desires, so that they would not disappear and idolatry would be strengthened. In history and modern times we find examples of Anabaptists and Enthusiasts[29] whose dreams only intend to bring about the worst crimes and heinous blasphemy!"

Professor Jung: When someone dreams of an *old* anima figure, he is infantile in his consciousness. When someone dreams of a sage, he is a fool. This is perhaps the dream of an infantile man, who was not in tune with his time, and who therefore had to resort to the old religious commandments. The taxus has red berries, the myrtle white flowers, a symbol of female innocence. The wood of the taxus is very hard, and the tree grows only slowly. White may stand for the virgin, red for servant or slave; the *servus rubeus*[30] is the sun.

The symbol is found between pairs of opposites, however. A maternal secret is hidden there: the old woman is a Sibyl.[31] Ancient sacrificial instructions are, therefore, the solution to his problem. The old woman

[29] Several Protestant sects of the sixteenth and seventeenth centuries known as Enthusiasts (God-possessed) were condemned by mainstream Protestants for fomenting political radicalism. In England following the Civil War and Restoration they were held in particular disrepute.

[30] Latin: red slave or servant. The alchemists spoke of the *servus rubeus* and the *femina candida* (white woman); their copulation produced the supreme union of opposites.

[31] The Sibyls (from Greek, *sibylla*, prophetess) were ancient seeresses who prophesied at certain holy sites, under the influence of a deity.

brings with her the *ancient mother ritual*. The ancient gods have to be reunited with Christian ideas. This is *the* problem of the Renaissance.

Another example is the *Hypnerotomachia*, Francesco Colonna's struggle with love in a dream (*Le songe de Poliphile*).[32] He dreamed of an adventurous journey in which he (a monk) searches for Lady Soul. In his consciousness he has grown uncertain: where will he find Lady Soul? At the court of Queen Venus! As soon as he gets there, he is wakened by the ringing of bells. What Venus is in the unconscious, Mary is in his consciousness. The connection with the unconscious has to be established again and again, in order to be regenerated: the abstractness of Christianity was too much for him, thus the regression to antiquity.

[32] F. Colonna, *Hypnerotomachia Poliphili* . . . (1499). *Le songe de Poliphile ou hypnerotomachie de frère F. C.* (1883). The first complete English version was published by Thames and Hudson in 1999, five hundred years after the original (*Hypnerotomachia Poliphili, the Strife of Love in a Dream*, trans. Jocelyn Godwin; paperback edition February 2005). A study by the Jungian Linda Fierz-David, *Der Liebestraum des Poliphilo*, long antedated this version, appearing as *The Dream of Poliphilo: The Soul in Love*, Bollingen Series 25 (New York: Pantheon, 1950. Reprint; Dallas: Spring, 1987).

B. The Enlightenment and Romanticism

CHAPTER 5

M. l'Abbé Richard, *Théorie des songes*

Paper by Dr. Alice Leuzinger

Ms. Leuzinger: I could find no references to the life of the author, Abbé Richard.[1] The *Théorie des Songes* was written around 1750, with the intention of destroying the ancient belief in the preternatural and prophetic characteristics of dreams, and of explaining them in terms of rational causes.

The formation of dreams rests upon the physiological basis of the *esprits animaux*,[2] defined by Descartes as follows: these are the most subtle and agitated kind of blood corpuscles, secreted from the circulation of the blood and absorbed by the nervous system. They are vitalizing and watering forces, which play a part in the psychic functions of imagination and reproduction. The starting points of dreams are always previous sensory perceptions; they are the factual material that dreams draw upon and comprise both the distant and the most recent past (day residues). With the help of the *esprits animaux*, sensory perceptions reach the brain. That is how visions of imagination are created. These are reanimated and renewed, when the *esprits animaux* flow back along previous channels; with their help imagination can recall images. The *esprits animaux* are, therefore, "collaborating forces" in both senses of the word. Imagination has a reproductive function. If images are potent enough, they reach the soul. The function of the soul is to choose

---

[1] Monsieur l'Abbé Richard, or Jérôme Richard (ca. 1720–18 . . .), *La Théorie des songes* (Paris: Les frères Estienne, 1766).

[2] French: animalistic spirits.

from and arrange the material, to leave out or accentuate individual parts and their connections. No clear boundaries, however, separate these two powers, soul and imagination; their spheres of influence are unstable, flowing into each other. When the soul gains the upper hand, imagination can become the *"faculté imaginative de l'âme."*[3]

Imagination on the one hand is rooted in the physical, because it is depends directly on sense perceptions and the *esprits animaux*; on the other hand it has a spiritual tendency, because it is under the soul's control.

"The imagination is the place where the soul forms images; the stronger the traces of the *esprits animaux* are—which the soul uses—the clearer the imprinting of images in the brain. The strength of imagination thus consists in the brain's disposition to receive deep impressions. The activity of the imagination, to grasp and portray things, always depends on the soul, with the collaboration of the organs and the basis formed by the *esprits animaux*" (Abbé Richard).

Each of these powers possesses its own intensity. The soul, whose activity never stops, does not know the physical state of exhaustion, to which the imagination—as something rooted in the body—is subject.

"Dreams are a repetition, sometimes an accurate one, more often a confused and obscured repetition of images of things, with which we were occupied in the past, and whose only connection with the future is the link found in the sequence and actions of the same individual" (Abbé Richard).

Professor Jung: At the beginning of the eleventh century, Arab scholars came to the Moorish universities and handed down the tradition of ancient Arab knowledge. That is also how the theory of the *spiritūs animales* entered European thinking. It goes back, however, to *Alexandrine* knowledge, and ultimately to the fragments of Pherekydes.[4] This is a kind of physiological dream theory. The *anima rationalis*[5] exercises ultimate control and masters the imagination to realize images. The dream is under the command of the *anima rationalis*.

---

[3] French: imaginative faculty of the soul.

[4] Pherekydes of Syros (sixth century BC), Greek philosopher, author of a book about the birth of the gods and the origin of the cosmos of which only fragments survive. He was one of the teachers of Pythagoras.

[5] Latin: rational soul.

Abbé Richard, however, has to represent orthodox church doctrine. The example of the princess[6] is of importance for church politics: it does *not* support his theories. The confessors, *"directeurs de conscience,"* were seriously interested in dreams and developed the art of rearranging the expressions of unconscious psychic life and interpreting them in such a way as to leave *orthodoxy* undisturbed. Dreams were arranged to be edifying.

But it was different in reality: the princess, who wants to begin a spiritual life, withdraws from conscious interests and tries to withdraw her expectations and desires from the sensual world. This libido is turned inward, the inner world gets enlivened, and all kinds of figures come to life in it. The dream shows the figure that arises in her: she is lost in the woods, that is, in the unconscious, and there she encounters someone, obviously a poor beggar, obviously no great intellect, but a simple, blind man in her unconscious. It is the so-called animus[7] figure, the princess's *thinking*, the thinking *peculiar* to her. This thinking is aimless; it is blind. And now something interesting happens: suddenly this thinking is a *prophet*, so to speak; he explains that he has the inner light, which fills her with joy. This has an edifying effect. But the *"directeur de conscience"* turned things upside down, so that she did not recognize her *own* thinking, because that would have led her out of the church. The dream was thus reinterpreted in a dogmatic way.

When a *beautiful* dream comes, we can be sure that the unconscious is making great efforts to bring *its idea* closer to *consciousness*. When we dream of something ugly, we are disgusted. That's normal. We then repress it, and that's right, because otherwise it would absorb too much libido. A beautiful dream means that one must view these manifestations of the unconscious as something positive. It was right, however, for this dreamer to withdraw. Not everyone needs to be fruitful; for some, death is the right thing. This shows in the dreams. They point in a direction that would be unintelligible to others. It is our sickness that we no longer perceive such simple and natural things.

[6] Obviously referring to a dream from the *Théorie des songes* quoted in the seminar, but not reported in the minutes.

[7] Re animus and anima, see C. G. Jung, CW 9/ii, ¶s 20–42; Emma Jung, *Animus and Anima* (G).

Niklaus von der Flüe[8] is an excellent example of dogmatic twisting. With great cunning he reworked his visions until they finally came out dogmatically domesticated. That was necessary in his day.

Nearly the same thing happened with Flaubert's *Tentation de St. Antoine*.[9] There, too, we're inclined to say that it's a real shame anyone would want to repress dreams or visions that told the truth. But it was the right thing to do at that time. It couldn't have been otherwise; the age was *antibiological* in its thinking.[10]

---

[8] Swiss hermit and mystic (1417–1487); he prevented fratricidal war between the confederate Swiss cantons.

[9] Gustave Flaubert, *The Temptation of St. Anthony* (Paris, 1874; New York: Random House, 2002). This was a lifelong work, thirty years in the making, which Flaubert considered his masterpiece. Based on the legend of the third-century saint who lived on an isolated peak in the Egyptian desert, it is a fantastical rendering of one night during which Anthony is besieged by carnal temptations and philosophical doubt.

[10] Jung's perspective here of course includes the benchmark year of 1859, which saw the publication of *The Origin of Species*, but also notes the persistence of a customary outlook on fantasy that runs from the Abbé Richard even to Flaubert, from 1750 to at least 1875.

—· CHAPTER 6 ·—

Franz Splittgerber, *Schlaf und Tod*[1]

Paper by Kristin Oppenheim

Ms. Oppenheim: The title alone, in which the author designates his work as apologetic,[2] shows the difference between him and scientific authors of our time. He has a certain agenda—namely, to strengthen the reader's adherence to Christianity or to convert him to it by proving the existence of a metaphysical connection between the soul and God. This tendency does not seem too questionable in our eyes, because the method is not affected by it, only the conclusions. As we shall see, his position is not far removed from today's psychology. He, too, teaches a connectedness between all souls, those living as well as those departed; the difference is only that he does not call this connectedness a collective but a divine one.

Historically speaking, he—just like C. G. Carus, whom he often quotes—espouses the side of *Romanticism.* Both vehemently attack the Enlightenment.

In his introduction Splittgerber stresses the importance of sleep and dream for the study of the human soul. The great progress Splittgerber and like-minded psychological thinkers represented lies in the fact that they do not stop their investigation of man at the point at which consciousness ends, but rather make it precisely their starting point.

---

[1] Franz Splittgerber, *Schlaf und Tod, nebst den damit zusammenhängenden Erscheinungen des Seelenlebens. Eine psychologisch-apologetische Erörterung des Schlaf- und Traumlebens, des Ahnungsvermögens und des höheren Aufleuchtens der Seele im Sterben* (Halle: Julius Fricke, 1866).

[2] Here in the sense of "serving as or containing a formal justification or defense."

Naturally, in such cases dreams are of great importance. Splittgerber expressed this, for instance, in the following words: "In dreams, when the soul is free from organizing reason, it descends into the depths where it starts a lively and increased activity of its own."

The following chapters discuss the fact that the soul does not cease its activity during the sleeping state, despite the body's dormancy. In sleep it returns to the innermost hearth of life, from which it gains new strength for the waking state afterward. This sinking down works in connection with a force that organizes external impressions; what seemed insoluble during the day finds its solution at night.

Professor Jung: This idea of the return of the soul to its source is also the basic principle of yoga. The practical form of yoga for creating "emptiness" is widespread throughout the whole East. It is contemplation with the goal of vitalization. The task is "to think nothing." It's the complete blocking out of ideas and images. The purpose is to empty consciousness so that energy can flow back into the unconscious.

Ms. Oppenheim: Furthermore, Splittgerber gives an account of the soul's life in the dream. As far as the intensity of sleep during dreaming is concerned, he is of the opinion that dreams arise only during dozing consciousness, never in deep sleep. Dreams are composed of day residues, although these are hard to interpret because organizing reason is missing in the dream. Although this statement rather seems to be derived from the Enlightenment, Splittgerber supplements it by pointing to the deep meaning of *fantasies*—without, however, going into more detail regarding the separate parts of fantasy.

Professor Jung: Usually dreams arise during lighter sleep. During deep sleep the images are completely converted into motor phenomena, as, for instance, in talking during sleep. One can hardly ever obtain such dreams.

Ms. Oppenheim: In the following, Splittgerber gives a classification of dreams. Like nearly all dream researchers before him, he speaks of meaningful and meaningless dreams. As far as the former are concerned, he thinks that "the eternally waking spirit expresses thoughts from the deep primeval basis of its being," whereas meaningless dreams contain images from the waking state, which pass by quickly. Modern psychology also knows of qualitative differences, of big dreams and lesser ones, but it does not attach value exclusively to dreams that are prophetic or have general importance. As far as Splittgerber is concerned, he accounts for this shift, it seems, because he is ignorant of symbols. Although he acknowledges symbols in theory, he simply ignores them in practice; out of the enormous number of daily dreams he discusses only those whose content comes true literally.

Professor Jung: With few exceptions, the romantics paid attention only to so-called big dreams. A big dream has a particular structure; it is a creation held together by a powerful *feeling tone.*

Ms. Oppenheim: Splittgerber describes the intensification of psychic life in dreams with the help of two different aspects.

(1.) The *metaphysical-intellectual* side: because of its being connected to some ultimate metaphysical ground, the soul is capable of *transcending* the succession and coexistence of *space and time.* Regarding this phenomenon, and the statement that it is caused by the soul's connectedness with God, Splittgerber quotes Schubert,[3] among others. "As long as the soul is moving in the dream, its ideas follow a completely different law of associations than usually. By a few hieroglyphic images strangely strung together, we express more in a few moments in dream language than could be expressed by ordinary language over the course of several days. And all this without any remarkable gaps, and with a coherence structured in itself, although a completely peculiar and unusual one."

Connected with the intensification of metaphysical capability are dreams of things long forgotten, as well as dreams of finding completely unknown things, sometimes in unknown places.

In one chapter of his book we learn about Splittgerber's view of *symbols.* They are interpreted in the conventional manner, sometimes with a special Christian twist. What is amazing and new, however, is his comment that in most cases dreams appear in symbolic form, in the form of images "which are by no means accidental, but on the contrary have the same visual characteristics in the most various peoples of the earth, and which constantly return nearly everywhere on similar

---

[3] Gotthilf Heinrich von Schubert, *Altes und Neues aus dem Gebiet der innern Seelenkunde,* 7 vols. (1817–59). Schubert (1780–1860) was an important Romantic naturalist and representative of mystical natural philosophy.

occasions. It even seems as if the soul's choice of images is based on a particular ingenuity."[4] As far as the increase in our *intellectual* capabilities is concerned, his view is probably still the one current today, for he states that such an increase could not exceed the most highly concentrated personal achievement in the waking state, so that there can be no question of supernatural mental achievements in dreams.

(2.) The *ethical-religious* side: because the dream portrays us less favorably than we believe we are in reality, our conscience stirs; we have the possibility of improving. "What does not slumber *within ourselves*, even if it be only a premonition or the faintest impulse, can never ever rise from the bottom of our soul."

Professor Jung: As for so-called ethical dreams, I would like to say the following. For example, someone dreams of doing something that shows his worst side. The dream, however, is a *product of nature*, it has *no ethical tendencies*. It's often the case that a dream will show the bad side. Even if we realize this, the dream may recur nevertheless, because its meaning is not ethical, but different. Dreams are like plants, natural growths. One *can* make an ethical, philosophical, or any kind of problem enter the picture, but it's not contained in the actual *dream*.

Ms. Oppenheim: In a further chapter, "The *turba*[5] of psychic life in dreams," Splittgerber discusses meaningless dreams. All dreams without a *clear* meaning he calls illusory dreams. They are made possible by the cessation of reason's activity and by the "unrestrained roaming" of fantasy. The content is made up mostly of *day residues*—namely, of what impressed us last or most deeply, of what most occupied us. Fantasy takes hold of the day residues; most dreams can be explained that way. A pleasant day brings a pleasant dream, a sad day a sad dream. The dream can be explained not only from day residues, however, but also from other causes, for example, *bodily influences* such as illness, headache, or things weighing heavily on one's mind. The ultimate and decisive cause of the *turba* in our mental lives, whether awake or asleep, can be found in the *moral depravity* of these lives, that is, in the sinful apostasy of our finite mind from the origin of its being, from the eternal divine spirit.

---

[4] This statement comes close to Jung's notion of archetypes (G).

[5] Latin: commotion, uproar, turmoil, tumult, disturbance.

Professor Jung: The *turba* is the babble of the devils, as expressed, among others, by the Church Fathers, for instance, Athanasius of Alexandria.[6] If we live alone for some time, we will hear voices from the distance, or the calling of names. These are simply *phenomena of solitude*.

According to the teachings of the Church, *turba* is devilish spirit. The Holy Spirit comes in silence (Athanasius), while the devils arrive in noise, even ringing church bells. The devil is apostasy from God. And this is actually correct. When we defect from the principles of instinct, we defect from the divine will, and thus inflict damage on ourselves by disobedience, ignorance, morbidity, and through not following our instincts. In theological terminology this defection is called "sin." It is couched in moral terms by theology. Its characteristic feature is that it presupposes our knowing what is good and what is bad. It naturally follows that a deviation from the original plan is bad, and adherence to it is good. But if we are in doubt, things become uncertain. There are cases in which we have to say that it is better to deviate from the original plan. Of course, one may always say that a deviation is quite bad. But if we are honest, we must admit doubting that we don't always exactly know what is good and what is bad. It actually demands divine powers to tell the final difference between good and bad. That's why mankind has always turned to divine revelations. We find the deepest doubts in ecclesiastical history about what is good and bad. These are very sensitive, fateful questions.

[6] E.A.W. Budge, ed., *The Book of Paradise: Being the Histories and Sayings of the Monks and Ascetics of the Egyptian Desert by Palladius, Hieronymus and others* . . . (Life of St. Anthony). For later collections, see Sr. Benedicta Ward, trans., *The Sayings of the Desert Fathers: The Alphabetical Collection*, and *Lives of the Desert Fathers* (both Kalamazoo: Cistercian Publications, respectively, 1975 and 1981).

C. The Modern Period

CHAPTER 7

Yves Delage, *Le Rêve*[1]

Paper by Hans Baumann[2]

Mr. Baumann: Delage was a biologist and a member of the French Academy. In his old age, eye problems forced him to interrupt his work for long periods, which gave him much time for introspection. Thus he could further elaborate his theory of dreams, which he had already written up in 1891, and publish it in 1920. The main part of the book is taken up by *physiological* explanations of dream causes and processes. The psychological interpretations he offers are based on *association psychology* and the *psychology of faculties* (*Vermögenspsychologie*).[3] With regard to the numerous dreams and parts of dreams, only descriptions can be found, and hardly any interpretations. On the other hand, Delage is not confined by a system of interpretation or any tendency toward mystification. He gives rational explanations in accord with his epoch and his scientific circle; his methodical approach shows him to be a clear-thinking scientist.

He distinguishes between three *methods* of dream research: the objective method, the experiment, and introspective observation. In his view, only the last method is fruitful. The *objective method* consists in

---

[1] Yves Delage (1854–1920), *Le Rêve: Étude psychologique, philosophique et littéraire* (Nantes: Imprimerie du Commerce, 1920). Freud takes note of Delage's 1891 paper on dreams in his *Interpretation of Dreams* (1899). Among his many achievements was the establishment of the function of the inner ear's semicircular canals. Under the pen name "T. Henvic," the eminent zoologist also published psychoanalytic fiction and poetry.

[2] Mr. Baumann's paper has been slightly abbreviated (G).

[3] A psychology that goes back to Aristotle's distinction between three basic, inborn human faculties (*facultates*): cognition, emotion, volition.

measuring depth of sleep, respiration, pulse, position of the extremities, facial expression, talking during sleep, etc. All such expressions are noted chronologically, and then the dreamer is asked about his dreams. Vaschide in particular used this method.[4] Another representative of this method was Heerwagen,[5] who conducted statistical surveys with the help of questionnaires that led to the following results, among others: out of four hundred people, for example, 24 percent are said to dream every night, 33 percent dream frequently, 38 percent rarely, and 4 percent once in a while. Delage opposes the view that one dreams during the whole night, as postulated, for example, by Hervey de St. Denis, whom he otherwise frequently quotes because of his rich material and his observations, above all in his book *Les rêves et les moyens de les diriger*.

Delage states that most contemporary dream theories are based on the views of Descartes, who writes: *"L'âme est de nature pensante, elle ne saurait pas ne pas penser . . . Supprimer la pensée, c'est supprimer l'âme elle-même,"*[6] and who also supposes that one would *always* dream. Here I would like to add that today something similar is put forward by Dunne in his remarkable book, *An Experiment with Time*.[7] As a counterexample, however, Delage mentions the dream of "Maury Guillotiné," often quoted in the literature: "The dreamer undergoes a long tribunal during the French Revolution, is convicted, and guillotined; then he awakes." This dream sequence is told at great length and in great detail. After waking, the dreamer realizes that the bar of the bed's canopy had fallen on his neck. He concludes that the "very long" dream can have lasted for only a fraction of a second—namely, between being hit by the bar and immediate awakening.[8]

[4] N. Vaschide, "Recherches expérimentales sur les rêves," *Comptes Rendus de l'Académie des Sciences* (July 1899): 183–86; *Le sommeil et les rêves* (Paris, 1911). P. Meunier and N. Vaschide, "Projection du rêve dans l'état de veille," *Revue de Psychiatrie* (February 1901) (G).

[5] F. Heerwagen, *Statistische Untersuchungen über Träume und Schlaf. Philosophische Studien* V, 301–20, 1888 (G).

[6] French: the soul is by its nature thinking, it cannot not think . . . To suppress thought is to suppress the soul itself.

[7] J. W. Dunne, *An Experiment with Time* (1927; reprint 2001, Hampton Roads). John William Dunne (1846–1949) was an English aeronautical engineer and designer of Britain's early military aircraft. A series of strange, precognitive dreams led Dunne to reevaluate the meaning and significance of dreams. His book, exploring the relationship between dreams, time, and reality, sparked a great deal of scientific interest—and controversy—in his new model of multidimensional time.

[8] Freud discussed this dream in *The Interpretation of Dreams*. For a recent discussion of "Maury Guillotiné," see Gordon Globus, *Dream Life, Wake Life: The Human Condition through Dreaming*

The *experimental method* consists in producing sensory impressions, such as tactile stimuli, fixation of the extremities, or moving a light before the sleeper's eyes. Subsequently, the dreamer is questioned about the dreams. Delage rejects this method, too, and considers only the *introspective method* to be fruitful. By this he simply understands the recording and observation of the dreams one remembers.

Delage classifies dreams according to their *content*. Of the ten categories he lists, I would like to mention only those of interest to us here, for instance, "les rêves généraux," *general* dreams. In those, a dreamer may fly or fall into an abyss, swim in water, or come to a narrow defile. We can in fact detect archetypes here, or rather *archetypal situations*. Delage explains them by bodily sensations, however, and the memory of these; in the case of flying, for example, by memories of exercises on the high bar, during which one actually flies rather high through the air. Another category is represented by the "rêves symboliques," *symbolic* dreams. They represent an *inner language*, whose meaning, however, he does not understand. For example, in one dream he held "a coin in his hand, on which he himself was symbolized, namely, by an extraordinarily corpulent peasant woman." In addition, there were still other little symbols. He then specifies, cloaked in materialistic-physicalist ideas, a correct core of the matter: that dream symbolism follows the law of the least necessary energy, uniting various important features in one object. In the category of the "rêves des doubles," he attributes dreamed *doubles* to the idea that the soul is a "double," which idea would be at the origin of many religious forms of belief. On the basis of numerous documents of primitive and mythological notions, we can acknowledge this idea, too, as absolutely correct.

With regard to more *formal* characteristics, Delage distinguishes between two categories, "les rêves représentatives simples," simple dreams, and "les rêves complexes," complex dreams. In *simple* dreams the time and locale of the dream events are consistent, even if there is a great deal of action. Here is an example from Delage's book:

The dreamer [Delage] is standing near the ocean, not far from his maritime laboratory, and hears the noise of an airplane, which he then sees. The body

(Albany: State University of New York Press, 1987) (a survey of Jung, Boss, Heidegger, Dennett, and others from the standpoint of transpersonal psychology).

of the airplane is a market basket. His colleague on the faculty, M. K., is sitting in it. Wings are missing, and only one big propeller, on a long stick at the rear, propels the machine rapidly out over the sea. A motorboat is rapidly approaching the coast. The airplane is now a heavy motorboat, which at the same time looks like a racing car. It still has the same big propeller. It falls vertically toward the sea, makes three loops, and after the last loop crashes into the sea. Water splashes high into the air.

We certainly would not call this dream simple, and we can recognize important things in it, clearly differentiating between two phases. Delage, however, sees only one reference to himself as the dreamer, that is, his amazement at seeing that M. K. is able to perform such complicated maneuvers as flying and doing loops without asking him, Delage, for advice. For in reality M. K. would only be a double of the dreamer's personality, who might be able to lend this figure a shadowy corporeality, but certainly not an independent soul. It is incomprehensible, therefore, how M. K. could make an independent decision without the dreamer's having been informed in advance. Such obscure thoughts about the meaning of dreams can be found frequently in Delage, although they do contain some correct notions, such as the idea of a "shadow," even though not more developed. His main focus is on rational, above all physiological, explanations.

He views the *composition* of dreams under the following aspects: (1.) setting and personae, (2.) plot, and (3.) role of the dreamer. As far as setting and personae are concerned, Delage states that these are entirely taken from the dreamer's memory, that is, from *external* perceptions, as well as from thoughts, ideas, notions, or words. Here is one example, the "rêve de l'homme à la tête de bois":[9]

Three painter apprentices; one pulls and two push a cart with their tools. Then a big wooden log approaches, floating in the air at face level; it is dry, cracked and burned, like the wood used in the cheminées.[10] It disappears, but instead one of the workmen has a wooden head of the same appearance. He looks at the dreamer [Delage] with terrible eyes.

[9] French: dream of the man with the wooden head.
[10] French: forge, hearth, chimney.

In this dream, too, which surely is very detailed, Delage interprets only the wooden log: he had seen a quite similar one the day before, and it had caught his attention. About everything else he has nothing to say at all. For him fantasy and imagination do not exist, as he explicitly states.

By way of compensation, he offers a detailed hypothesis about the "*cérébration créatrice*," from the point of view of his analytic-rational attitude, according to which all the more complex impressions, images, and notions are broken down into their "*éléments constitutifs.*" Our whole inner world is then rebuilt from these basic elements, in an infinite number of possible combinations. Such constitutive elements of an image or thought include the position in mental space (*espace mental*)—thus, for example, the word "Danube" immediately makes us place the Danube in an imagined space. For an "element," it seems to me, this spatial image is very complicated. Further elements are form, color, taste or smell, feeling, the object's name, the time (this is similar to mental space: the "French Revolution" is situated at a specific point in historical time), and bodily sensations. The latter can be sensations from either motor activity or the bowels. We are better able to understand such a connection with the vegetative system, construed as a constitutive element, than we can certain others.

As far as breaking down an image or thought into its elements is concerned, Delage states that this can amount, so to speak, to a reduction of ideas to their atomic components. These smallest components then reassociate into new images, whose original source can be recognized only rarely. Delage rejects the view that a creative fantasy is at work in this process, because the only thing at work would be "*l'énergie de reviviscence et l'association des idées.*"[11] He immediately proceeds to put this theory on a physiological foundation. The great number of single elements of all our ideas and images corresponds—as far as its order of magnitude is concerned—to the number of neurons in the brain. Upon this idea Delage bases his theory concerning the origin of dream thoughts and of thought associations in general, always giving priority to the physiological side.

[11] French: the energy of revivification and the association of ideas.

After a critical view of various explanations of dreams, Delage makes use of Lapique's hypothesis.[12] It is based upon the notion of *chronaxy*.[13] This is the minimal duration of time required by a minimal electric current to provoke an excitation in a muscle or nerve. This duration is very short, and therefore successive electrical impulses, if applied in the intervals of chronaxy, can stimulate the nerve most. Lapique discovered that each sensory nerve and muscle has a *specific* degree of chronaxy, and thus a specific mode of vibration. . . . Lapique postulates the hypothesis, yet to be proven, that this applies not only to the motor but also to the sensory nerves, as well as to neurons of the cerebral cortex. Delage builds his association theory on this hypothesis, although he expressly stresses its hypothetical character. As we have seen, he assigns, so to speak, one element of an idea to each neuron of the brain. Thus the association of different ideas, whether in consciousness or in the dream, is also caused by a vibrating interaction between certain neurons.

In the waking state the sensory impressions rapidly follow each other, but the ideas and their associations are carefully chosen by directed thinking and the criticism of waking consciousness, so that a great deal of sensory impressions and ideas is immediately repressed again from consciousness. Each element, or each idea, has a certain *potential energy*, by which it can be revitalized. In this process the repressed or inhibited ideas accumulate a very high level of energy, because they are dammed up against the gradient. The discharge of energy can happen only in the *dream*, when outer impressions and inner ideas have ceased. This creates a void into which the dream images flow to complete their discharge of energy. The physiological explanation Delage gives for the recommencing of the vibrations after the cessation of inhibitions of the waking state, however, is a weak one: its origins would lie in the body, for example, in the "*lueurs entoptiques*" (luminescence of retinal images), a theory developed by Bergson in particular. In the above dream of the airplane, for instance, the image of the glowing sea, where Delage's laboratory is situated, would have resurfaced in the dream due to such luminescence. For the sequence of images that follows it, however, Delage has but one explanation—*coincidence*: such lumines-

[12] L. Lapique, "Principe pour une théorie de fonctionnement nevreux élémentaire," *Revue Générale des Sciences pures et appliquées* 21, no. 3 (1910): 103–17.

[13] Also called *chronaxia* or *chronaxis*.

cent images cause the development of groups of ideas, which lead, by accidental vibrations of neurons, to further associations of images. . . . The unspent energy of the neurons is also absorbed by certain substances in the blood, which can then discharge it during sleep.

These theories remind us of those brought forward by Peucer and Abbé Richard: since antiquity an *intermediate substrate* between the physical and the psychical had been postulated. Peucer speaks of a "mixture of primary qualities," which would cause a "state of warmth or tension." The doctors against whom he fought called this the "intermediate substance." Abbé Richard invokes Descartes's theory, according to which certain kinds of blood corpuscles are carrier substances for the psychic factor. For Delage, too, speaks of certain substances in the blood or the vibrations of neurons, the *"énergie de reviviscence"*—likewise an oscillation between material and energetic substrates.

Delage investigates the three parts of dreams mentioned above on the basis of these physiological theories. Regarding the *scenery and the personae*, he asks: which of the ideas and images that fight for their appearance in dream consciousness take precedence? The balance is turned by the sum of three factors: the potential energy of revivification, the strength of the associative link, and the dreamer's emotional state. These three factors always act together, with the understanding that at times one or the other is stronger. He puts his main emphasis on the *emotional state*, which also contributes to the first two factors, in that emotion increases the revivification energy in individual images. Furthermore, they try to make those emotions form associations, which were, or still are, made by the dreamer. As an example, Delage cites meditative daydreaming, which opens the floodgates to the emotions with their fine nuances.

In our discussion of the composition of dreams we now come to the second element, the *plot*, the play among the actors. This, too, is determined by the dreamer's emotional state, in that the dream figures perform those actions, or make those gestures, which express a given emotion. This play among the actors also has the function of establishing a link between individual images of the dream, which Delage views as only very loosely connected. Furthermore, certain thought processes can be personified by the dream figures. Delage sees this as particularly important; in any case, he supplies a large number of examples. In dreams there appear different, mutually contradictory thoughts, whose dialectic is played out between the various figures speaking with each other. . . .

The contradictory interpretation of the flying dream, in which colleague M. K. flies around in his wingless market-basket-airplane and falls into the sea without being prompted by Delage, is left open by him. He attributes no personal meaning to it. In my view, his contradictions run as follows: if a dream figure performs an obviously *negative* action, it will be the figure's own fault, acting autonomously, and the dreamer will wash his hands of the matter, in all theoretical innocence. If, however, there is a "serious" discussion—as in another dream of his that he quotes—then the other figures will also be parts of himself.

But Delage does not explain, regarding either thoughts or emotions, why they are represented by *specific* figures in the dream, and what the dreamer's own actions stand for. He attributes all this to coincidental associations, explaining it as follows: dream memory oscillates, so to speak, between various ideas and figures, until somewhere it accidentally clicks into place, often resulting in "meaningless" combinations. As an example Delage quotes, among others, a dream of his own. The main content is his conversation with a tiger cat in the basement of his house, amid wine and coals. In the end the animal tells him confidingly: "I'd like you to call me *Mistress Toutmuss*." The dream is told in great detail; naturally, we'd be able to find significant instinctual and anima problems in it. But Delage finds only the expression "Toutmuss" remarkable, and reconstructs it from his memory of a remark made by an American woman on a sea voyage: "The sea is so smooth!," and of a "tooth,"[14] the combination of which is "Tootmouth." In the dream this becomes the French *toutmuss*,[15] a "meaningless" association, as he says. Just like ourselves, Delage looks for ex post facto *associations* to individual dream objects; in following our method, however, we cannot view these associations as meaningless, but as ideas and meaningful context. For that American woman on the sea voyage, and the tooth as a sexual symbol, excellently correspond to the rest of his tiger dream.

In order to cope with such possibilities, of course known to him from Freud's theory, he advocates the view that many actions, which link

---

[14] These expressions in English in the original.
[15] Which is not a French word, *bien entendu.*

the individual images in dreams, are only amended in the act of reproduction, because of man's unconscious need to find a causal and logical
connection between everything that happens. Thus the dream action
is always falsified a bit! He mainly draws on Foucault,[16] who even states
that the sequence of dream images is completely uncontrollable, and
that one may even assume that they appear in an order that reverses how
they are narrated afterward. Delage rejects this, however, as unproven.

According to Delage, the connection between single dream passages
can follow a logical or moralizing principle. He is rather ignorant about
what dreams mean to the dreamer; otherwise, he would not report his
own dreams, of all things, in such great detail. In his opinion, dream
contents are by no means fundamental, although he says that he was
able to realize finer nuances of his attitude toward other people, as well as
to make more sublime observations and draw better conclusions. In any
case, he arrives at the idea of a second ego, or a *little ego*, which seems to
confront, out of the dream, the *great ego*, that is, ego consciousness, and
which seems to represent something completely different, something
unknown and also uncanny. But the key to this background of ours is so
well hidden that we can no longer find it. Only the dream lets us steal
a brief look at this realm.

Can Delage himself benefit in such a way from dreams? We must
answer in the negative, as was shown, for instance, by his tiger dream.
On the one hand, he is too exclusively a rationalist, while on the other
he is unconsciously too much of a Freudian to realize, for example, the
anima problem. This situation in particular is made evident by him in
a long dream that is of the greatest interest to us, and which I would
like to call a *great* dream. Probably because he senses its importance to
himself, as he reports it *in extenso*, without being able to say anything
about it, he calls it the *"rêve du prophète"*:[17]

> On his wife's insistence, he is swimming with her through long channels to a
> patriarch, who teaches him, so to speak, "common sense"[18] about sexuality,
> education, etc., all this in a ritual, and in a voice that is not heard out loud,
> but internally, always in the company of the wife.

[16] Marcel Foucault, "L'évolution de rêve pendant le sommeil," *Revue Philosophique* 57 (1904):
459–81. *Le rêve: Études et observations* (Paris: F. Alcan, 1906) (G).
[17] French: dream of the prophet.
[18] This expression in English in the original.

In addition to this dream I would like to mention an experiment made by Mourre,[19] in which he let ideas be associated freely, resulting in meaningless correlations, as he sees it. Such a "pseudo dream"—we would call it active fantasizing[20]—goes as follows: "I think of Cap Misen, from where I look at the sea. I am in Capri, on Monte Solaro. I look at the sun; in it I see two black spots with arms and legs. A long rope is stretched between the sun and the earth . . ." and in this vein the sequence of visions continues. Only to the two last images can we supply known parallels: the black spot on the sun with the arms and legs is strongly reminiscent of the reverse side of the magic mirror that we encountered in a previous seminar.[21] And the rope from the sun to the earth parallels the vision of the mentally ill man described by Professor Jung,[22] who sees a phallus hanging down from the sun[23] as the origin of the wind.[24] A more recent mythological parallel to this image is the tube that goes down from the sun and ends in Mary's womb. Naturally, Delage can make nothing of this very interesting series of visions, just as he can make nothing of the abovementioned category of symbolic dreams.

Delage dedicates a separate chapter to the dreamer's psychological condition. He says that the soul's faculties, such as volition, emotion, discerning memory, and power of judgment, are present only on a low level in dreams: little attention, generally only impulses, no directed volition, and disordered imagination. Still, he contrasts impulsive will with certain phenomena such as Hervey de St. Denis's "free will in dreams," according to which one can direct dreams. Delage himself gives examples of the fact that one is able to be deliberately passive in

[19] C. Mourre, "La volonté dans le rêve," *Revue Philosophique de la France et de l'Étranger* (May 1903).

[20] Not to be confounded with the notion of "active imagination," which is a directed movement within inner images, with the involvement of consciousness. Cf. B. Hannah, *Encounters with the Soul: Active Imagination as Developed by C. G. Jung* (Boston: Sigo, 1981; Wilmette, IL: Chiron, 2001) (G).

[21] Cf. volume 1, chapter II, B, 4.

[22] C. G. Jung, CW 5, paras. 151, 154; CW 8, paras. 317ff. (G).

[23] In the Mithraic parallel (see note following), the sun dangles something else: "And in like fashion also [shall be seen] the Pipe, as it is called, whence comes the Wind in service [for the day]. For thou shalt see as though it were a Pipe depending from His Disk; and toward the regions Westward, as though it were an infinite East Wind." G.R.S. Mead, *A Mithraic Ritual* (London and Benares: Theosophical Publishing Society, *Echoes from the Gnosis*, vol. 6, 1907), 22.

[24] Also found in the Mithras liturgy; see C. G. Jung, CW 5, paras. 149–53 (G).

dreams in order to see what will happen. Thus, in a dream he deliberately lets himself fall from a rock down the precipice, but is carried by the air.

The dreamer is said to believe in the objectivity and reality of the dream, because there would be no reason not to. After all, all critical faculties are missing in the dream. Power of judgment, however, plays a special role, because frequently judgments or considerations are made in dreams, although in most cases they are wrong or illogical. Basically, even in the case of reflections in dreams, nothing but coincidence and uncontrollable associations are at the dreamer's disposal. One could describe this state as follows: the dreamer can focus only on single objects, but cannot see clearly peripherally at the same time. . . . Due to the lack of such peripheral material for comparison, it is impossible, therefore, to verify the correctness of the central ideas and thoughts in dreams. Only amnesia would exist, although actually as a kind of hyperamnesia.

Delage then also mentions dreams in which the thinking was *correct*. The mathematician Henri Poincaré, for instance, dreamed the solution of many mathematical problems, and the composer Tartini even dreamed the whole of his famous *Devil's Sonata*. Here I would like to remind you of the solution that came to the chemical problem of the benzene ring, seen in a dream by its discoverer[25] after long and fruitless efforts. The machine that makes perfectly round billiard balls was also dreamed by its inventor, down to the last detail.[26]

Next, Delage discusses the value of dreams in *medicine* and gives a whole series of interesting examples. A man dreams, for instance, of being bitten in the leg by a snake. A few days later a carcinogenic sore actually appears in that spot. Delage himself dreamed of his eye complaint before it appeared. In *philosophy* dreams have played a very great role in ideas about immortality and the whole pantheon of gods. Dreams are also said to be important for spiritual problems. There are many interesting examples in the literature.[27]

---

[25] A. Kekulé of Stradonitz (1829–1896). His dream vision of a snake eating its tail gave him the key to understanding the chemistry of the benzene ring, a basis for the whole of organic chemistry and thus our modern industrial culture (G).

[26] Another example: in 1913 the physicist Nils Bohr discovered the highly important atomic model, later named after him, in this way.

[27] Émile Durkheim, "Origine de la pensée religieuse," *Revue Philosophique* (January 1909). C. Flammerion, *L'inconnu et les problèmes psychiques* (Paris, 1900). P. Janet, *L'Automatisme psy-*

A further chapter is devoted to a detailed description and criticism of dream theories, such as those of Bergson[28] and Freud. His criticism of the claims in Freud's theory is the same as ours: first, that there should be a hidden meaning behind the dream's manifest content; second, that a dream is said always to give expression to an infantile wish; and third, Freud's obstinacy in trying to generalize his theory, often resulting in artificial conclusions, in "*tournures d'esprit.*"[29]

Delage's book is an attempt to develop a theory of dreams on the basis of typically materialistic views. It contains, after all, a great number of contradictions. Because of his attitude as described above, Delage has to reject a deeper psychological meaning in dreams, something to which Freud's theory may probably have contributed. On the other hand, he senses the *individual* importance of dreams, concerning which he beats around the bush, particularly in the case of those dreams of his own that greatly preoccupy him. Consequently, he is unable to conceive the notion of a *collective-psychic origin* of dream images.

Delage's relative impartiality in scientific matters, however, should be emphasized, as well as his pointing out that he views his own theories, and also those of Lapique, as provisional hypotheses.[30] The great number of viewpoints discussed, as well as the 173 examples of dreams, make this an interesting book despite its shortcomings.

---

chologique (Paris: F. Alcan, 1899). A. Maury, *Le sommeil et les rêves*, 4th ed. (Paris, 1878). "De certains faites observés dans les rêves et dans l'état intermédiaire entre le sommeil et la veille," *Annales médico psychologiques* 3 (1857). T. Smith, "The Psychology of Day-Dreams," *American Journal of Psychiatry* 15 (1904): 465–88 (G).

[28] H. Bergson, "Le rêve," *Bulletin de l'Institut géneral psychologique* 1 (1901): 103–22; and *Revue Scientifique* 4ᵉ s. 15 (June 8, 1901): 703–13 (G).

[29] French: twists of the mind.

[30] Lapique's ideas, by the way, have been more and more confirmed, and are one of the most important bases of biological and neurological research today (H. B.).

CHAPTER 8

Discussion of Paul W. Radestock,[1] *Schlaf und Traum* (*Sleep and Dream*)[2]

Paper by Dr. Alice Kitzinger[3]

Professor Jung: This book offers an interesting insight into a psychology characteristic of the 1870s. At that time *materialism* flourished. The physical was seen as what was really essential. Basically, therefore, psychic processes were traced back to the organic and physiological nature of man. Medical psychology degenerated into brain mythology. So the sleeping and waking states, for instance, were explained by the contractions of the nerve processes of brain cells: during the waking state the processes touch each other, resulting in a circuit. In the sleeping state these processes withdraw, and then consciousness is obliterated. No person had ever seen such a thing, but everyone was happy to have this idea. After all, a couple of things could be explained that way! One wasn't able, however, to get to know the real nature of the soul that way. It was basically a *psychology without a soul*. But as there was still the wish to understand or comprehend the psychical, an intense preoccupation with consciousness developed, because consciousness was the

---

[1] German psychologist of the late nineteenth century, author of *Schlaf und Traum: Ein physiologische-psychologische Untersuchung* (1879), *Genie und Wahnsinn: Eine psychologiscche Untersuchung* (1884), and *Habit and Its Importance in Education: An Essay in Pedagogical Psychology* (1886), trans. F. Caspari, intro. G. Stanley Hall (Boston: Heath, 1897). Jung's discussion credits Radestock not only with ethnological acumen about dream motifs but also with crucial anticipations of the compensatory function of dreaming and the collective unconscious.

[2] Meeting on November 15, 1938 (G).

[3] Parts of Dr. Kitzinger's paper are included in the proceedings of the seminar (G).

only thing one actually knew about the psychical. Grandiose notions about the nature of consciousness were conceived—and it was indeed necessary to strengthen consciousness; the time when consciousness was still an endangered variable was not so long ago at all. The greatest superstition lurked directly behind the intellectualism. The most absurd scientific theories were happily believed, as already mentioned. People did not at all notice how unscientific they were. With the help of the theory, they felt protected from the fact that there were still other things that existed in the psyche. The great danger was to regress to the Middle Ages, and perhaps to discover God, that is, something that we "no longer" master. The fear was that the old superstition might turn out to contain a grain of truth after all. People could not distinguish between a psychic fact and either concrete metaphysics or a regression to the Middle Ages. The result was that consciousness was overestimated. One tried to explain "downwards" from consciousness, that is, the unconscious was derived, in a very anthropomorphic way, from consciousness. For scientists of the 1880s and 1890s, it would have been a tremendous endeavor to think as we are able to do today without any effort—namely, *that consciousness is based upon the unconscious.* If we assume that consciousness emanates from the unconscious, then the unconscious will gain much greater importance, and will somehow become ominous for our consciousness. [In the '80s and '90s] one really couldn't go back on that onerously achieved position of consciousness, which one had become so proud of!

Even at that time, however, there existed other opinions. Carus[4] had lived not long before; and von Hartmann,[5] who elevated the unconscious to Absolute Spirit, was a contemporary of these brain mythologists. He anticipated today's viewpoint that unconscious functioning is the actual psychic activity, and that consciousness develops out of

[4] Carl Gustav Carus (1789–1869), German doctor and natural philosopher of the Romantic era. His philosophy attributed great importance to the unconscious. He postulated that everything natural was produced by ideas, which makes him a forerunner of the theory of archetypes (G).

[5] Karl Robert Eduard von Hartmann (1842–1906), a German philosopher greatly inspired by Carus. His main philosophical work is *Philosophie des Unbewußten* (Berlin, 1869; 11th ed., 3 vols., 1904). The object of his philosophy was to unite the "idea" of Hegel with the "will" of Schopenhauer in his doctrine of the Absolute Spirit, or, as he preferred to characterize it, spiritual monism. He held that "a will which does not will something is not." The world was produced by will and idea, but not as a conscious matter; for consciousness, instead of being essential, is accidental to will and idea, the two poles of the unconscious.

it only secondarily. Only recently Carus and also Bachofen[6] have been rediscovered. I lived in Basel when Bachofen was still alive. I knew him, and I remember that everybody made fun of the quaint old man. He was not taken seriously. It was not realized how brilliant he was. Burckhardt,[7] too, spoke very critically of him. He was just as much laughed at as Nietzsche.[8] It was just that Nietzsche was even stranger and provoked more gossip, so there was more talk about him. Bachofen had no audience.

No one can be personally held responsible, however, for this negative attitude. It has to do with the general resistance to relinquishing the overestimation of consciousness, and accepting that we are not the only masters in the house, that we are at the mercy of another one. There can be no doubt about this power of the unconscious. Our everyday life is full of examples: we'd like to introduce someone, for instance—and his name escapes us. Indeed we know the name, but we don't remember it at that particular moment. When the unconscious does not cooperate, we are at a complete loss. The effect of the unconscious is demonstrated most clearly in mental disturbances and neuroses. I once was very impressed by the following case:

> A philosopher had the hypochondriacal idea that he suffered from stomach or intestinal cancer. He said that he had already been to numerous doctors who naturally had not found anything. Even though he was certain that he did not have a carcinoma, he could not surmount his fear of having one nevertheless. So obviously he was completely incapable of fighting that idea. In his theories, of course, the unconscious did not exist at all. But that's exactly why it played this trick on him!

True, we must be prudent and not needlessly personify the unconscious. It is indisputable, however, that consciousness depends on the unconscious in all important expressions of life. In evolutionary terms, too, consciousness is a product of the unconscious. Children start off in

---

[6] Johann Jakob Bachofen (1815–1887), Swiss historian, known for his theory of matriarchy (*Mother Right: An Investigation of the Religious and Juridical Character of Matriarchy in the Ancient World*, 1861). He assembled documentation meant to demonstrate that motherhood is the source of human society, religion, morality, and decorum.

[7] Jacob Burckhardt (1818–1897), Swiss historian and art historian, best known for his works on the Italian Renaissance and on Greek civilization.

[8] Nietzsche had been his colleague at the University of Basel, and had called Burckhardt "our great, our greatest teacher."

an unconscious state and grow into conscious states. We can observe how these islands of consciousness grow together, until continuous consciousness develops. At first children call themselves by their own names, as if they regarded themselves as objects. But this is only quasi-objectivity, based on a nondifferentiation between subject and object. Only gradually does the child emerge from this unconscious state and learn to say "I."

Radestock gives a mainly external description of phenomena, and tries to coin terms for what he observed. As you have heard, he wants to demonstrate the continuous relations between physical and psychic processes.

(From the paper:)

> In his foreword he writes: "In my physio-psychological study I wanted to demonstrate the continuous relation between physical and psychic changes, and to prove the importance of dream images in the mental life of the individual, of peoples, and of the whole of mankind."

The psyche becomes derivative from the organism. According to the spirit of his age, he mainly drew upon consciousness to come to an understanding of the psyche. With all his knowledge of the dream processes, he lacked the insight—the first discovery of which we owe to Freud—that dreams have an inner continuity of meaning. This discovery of meaning is actually the basis for the whole later attempt to understand the unconscious. Nevertheless, already in Radestock we find certain ideas that are ahead of his time: among others, the idea of a *compensatory* meaning in dreams, the idea that they stand in a certain balancing relation to consciousness.

(From the paper:)

> The dream can have different effects on the dreamer. It can have a balancing and healing effect; it can cause apparently inexplicable affects, feelings of sympathy and antipathy, and it can have a stimulating effect on mental productivity, a fact Radestock discovered with the help of a compendium of his own dreams, and based on the reports of various artists.

You see that this notion of compensation was already held before our time. We also find in Radestock the idea that the images appearing in dreams can also be found everywhere in ethnopsychology.[9]

---

[9] Art historian Michele Facos, with reference to Paul Gauguin in particular, enlists Radestock's pioneering views in relativizing the barriers between civilized/uncivilized and conscious/unconscious. "In *Sleep and Dream* (1879), Radestock observed that many indigenous peoples believed

(From the paper:)

He describes the influence of dreams and related, i.e., visionary states, on the coming into being and development of religious ideas. . . . As the figures of the dead often appear in dreams not only in a favorable but also an un-favorable light, one tried to appease them; ancestor worship developed, the deification and demonization of these figures. . . . Visionary states, like those of the shamans, for example, and images emerging in meditation, have par-ticularly contributed to the consolidation and spread of religious ideas.

This already anticipates the idea of what we call the *collective unconscious*,[10] the existence of which is always so fervently denied. Thus the idea of the collective unconscious is not so new either. Bas-tian[11] already described the phenomenon of collective images in detail. Then again we find similar ideas in Nietzsche, who surely had not read Bastian or our good old Radestock, when he writes, for instance, that the dream would repeat the *pensum* of ancient mankind, that it would traverse the whole spectrum of ideas that our ancestors had already trav-eled. This is a probable assumption; our bodies also bear traces of the past. Why should it be otherwise in the psyche? Because our psyche is being formed by the newspapers and the radio? Our psyche has remained exactly the same, only the surface has changed. The basic contents have always been there; otherwise we would not be able to understand for-eign cultures in their strange ways of thinking. In ethnology, for exam-ple, one was content for a long time to point out that primitives were different. Lévy-Bruhl[12] still speaks of an *état prélogique*. But primitives think as logically as we do; only the premises are different.

---

that the dead were constantly present although they appeared to the living only in dreams. Rade-stock's notion of cultural differences in what people dreamed about relied on the racialist theories of Arthur de Gobineau's four-volume *Essay on the Inequality of the Human Races* (1853 & 1855)" (*Symbolist Art in Context* [Berkeley: University of California Press, 2009], 18).

[10] C. G. Jung developed the notion of the collective unconscious in *Symbols and Transforma-tions of the Libido*; cf. CW 5, preface, 2nd and 3rd editions, and chap. 2, B, 4, footnote 66 (G).

[11] Adolf Bastian (1826–1905), known as the founder of ethnography, was broadly educated in law, biology, and medicine, and traveled widely in carrying out ethnological studies. As Jung notes here, his archetypal hypothesis takes Bastian's notion of *Elementargedanke*, or elemental ideas, as one of its chief antecedents.

[12] Lucien Lévy-Bruhl (1857–1939), French philosopher, sociologist, and ethnographer, inves-tigated the collective consciousness of primitive ethnic groups and concluded that the mental activity of such societies can be explained by the "law of participation" (*participation mystique*). In the occult powers of the totem he recognized the effect of archetypal images (cf. chapter 10 herein; late in his career, Lévy-Bruhl withdrew support from his formulation of this idea) (G).

CHAPTER 9

Discussion of Philipp Lersch, *Der Traum in der deutschen Romantik*[1] *(The Dream in German Romanticism)*[2]

Paper by Dr. Charlotte Spitz[3]

Professor Jung: Do you see a connection between *Romanticism* and *psychology?*

Participant: Yes, in the relation to the unconscious, particularly to the *collective unconscious.*

Professor Jung: Is the Romantic's idea of life in general identical with the idea of the collective unconscious?

(From the paper:)

> The way individuality recedes in the dream is correlative to the emergence of collective psychic life. Hence the assumption, so important to us, that the individual is rooted in life in general, in a general psychic life. The dreaming human being receives the contents of life from these roots.

Participant:[4] No, collective life is unformed life as such. It is based on a connection to the environment that is established by inner perception.

---

[1] Lersch's dissertation at Munich (Munich: Hueber, 1923). Lersch (1898–1972), a disciple of Wilhelm Dilthey, published studies of emotion, its expression in body language, and the "Vital Unconscious" and "Biocentric Principle" and did early work in military psychiatry. During the National Socialist era, he took the academic loyalty oath, although not a party member, and held professorships at Leipzig and Munich. Following a denazification trial after the war, for his support of euthanasia, he continued to teach.

[2] Meeting on November 29, 1938 (G).

[3] Parts of Dr. Spitz's paper are included in the proceedings of the seminar (G).

[4] Reacting to Jung, not to the quote from the paper.

(From the paper:)

> The Romantics stress the capability of remaining in contact with the environment by an inner connection, despite a complete elimination of the natural senses, to know the environment with an intensity of inner perception which sensitivity in the waking state falls short of by far.

Professor Jung: The idea of collective life is a general view of life as such. The collective unconscious is quite different from that, however: in a certain sense it is even excluded from collective life. But don't the Romantics perhaps believe in something similar to the collective unconscious after all? Didn't you notice something? Didn't you come across passages in Romantic literature that confirm this presumption?

Participant: The interest in *mythology* and the ideational world of *primitives*.

Professor Jung: Yes, the idea of the collective unconscious finds an expression in the preoccupation with mythology and folktales. But the ideas aren't specified or made clear anywhere. It's all *feeling* and *sentiment*. Romanticism is characterized by emotional ecstasy, by something phantasmagoric, enthusiastic, by an indescribable mix of feeling states.

(From the paper:)

> The actual attitude of the Romantics toward life is that they do not want to grasp the world as an object, but to experience it as a state. Here lie the roots of romantic subjectivism, which is nothing other than a desire to remove all objective, spatial existence, the dimension of the object. The final and climactic point of this way of life is in mysticism, which also does not want to possess "the loved object," as Lersch puts it, but wants to be the object, to merge with it, melt into it. . . . Feeling is the organ with which the world's existence is perceived; conceived as a spiritual experience, it is the criterion of what is real.

How do you explain this?

Participant: In a certain sense as a contrast to the Enlightenment.

Professor Jung: That would give rise to the idea of a deliberate reaction, as was the case in the French Revolution, for example. There the meaning of spiritual values, of ethics and religion, was crushed. Is that how we have to see it?

Participant: No, it's that what erupts had been neglected before.

Professor Jung: Yes, this is an involuntary state, a kind of inner movement. How do you explain this strange dizziness, this state of movement?

Participant: By the approach of the unconscious.

Professor Jung: When the unconscious is constellated, that often leads to such a state, to being strangely dazed. What is the reason, why does the unconscious have this effect?

Participant: Because contents of the unconscious are forced upon one, and one does not know how to deal with them.

Professor Jung: Yes, contents become tangible. What do they cause in consciousness?

Participant: A fascination.

Professor Jung: The contents are fascinating, that's right. In general, when we read myths or folktales, we are mildly interested. We remember blessed childhood states and find all that quite nice, but we are not fascinated. We don't become enraptured. It is something completely different if mythology *happens* to one! That is exactly what happened to the Romantics. Vital contents that had got lost through the Enlightenment were forced upon them with such force that they exerted a heating and vaporizing influence on consciousness. That caused the intoxication! When images come out of the forge of the unconscious, such strangely dazed states develop. It becomes dangerous when they become collective movements, then they can generate real epidemics!

Participant: Isn't the intoxication also due to the fact that single contents are contaminated with the whole of the unconscious? The whole unconscious infiltrates consciousness; confronted with this, consciousness is not yet ready to make all the constellated contents conscious.

Professor Jung: Yes, one isn't able to integrate them, to really clarify them. All kinds of connections impose themselves and can't be cut off. What do we call such a state?

Participant: It is a state of disintegration, a schizophrenia.

Professor Jung: Yes, consciousness covers a certain area, and is limited to a certain area that allows for only a limited number of contents. We are unable to clearly conceive of two contents at the same time. It is in the nature of archetypal images that they push their way simultaneously into consciousness in indeterminate numbers. Consciousness has to expand excessively to be able to "think" archetypes. When this fails, it loses all lucidity; the images become dark, and can even get torn apart. When everything falls apart, we speak of a schizophrenic state.

Participant: Viewed in the context of this mental split, is the *blue flower*, the allegory of romantic desire, a symbol of wholeness, or of spiritual unity?

Professor Jung: The image of the blue flower is an attempt to integrate the multiplicity into a whole, into a *unity*, and thus create a counterweight to the chaos of intruding archetypes. This was precisely the problem at that time, which to a great extent was infected by the French Revolution and bore the mark of intellectualism. The situation was extremely uncomfortable. The clear, tidy connections of consciousness were abruptly severed by the intrusion of the unconscious. They did not know how to deal with the unconscious; they no longer had forms in which to express themselves, except in lyrical poems, folktales, or fantastical stories, such as those E.T.A. Hoffmann wrote.[5] A real attempt to conceptualize these things was never made. Have you noticed other features that are characteristic of Romanticism?

Participant: The emergence of events long forgotten by consciousness, for example, in dreams.

Professor Jung: In the Romantics, we can clearly see *how* the unconscious operates. Not only do the forgotten contents come to life again, but also completely new images emerge from the depths of the unconscious. As it is, the psychical not only depends on our opinion, it is not something arbitrary, but something that happens, a phenomenon. I have coined a term for this fact that many people don't understand.

Participant: Psychic reality, the *reality of the soul*.

Professor Jung: Yes, that's what it's about. The Romantics perceived the reality of the existence of these inner states and contrasted it with outer reality. Have you noticed anything else with regard to Romanticism?

Participant: The *dream* is seen as an essential part of psychic life. (From the paper:)

Novalis[6] writes: "The dream teaches us, in a strange way, how effortlessly the soul can enter into each object, and can at once turn into each object." Thus, the dream is the world adequate for the Romantic

---

[5] Ernst Theodor Amadeus Hoffmann (1776–1822), German jurist, writer, composer, and visual artist. Jung refers above all to *The Devil's Elixirs* and *The Golden Pot* (G).

[6] Pseudonym of Friedrich Leopold, Freiherr von Hardenberg (1772–1801), important German poet and novelist in early Romanticism. The fragment *Heinrich von Ofterdingen* describes the hero's search for the mysterious "blue flower" (G).

attitude toward life. In the dream there is no objective comprehension of the world; its essence lies in a deepened, saturated feeling of the present state. . . . Its meaning lies not in the outer appearance of single images, but in the quality of feeling, in the atmosphere that is evoked in us by the whole of the dream events. . . . But the experience of a dream is not only livelier and deeper as far as the affects are concerned, but also richer in contents. It not only supplies wish fulfillment, but also brings to life impressions of objects, people, and events that are hardly touched by waking consciousness. . . . The realm of the unconscious is opened up.

Participant: The inner contents are heavily projected onto the world.
Professor Jung: Did Romanticism really project its contents onto the world? Envision how the Romantics experience the world!
Participant: We can't actually say that the Romantics projected. If they did, there wouldn't be so much talk of sober awakening.
Professor Jung: Yes, the fact is rather that the Romantics *introject* the world. It may happen occasionally that they project their inner constellations onto the world, so that what is real takes on a symbolic role. In general, however, there is a clear distinction between inside and outside: one is afraid of existence, outer existence, which unfortunately does not correspond to this beautiful reality inside, where one is able to make a dumb bourgeois interior revert to a Gothic style, or to breed artificial cobwebs. . . . *Yearning backwards* is a movement away from this odious reality. So consciousness of reality as it really is did exist in Romanticism, but that reality was transferred into the sphere of folktales. That's introjection. In *projection* inner images are moved outward, so that reality is veiled. It then appears in an altered form, precisely because what had been released from the inside is experienced and seen on the outside. In introjection the world is swallowed and spun into an inner web. Although the outer world is seen as it is, the current moves away from it.

(From the paper:)

The difference between the waking state and the dream is perceived by the Romantics, therefore, in the following antitheses: out there, a foreign, rigid, hostile world, gray and dull; in here, a lively, dear and intimate, colorful one. There banality and boredom, here beauty and rich experience; there finitude and here infinity. . . . The Romantic has a strong desire for the realm of the dream and the age of myths, when the living bond of the individual with the environment was realized; the world as it is here and now, however, is inconceivable for him as a reality.

Participant: Is the attitude of introjection introverted?

Professor Jung: There are extraverts as well as introverts among the Romantics. Romanticism is a time style in which both types partici-pate. Introjection need not be connected to the attitude of introver-sion. A Romantic could be extraverted without *eo ipso* being an adher-ent of the French Revolution, for example. Goethe wasn't a fanatic of the Enlightenment either! Do you see other crucial features in Roman-ticism? It was stressed in the paper that the Romantics interpreted the notion of *appearance* as an *illusion.*[7] Is appearance illusion?

(From the paper:)

> Kant's philosophy was used as an intellectual justification, by mistakenly interpreting his notion of "appearance" as "semblance." It is Romantic to view life as if through a veil, with a doubting "maybe" over every-thing, and an ultimate "ungraspable" behind everything. Reality is a dream drifting past, which cannot be seized; its existence and meaning will forever remain alien to humans.

Participant: It depends on the perspective. If we assume that the psy-chical is reality, then from this viewpoint appearance is an illusion, that is, only an accidental form bound by time and space, which has no essential meaning with regard to the other reality.

Professor Jung: Yes, this view arises when we experience the world with our feelings! For Kant, too, the world of appearance was not what was actually real. Real were the *noumena,* imaginary objects. We can-not say about Kant, however, that his conception was based on emo-tional experience. For him, moral judgment was the creative root of the actual, ideal world. It was the idea of the reality of *noumena* that influenced the Romantics, although they comprehended Kant through the organ of feeling. It was precisely the infiltration of philosophy by

---

[7] In the original: *"Erscheinung als Schein." Scheinen* originally meant "to glow," "to glimmer," "to shine," and only later took on the meaning of indicating a deceptive outer image that does not correspond to reality. *Erscheinen* is "to show itself," "to become evident." The noun *Erscheinung* can also stand for "appearance," "event," "fact" (Duden, *Das Herkunftswörterbuch*).

feeling that significantly contributed to the development of the intoxicated state that we have just spoken about.

Participant: Doesn't the view that appearance is mere illusion stem from the fact that we do not look at things under the aspect of their intrinsic origin? Spinoza,[8] for instance, speaks of *"natura sive deus."*[9]

Professor Jung: When Goethe says, "We live our lives in reflected colors,"[10] he expresses approximately the same opinion as that of the Romantics: reflection is a reality, illusion is reality. This corresponds exactly to the Eastern conception of *maya*. The word *maya* is derived from the stem *ma*, which means material, building material. When somebody says *maya* he means something real, although it is only an illusion. In the East, therefore, they speak about the real illusion of forms. Thus our simple translation by the term "illusion" is wrong. We should rather say real illusion, which emanates from something unknowable.

What else strikes you in Romanticism? Can influences be discerned, for instance, which Romanticism had on the later development of psychology? What is the historical bridge that connects the modern spirit with Romanticism?

Participant: Carus.[11]

Professor Jung: Yes, and who was influenced by him?

Participant: Eduard von Hartmann.[12]

Professor Jung: Yes, he is in fact the bridge between modern philosophy and Romanticism. He was deeply influenced by Carus. He himself acknowledged in his foreword to *The Philosophy of the Unconscious*—

---

[8] Baruch (Benedict) de Spinoza (1632–1677), influential Dutch philosopher and ethicist. Spinoza is best known for *The Ethics* (1677), a work that presents an ethical vision unfolding out of monistic metaphysics in which God and Nature are identified. God is no longer the transcendent creator of the universe who rules it through providence, but Nature itself, understood as an infinite, necessary, and fully deterministic system of which humans are a part. Humans find happiness only through a rational understanding of this system and their place within it.

[9] Latin: Nature or God, i.e., Nature is as important as God.

[10] *Faust II*, Act I.i.4727 ("Am farbigen Abglanz haben wir das Leben"). The context also includes refraction, in the rainbow hues of sunshot spray. Newtonian refraction—Brechung or Refraktion—was not Goethe's way with color, but since prismatic refraction marks the context, translator David Constantine nods toward both meanings: "That is the image for this striving life of ours. / Think more of that and grasp with more exactness: / We have life only in its flung-off colors" (*Faust Part II* [London: Penguin, 2009], 6).

[11] See above, 70.

[12] See above, 70.

although it was embarrassing for him—that Carus had anticipated him. His main metaphysical ideas can already be found in Carus, and Carus is a Romantic through and through! The fact that we speak about the *unconscious* at all is a direct *inheritance* from the Romantic spirit. We have not been able, however, to adopt other constitutive elements of Romanticism in the present.

CHAPTER 10

Discussion of Jackson Steward Lincoln,
The Dream in Primitive Cultures[1]

Paper by Dr. Kenower Bash[2]

Professor Jung: Lincoln, who wrote this book, is actually an amateur in psychology and ethnology. I know him personally. He has worked very diligently, but, as is so often the case, his knowledge of psychology is lacking. After all, one must have experienced the psychic facts to some extent in order to understand the ideational world of primitives. One will never be able to know, for example, what a primitive means by a great dream if one has not experienced for oneself what a great dream is. For a Negro it means everything when he says, "The Great Vision."

Primitives are all quite natural psychologists, precisely because they are not "psychologists." It happens to them. Unfortunately the views they hold correspond to my views; that's why people think that I'm a primitive and that I practice demonology. That's what the representatives of science accuse me of. When I prove, for instance, that primitives have the same mythological ideas as civilized man, or that some civilized people have the same ideas as primitives, that is no demonology. One cannot say that such views are merely theoretical; these correspondences do exist. I will give you examples that show that primitives make assertions that can also be found in Latin texts from the Middle

---

[1] *The Dream in Primitive Cultures*, introduction by C. G. Seligman (London: Cresset Press, 1935). Meeting on January 10, 1939 (G).

[2] Parts of the paper—with Bash by this time having earned his MD—are included in the proceedings of the seminar.

Ages or in ourselves, and in present-day civilized man—without being in the least interdependent. When Negroes say, for example, that souls leave at night and enter another person in the form of a fireball, we can find precisely the same idea in the Middle Ages. Caesarius von Heisterbach,[3] who lived at that time, tells the story of a nun—the text is from the thirteenth century—who had seen the soul in the form of a fireball. The Negroes certainly did not read this story, and the nun knew nothing about the Negroes either. The same image can be found in Jakob Böhme,[4] who was a shoemaker, a completely uneducated man, and who certainly hadn't read Heisterbach either. Or you can take as examples contemporary persons who are preoccupied with their souls and bring to the doctor drawings of fireballs as a soul symbol. Or think of Greek natural philosophy, which also entertains these ideas. It really can't be assumed in all these cases, which exist completely independently of each other, that the shared ideas are based upon tradition. We simply have these images within ourselves—but one must have experienced this. Lincoln doesn't know this; that limits his judgment.

He is also somewhat incautious in applying Freud's theory rather inappropriately. For example, he adopts the view of the dream as a wish fulfillment. When we talk about an unconscious wish, we have already said too much. We don't know what the unconscious does. We can only see what the unconscious produces. We don't know what it wishes. It's quite cheap simply to impute a wish to the dream text. Just have a look at how that is done! Suppose I dream of a beautiful apple tree full of fruits. Nobody can forbid you from interpreting the dream in such a way that the unconscious wishes for the apple tree! You are helpless against such an interpretation, because you can neither affirm nor deny it by means of the dream text. Or take this: how can you speak of an unconscious wish, for instance, when you have a dream in which the father died—and the father already has been dead for a long time? How should this be an unconscious wish? There's absolutely no evidence for such an assumption. We have only the dream text and nothing else.

---

[3] Caesarius von Heisterbach (1180–1240), theologian and writer in the Cistercian monastery of Heisterbach. He collected valuable documents concerning the history of culture and morals in his *Libri Miraculorum* (G).

[4] For the mystic Jakob Böhme (1575–1624) God was the origin of all things, even of evil, which is necessary to create the good. Similarly, the good in man only shows on the basis of evil; man would be able to freely decide between the two (G).

Everything else is theory. So this is exactly why Lincoln was unable to do justice to the nature of primitives, because he viewed the dream as a wish fulfillment. We have to put ourselves in the position of primitives if we want to understand them. Take a dream a primitive told me, as an example.

> There was an old chief who had made friends with me.[5] He had many head of cattle that were looked after by his slaves. Among the cattle was a white-and-black spotted cow. He dreamed that this cow was going to calve. In the same night in which he dreamed this, the cow actually did calve. He had not known, however, that this cow had been pregnant. Of course this was his wish! But what does this mean for the dream? One could argue that the man could have observed, after all, that the cow was pregnant. There are indeed such cases. But this supposition is completely unnecessary for understanding the dream.

Such a dream can be sufficiently explained as *participation*. And by this we get much closer to the life of primitives than by all kinds of theoretical constructs.

Primitives, as it is, live in partial identity with the animal. There are few differences between animal and man. For the primitive, it is only by coincidence that the animal has taken the form of an animal. Primitives generally speak as if they were talking about humans when they talk about animals. They might say, "Then an elephant found something and put it into its pocket." Or they imagine the spider asking her children, "Where is the snuff box?" Animals are humans. They speak human language, and therefore a magician can also understand animal language. Primitives often regard animals as their ancestors. They also address them as such; a dog can be the mother, a bull the father. An animal can be my ancestor, and insofar as I am also my ancestor, I am his brother. Primitives may even think that objects are their ancestors. These are the so-called *totem objects*. Take the example of the arrow-bow: this is an object that the primitive makes himself. But he is of the opinion

---

[5] Apart from many other travels to peoples who had remained aboriginal, in 1925 Jung also visited Kenya in Africa (cf. *Memories, Dreams, Reflections*). There he became friends with the chief of the still-primitive tribe of the Elgonyi, who lived in the rain forest of Mount Elgon and were partly still cave dwellers. Cf. C. G. Jung, CW 18, ¶s 1288–91 (G), as well as Blake Burleson, *Jung in Africa* (New York: Continuum, 2005), in the references to Tendeet, the Elgnoyi headman.

that he wouldn't be able to make an arrow-bow if he didn't have arrow-bow ancestors. The arrow-bow is an arrow-bow man, perhaps it's the great-grandfather, who happened to have the form of an arrow-bow. The latter has a head on top and feet at the bottom. And where the strings are wound around the bow there is the neck, and the two buttons above are the eyes. The strings of the bow are a bit frayed, that's the hair. And the string that hangs on it is the woman, who clings to his neck. It's the ancestral couple.

Or take the rain totem: how can rain be an ancestor? He is simply the rain man—the clouds are his head, the hanging fog shadows are hair, and the rain coming down the legs. Where rain hits the earth, there are the feet. This is not what I think; this is what primitives think. The rain ancestor has the form of rain, but in reality he is a man.

You see, what is essential in the totem is the idea of the *archetypes*. This idea is so suggestive that even Lévy-Bruhl, who can certainly not be suspected of espousing my psychology, says: "Ce sont des types, vraiment des archetypes."[6] Most often these totem beings are half human, half animal; they are the ancestors. This whole experience is a memory of the time when man was half animal, half human: *aljira*[7] or *bugari*. These terms mean totem ancestor, totem animal, and so also the place or the world where these ancestors still live, the time in which they lived. This *aljira* is "the time in which time did not exist yet," but which is always there—alongside the time that has become time. But the world in which time does not yet exist is the world of the unconscious, and this world is always—alongside. We are indeed able to go to *aljira* in the dream, and to put ourselves into the *aljira*, because *aljira* also means dream. When a primitive tells a myth, and does not tell it correctly, another primitive will say, "He can't tell it correctly, he didn't dream it correctly." The dream is the informant about the *aljira*; it is the *aljira* itself. What he hears in the dream is a piece of exact information about the archetypes. "*Les éternels incréés*," the eternally uncreated, it couldn't be expressed better.[8] These are simply the Platonic ideas; this

[6] French: these are types, real archetypes.

[7] See the discussion of the "Dream of a five-year-old girl of the death masks of her parents" in *Children's Dreams Seminar*, 151.

[8] The phrases from Lévy-Bruhl in this paragraph stem from several writings Jung absorbed beginning in 1910. For a compact survey of Jung's debt to Lévy-Bruhl, see Shamdasani, *Jung and the Making of Modern Psychology: The Dream of a Science* (Cambridge: Cambridge University Press,

is Platonic philosophy on a primitive level. That is, it is not philosophy, but experience. You will experience this in dreams. *"Les éternels incréés"* are the archetypes, the primeval images, without which nothing at all can happen. This is also the reason why the primitive can see the primeval parental couple in the arrow-bow. From there stem the myths, the chants, the dances. They are taught by the ancestors, those uncreated and eternal ones, in the dream. In view of this primitive state of the soul, it is really unthinkable that we might apply Freudian psychology to it.

Participant: What is your position regarding Lincoln's rejection of the collective unconscious?

(From the paper:)

> Here Lincoln contests Jung's alleged assertion that the dream symbols were creations of a collective unconscious, shared by all humankind, but thinks that the symbols of the great dream visions would at most be collective creations of the tribe. . . . They are thought of as an expression of tradition, not of the memory of the race.

Professor Jung: I can only say that the good man simply doesn't understand it better. He cannot deny that the functional system, which lies at the base of human nature, is approximately the same in all people. The similarity of mythological forms, which can be observed all over the world, is an expression of this commonality in the psychological foundations. People always function the same way, even where there is no tradition. This has led me to the opinion that there has to be an *unconscious system*, which is *the same in each human being* and which gives rise to the same problems. Lincoln repudiates this idea of the collective unconscious, because he thinks there would be an independently existing spirit that had spread throughout humankind. There can be no question of that, for this is about the fact that the psyche functions in the same way in all humans, just as the function of the heart is the same in all humans. He himself talks of individual

---

2003), 288–97. On internal experience rather than philosophical formulation, see 297: "Jung also claims that what was important was the similarity of the content of the act, and not just how it was done. . . . One can conjecture that it was through combining key concepts of Bastian and Lévy-Bruhl that Jung came upon the conviction of the existence of that which he would subsequently call archetypes."

experiences, although they are supposed to have been caused by phylogenetic heredity. But so far nothing is known about psychic experiences being transmitted through heredity. I am occasionally accused of such a statement, although I have expressly repudiated it. Instincts have not been acquired, and archetypes are forms of instincts, modes of functioning that exist, a priori. But we cannot prove that we can also transmit acquired features.

You have learned from the paper that Lincoln, despite his repudiation of the collective unconscious, cannot deny that we can detect a *similarity of psychic contents* in different tribes and cultures. It's only that he tries to account for this fact upside down. He is inclined to explain the similarity of psychic images from the similarity of social conditions. He directly postulates that there have to be similar social conditions; there have to be similar cultures!

(From the paper:)

> The symbols in such dreams [great dreams], insofar as they are universal and have the same latent meaning everywhere, are no evidence of a collective genetic constitution. They are cultural products and indicate that there have to be cultural conditions that eternally remain the same. Such a similarity of symbols is probably due to certain universal, similar characteristics of the family group.

I'd like to put a question mark after that, however. We can't offhandedly prove this similarity of cultures. On the contrary, we are deeply impressed by the diversity of cultures, and the diversity of laws and moral views. The diversity of cultures stands in no contradiction to the thesis of a collective unconscious. It is, on the contrary, a characteristic of the basic images in the human psyche that they can assume the most diverse concrete forms, be it in single individuals or in various cultures. The idea of a mediator (*Mittler*), for instance, is a primeval idea that you can find everywhere; but the concrete forms in which this idea materializes are completely different. In one case it is the highest character of a people, in another case an ox or a snake. . . . That's simply how archetypal ideas work!

Lincoln's hypothesis that there have to be similar cultures is just a makeshift idea. He cannot explain the diversity of symbols in single individuals and in cultures. He follows Freud, therefore, who deduces all symbols from one and the same root, that is, the *father complex*. For Freud, the totem—and the totem is the epitome of archetypes—is simply the father, as such. Totem animals and totem objects can all be traced back to the totem ancestor,[9] the father. With this concept, however, he does not at all do justice to the facts. The totem ancestor is by no means always the father, but also the mother. True, we can reinterpret everything, but the question is only if this is so in reality as well. It's not mentioned that there are female totems, nor is anything said of those cases in which nothing can be achieved by this reduction of the totem to the father. Just take as an example the notorious *castration complex*! Circumcision is clearly a castration, which makes sense in a man. Moreover, castration is performed only on men. But what if women were also circumcised? Would that mean that the girl wants to sleep with the mother? Not a bit! What good would it do anyway to circumcise a girl? She could still sleep with the father. The castration complex is not *the* complex at all! Still it must be very tempting to deduce cultural processes from the castration or the Oedipus complex. Lincoln at least is of the opinion that religion, ethics, and the arts are rooted in the Oedipus complex.

(From the paper:)

> According to the author, religion, ethics, society, and the arts are rooted in the Oedipus complex. This complex seems to be intrinsic to the universal primal group of the family, in that it arises from the child's instinctive, antisocial tendencies toward the family. It is not necessary to presuppose a collective unconscious as the carrier of these tendencies.

Nor can Freud's *incest theory*, which Lincoln also espouses, be maintained! If incest can allegedly be found everywhere, we'd have to assume that it once played a truly enormous role in former times. Actually, one historian does contend that once the whole of mankind had to pass through the incest stage. The children of Adam and Eve are said to have been brothers and sisters, and mankind would have developed by their reproduction. This is what a professor says, one Herr Geheimrat[10]

[9] This expression in English in the original.

[10] The title of the highest official of a German royal or principal court. It has its roots in seventeenth-century Europe when governmental administration was established. The English-language equivalent is Privy Councillor. The title disappeared after the destruction of the German Empire in 1918, when the various royal courts in Germany were replaced by the Weimar Republic.

Lamprecht[11] of Leipzig! He writes about the "incest age" of mankind. Here you see where such ideas come from—from fairy tales and memories of Genesis. But they aren't even biblical. From where, according to the Bible, did the first men get their wives?

Participant: They took the daughters of the earth,[12] who had already been there.

Professor Jung: Yes, so not even in the Bible does incest occur, but only in the minds of certain people. We have no evidence that incest once played a role. If incest meant such a lot to primitives, they would also practice it. But they don't. They consider it as something unusual. They don't practice it because it is incest—they could also practice cultic incest—but it's a horror because it's an exception. Their horror is as great as if an anteater would show up during the day. It is dangerous because it's unusual.

> The anteater can be observed only at night. When it appears during the day, that is bad. Then they all gather, coming together from four to five villages. The anteater is then dug out and killed. The man who had been the first to see the anteater is impure, because he had seen the unusual. He is a threat to the neighboring villages. Therefore he has to go down into the pit. Now the relatives come. The eldest brother of the mother has to provide a fine bull, which is slaughtered. The first piece is given to the man in the pit, the second piece to the uncle, then it's the mother's turn, etc. As soon as all have eaten a piece of this bull, everything is all right again, and the man is allowed to come out of the pit. The danger has been averted, and the unusual atoned for.

There is no moral indignation at incest among primitives; it is simply thought that nobody would do such a silly thing. Incest is not even prohibited, but it is shocking because of its strangeness. It is even imperative under certain circumstances! Kimon of Athens married his sister.[13] In ancient Egypt the Pharaoh married his sister, his daughter, and then also his granddaughter, not to commit incest but to be particularly

---

[11] K. Lamprecht (1856–1915), German economic, cultural, and social historian (G).

[12] This alludes to Genesis's prelude (1–8) to the story of Noah, in which two groups, the pious *ben elohim* and the rebellious *nephiylm*—sons of God and giants—both "came in unto the daughters of men," with the ultimate consequence of divine retribution on the human race.

[13] In Plutarch's *Life of Kimon*—Kimon was a general and admiral prominent at both Marathon and Salamis, and Perikles's chief political opponent (510–450 BC)—Plutarch relates that after the death of his father Miltiades in prison, Kimon was accused of cohabiting with his sister

noble and of the finest blood. It was all about the exclusiveness of the royal marriage. You see that the primitives have other moral views than we have. The only question for them is: is it common or not? Does it happen as a rule, or not? If not—if it is not a natural rule—it will mean something bad. I observed the facial expression of people when I inadvertently used the word for "spirit." That's very dangerous. They all made a face just like people in English society when someone has told a tasteless joke in the drawing room.[14] Then everybody will be terribly shocked and look out the window. There will be an embarrassed silence, and after a while someone will say: "Isn't it a nice day!" That's exactly how it was. My headman came running toward me and told me, for heaven's sake, never to say such a thing again. Not because the spirits are evil or unsavory, but because they are dangerous.

When someone does something unusual, then he is a magician. Then it gets uncanny, dangerous. One recognizes the magician by his use of unusual expressions. If somebody says, for example, "A flea is dancing, a mouse played on the flute, a rat is singing," the primitives will say, "If he says such things, he must be a magician." In witch trials, too, it was incriminating evidence that somebody expressed herself in an unusual way. The idea that the unusual is uncanny is widespread, by the way. It is also unusual, for instance, that someone can keep a secret. He has to spill the beans immediately. If he keeps a secret nevertheless, there will be a thunderstorm, or lightning will strike, or there will be an epidemic. Then he will have to confess at once. In the case of a thunderstorm or something similar, he will say by way of propitiation, "Was it my fault, because I said or did something? I will confess at once."

That is also how primitives experience their dreams. They talk about their dreams just like patients in analysis who take a walk together and naturally have a conversation about whether their dreams are favorable or unfavorable! Suddenly they come to the conclusion, "The dream is unfavorable." Then they call it a day. Nothing more is done. My own Negroes on my trip to Africa never carried it that far. But every morning my boys[15] gathered and sat behind the tent and talked for half the

---

Elpinike, but in any case betrothed her to Kallias, who offered to pay off the still-pending debt Miltiades owed to the state.

[14] This expression in English in the original, as well as the following quote and the word "headman."

[15] This word in English in the original.

morning, or all morning, about their dreams—are they favorable or unfavorable? It turned out that they had an Arabic dream book. Usually there was nothing in it about their dreams, because dreams don't think very highly of dream books. So when they didn't come to an agreement, they came to me. I was the man of letters, because I proved my worth by my knowledge of the Koran. It turned out that my views were quite compatible, even coincided, with theirs. For primitives, dreams are a first-rate source of information. The medicine man assumes supreme leadership of the tribe because he hears the voice of the deity in his dreams. This is revelation, and the people live with it. That's why the "M'ganga," the magician, told me that the medicine man hadn't had any dreams since the English had been in the country—because the political leadership had been transferred from the tribe to the district commissioner.[16] The initiation dreams of primitives are important, too. As far as they are known and understandable to us, they are excellent examples of individuation dreams. Black Elk,[17] an old Indian chief, tells of an initiation dream he had. This is a dream as it should be, strictly according to the rules: it has the four directions, the mandala, anything it takes for the job. It was an actual dream of vocation expressed on a primitive level. Such dreams make an enormous impression on those people. If we understand these dreams, they will impress us too.

You see that the unusual always has a special effect, and that it has an uncanny character. Thus it becomes understandable that one does not do the unusual thing, which is precisely the case in incest. It's simply a preconceived opinion of Freud and his disciples that incest necessarily plays a great role. One can reinterpret and read one's theories into everything. The question is only if what we read into it is what was *really* meant. If you make a sexual premise, you will of course be able to read it into each dream, but that does not at all prove that your premise is really contained in it. You can interpret every sentence one way or another, but this is still no proof of the correctness of the interpretation. Is it to be believed that primitives sit together and interpret the Oedipus complex with each other? This is not so. We can't just

---

[16] This expression in English in the original. Cf. C. G. Jung, CW 18, para. 1291 (G).

[17] Black Elk, the chief of the Sioux, had a vision in which twelve black horses stood in the West, twelve gray horses in the North, twelve chestnut roans in the East, and twelve dun horses in the South. Cf., J. G. Neihardt, *Black Elk Speaks: Being the Life Story of a Holy Man of the Oglala Sioux* (Lincoln: University of Nebraska Press, 1988), 23 (G).

say, "If something is cut off, this is a castration." Why should it be a castration? We have to ask what it is in reality. The accent on the idea of incest emerged only when sexuality had become interesting. This could develop only in a culture in which sexuality was a problem; in a different culture that wouldn't be the case. One could argue that primitives themselves point out that incest is important. But that is misleading. When you ask a primitive something, he will never tell you what he means, but give you the answer that suits you. Winthuis,[18] for example, was interested in the idea of the hermaphrodite. And of course it was handed to him everywhere on a plate! From the answer that a primitive gives you, you can only learn, at the most, if he likes you or not. Primitives hold Europeans in such high esteem, and fear them so much, that they always try to propitiate them. They don't want to say anything that might insult someone else. They are so polite because the other could well be a witch doctor, and if he is told something offensive things might turn out badly. One never knows. Therefore all clever people are very polite and careful. That is a fact to be reckoned with. If somebody comes along and asks, "Is it this?," then naturally it will be this. In Italy, too, you won't be able to get a normal answer. There people know how to deal with tyrants. You will never hear the truth. You'll have to wait for a long time before people will spontaneously tell the truth. The English have found out that all of the allegedly ethnological material quoted by Frobenius was also produced ad hoc and told to him. The Negroes often told me: "Well, if you like, if it pleases you," in order to oblige me. So such statements are extraordinarily difficult to understand, and it is very dangerous to accept them unchecked.

You see from all these examples that we can by no means transfer our cultural conditions onto primitives, as Lincoln does. That's nonsense, of course. But the most striking feature, as we have seen, is the assertion—derived from Freud's work on totem and taboo—that the totem is always the father. That's wrong. Thus Lincoln's attempt to declare the Oedipus complex, which is based on the father complex, to be the root of the family group and eventually of all tribal culture, is invalid. After all, as we have seen, *there isn't just one single root for symbols!* Besides the father, the mother plays a great role. One must not only look

---

[18] J. Winthuis, *Das Zweigeschlechterwesen bei den Zentralaustraliern und anderen Völkern* (Leipzig: Hirschfeld, 1928) (G).

at the son's complex. Where is the complex of the daughter? It also exists, after all. There are also matriarchal cultures in which the mother is much more important than the completely unimportant father. *"La recherche de la paternité"* isn't even *"interdite"*![19] It doesn't matter at all who the father is. Within certain limits, by the way, Lincoln concedes that tradition plays a role in spreading symbols. Of course, many things are handed down that way. That is true for language, habits, and customs. If we have Christmas trees in Switzerland, for instance, we must not believe that this custom also developed here. It goes without saying that there has to be a certain archetypal disposition, but we have taken over this idea through migration from Alsace.[20] Without doubt, cultural continuity is an essential factor in human development. But it does not suffice to explain the appearance of similar psychical images in different places! Go to the Burghölzli![21] Take simply any case history of a paranoid dementia[22] you find there! In dreams and fantasies you will find symbols that have certainly not been imparted. There are many examples of this. Then we must consult ethnopsychology and the history of comparative religions to find out what these symbols mean. These phenomena can be explained only with the help of the idea of the collective unconscious.

[19] French: the determination of paternity is prohibited; Article 340 of the "Code Napoléon" of March 20, 1804.

[20] The Christmas tree is a form of the age-old, widespread *Wintermaien* (literally, wintry May); a Germanic custom, practiced at winter solstice, of putting branches into the house and letting them blossom—a fertility and health symbol. From the sixteenth century onward, the branches were more and more replaced by trees.

[21] The psychiatric university clinic in Zurich, where Jung had been assistant medical director.

[22] I.e., schizophrenia.

CHAPTER 11

Discussion of Eugène Marais, *The Soul of the White Ant*[1,2]

Paper by Carol Baumann[3]

Professor Jung: You can imagine, after the very informative review of the book, how mysterious the life of termites is. In the tropics one is forced to deal with them intensively. They are a terrible plague there. When you pitch a tent somewhere, you have to check the posts every eight days and look for tracks of termites, which can be detected by a small, half cylindrical mound.

The following once happened to an Englishman who lived in the tropics.

He went to Europe for three months and entrusted his house to the servants. He owned three beautiful old etchings, which he had sent to him from England. When he returned from his trip, everything seemed to be in perfect order. But on entering his living room, he found that all the etchings were gone; only the empty frames were left. The frames were there, the glass was there, but the etchings were gone. He looked into the matter and discovered that termites had carefully eaten the etchings out of the frames, hollowing them out until only a thin layer

---

[1] *Die Siel van die Mier* (Afrikaans, *Soul of the Ant* [termite]) appeared in Pretoria, 1925. Nobel Laureate Maurice Maeterlinck plagiarized it extensively, perhaps contributing to Marais's suicide in 1936 (Marais, born in 1871, died at sixty-five). His unfinished study of baboon life was published in 1969. Robert Ardrey dubs him the pioneer founder of ethology. Marais also practiced law and was en eminent poet in Afrikaans. The English version of his termite study appeared in 1937 (reprints 1973 and 2009), translated by Winifred de Kok.

[2] Meeting on March 5, 1940 (G).

[3] Ms. Baumann's paper is missing (G).

remained, so that they collapsed at the lightest touch. What was amazing was that they glued the glass to the wall, so that it could not fall down.[4]

It was discovered that termites hollow out beams in such a way that they barely hold the weight. The parts carrying most of the weight are not eaten through, and from the outside one notices nothing at all. Often they also hollow out trees in this way, so that they remain standing as if in perfect condition. Then comes a storm, and everything collapses. So when you pitch camp under a tree, you must always check to see if there aren't any termite tracks, otherwise the tree could land on your head. The landscape is strangely transformed by the termite mounds. Thousands of old mounds make it a "*paysage mamelonné*."[5] The fresh mounds are jagged, spiky structures; usually their height exceeds their width. They are built parallel to the north–south axis. As an explanation it has been argued that termites are influenced by the earth's magnetic field. There are still other strange and unexplained phenomena. One of the greatest riddles is how the queen gets from one chamber to the other. The chamber walls are hard as stone, so that even with a pickax they can be broken only with the greatest effort. Hardly anything splinters off. The exit is formed by a tiny little hole, but the queen is far too big to get through it. In addition, termites are not able to carry her because she is much too heavy. But then one day she is in a larger chamber, as if she had dematerialized for that journey. It is also marvelous how both chambers of the termite mound went on functioning in exactly the same way after Marais had split it in two with an iron plate. It seems as if a *fluidum* ran through the plate, and as if something somewhere else was at work keeping everything alive. It's like an ideal state par excellence, in which everything has its place and does what it has to do quite naturally. Everything is in utterly strict rapport with everything else, as if each single creature were connected with the center by a nerve cord.

The termite nervous system is a sympathetic nervous system, as in all insects. In order to understand it properly, we had best go back to the earlier phylogenetic level in animals, that of the worms. In worms the paired segmental ganglia ("rope-ladder system") can be observed

---

[4] The source for Jung's redaction is not known.
[5] French: landscape full of warts.

particularly well. It consists of two intersegmental connectives of conducting fibers and ganglia, arranged segmentally commensurate with the worm's body structure. Worms are colonial animals, so to speak, composed of single segments and ganglia, and leading a kind of collective existence. We can find the rope-ladder system in all animal species, humans included. The sympathetic nervous system forms a system of the interior, so to speak. It controls the vegetative processes. Insofar as a being's life is governed by the sympathetic nervous system, it lives largely out of itself, self-directed, and scarcely influenced by the outside.

For a long time we approached psychology with the primitive view that everything would come from the outside and would then be mirrored in ourselves. The psychology of the past two centuries has essentially been a *sensory psychology*, that is, it explained everything with the help of the senses, as if the soul's contents were mere reflections. Thus it was basically a psychology of the cerebro-spinal nervous system, which to a great extent is an outward-directed sensory system. We also find this view of the soul in the Catholic Church. It speaks of miracles in instances that are actually psychic processes, for instance in the case of transubstantiation. Something quite similar happens in personalistic psychology. It covers only the field of what can be explained by the *person*, that is, by its relation to the environment. In contrast, the exceptionally important creative activity of the soul, which is directed from the inside outward, hardly gets any attention. A part of the soul is always overlooked, that part which lives out of itself, analogous to the autonomous nature of the sympathetic nervous system—the *unconscious*. There the *archaic images*[6] are rooted, and—unaffected by any outer influence—exist as collective structures. If disorders develop in the sympathetic nervous system, they can be redressed by treatment

---

[6] Archaic images correspond to *archetypal* ideas. These are motifs that appear again and again, in all times, in the same form, e.g., in the myths and folktales of all the world's peoples. The same primordial images also govern our contemporary dreams, fantasies, and ideas. Most often such ideas are accompanied by an intense feeling tone, and thus exercise a frightening or fascinating influence on the individual. Archetypes are transcendent and are determined not by their content but only by their form; they represent an idea's potential form, given a priori, and are capable of becoming conscious only to a very limited extent. The forms, not the ideas, are inherited. Archetypes are thus the counterpart to instincts. An archetype is the expression of unconscious, collective contents, but not of all contents, only of those constellated at the moment. Cf. the glossary in *Memories, Dreams, Reflections*, and C. G. Jung, CW 6, paras. 759ff., etc. (G).

of the unconscious. Healing occurs when the corresponding collective contents become conscious.

We would be mistaken to assume, however, that collective images, because they are independent of environmental influences, remain enclosed in the soul to no effect. On the contrary, they exert a strong influence, which creates a remarkable connection between people.[7] At our last meeting I spoke about religious experiences shared by the community, which are based on such deep excitations of the psyche by collective images. We also know that certain telepathic phenomena come from the unconscious. These are processes that can only be explained by *sympathy* (Greek *sympathein*: to suffer together). There a transmission without words and visible signs takes place; the contents go directly from one unconscious to the other.

Such a living out of "sympathy" is extremely pronounced in termites. One could integrate the multiplicity of individual termites and imagine them as a single being. From this point of view, certain analogies between the life of this community of termites and the human sympathetic nervous system become visible.

As Ms. Baumann told us, the queen plays a paramount role in the community of termites. She is a bulky, completely helpless being: a tiny little head and a colossal belly full of eggs. She is the organ of propagation for the community, an incredible uterus, which constantly produces fertilized eggs. The role of the king seems to be quite doubtful; it cannot be proven that he has any relations with the queen whatsoever, so that it actually seems as if the queen were an androgynous being. Astonishingly, we find that those deities who represent creative principles are nearly always portrayed hermaphroditically. They are capable of reproducing themselves by fertilizing themselves. So Atman, for instance, says of himself that he is one and has made himself two. For Atman would be "as big as a man and woman joined together; he divided himself into two, and thus husband and wife were born."[8]

The queen is not only a reproductive organ, however; it also seems as if she actually represented the soul of the whole community. Ms. Baumann has quite correctly pointed out that in human beings, too, the

[7] Cf. C. G. Jung, CW 9/i, para. 41 (G).
[8] C. G. Jung, CW 5, para. 227; P. Deussen, *Die Geheimlehre des Veda*, 23ff. (G).

group soul plays an extraordinary role. We find it, for example, in the medieval idea of the *anima mundi*. It is said that it carries and conserves the universe in its body. It surrounds it, so to speak, while simultaneously permeating it. That's how we must conceive of the termite queen: she doesn't simply live in a cell, but in a way spreads out over the whole population by invisible sensory organs. Apparently she can even reach far beyond the boundaries of the actual mound to the workers in her community that are busy far away. She possesses something like an *invisible presence*, which pervades and surrounds everything, carrying everything within it.[9] Seen from the outside, the queen seems to be simply a bulky form, dwelling several meters below ground; in fact, however, she is diffused over the whole population and is present everywhere, like a little world soul. That's how it seems, at least. In reality the queen might well be not the center, but another instrument herself.

We find many similarities between termite communal structure and the social structures of human beings. Just think, for example, of the role of the king in a monarchy; his health is extremely important for the people, and a kind of *tonus* radiates from him throughout the whole country. When the king dies, his people in effect die with him. On the other hand, he is held responsible for crop failures: because he was ill, the crop was no good. Poor crop—poor king! Think of the Grail myth: the whole country is made desolate because the king is wounded. In Nordic regions the kings were killed when the crop fell short. A Negro king is killed at the first signs of impotence. As long as he is in power, he is given any number of women, because he is the one who fertilizes the whole country. He has to be kept in a good mood, so that everything goes well—just as you've heard it said about the termite queen. The idea of the blissful, fertilizing, and lifeguarding presence of the king also lives on in a strange Indian custom that exists to this day. The citadel in which the raja lives is surrounded by fortress-like walls (and is also called "fort"). There is a special drum house, a superstructure that is most often built above the main gate. As long as the raja stays in the fortress, the drums are beaten day and night. When he leaves, the drumming stops. The drumming has a strangely upsetting

---

[9] There is a picture in the *Historia naturalis* by Albertus Magnus, in which the *anima mundi* is depicted as a female figure, who carries the universe in her belly. (Apparently Jung's additional comment: G.)

and suggestive effect on the nervous system. One actually vibrates and is constantly held in a state of tension. I heard it myself and had to think of the termite community. Just as from the termite queen, here, too, an influence radiates as if from a "life center" and pervades the whole town. When the drumming stops, something is missing in the atmosphere, and one feels as if one were in a town in which all life has stopped, and nothing can be heard: no trams, no people. . . . But when you hear the drum, everything stays oscillating and rhythmical. One knows that the raja is alive. There is also another custom that shows the effect the raja has. Every week he must appear before the people, so that they can see that he is alive. If that is so, then everything will be all right.

Once I came to the famous ruins of Fatehpur-Sikri.[10] Only the birds of the skies still live there, and wild dogs, and a handful of mortals who guard the grave of a holy man. But each Friday there is drumming from sunrise to sunset, in memory of the fact that Akbar the Great lived here. By chance I came there on a Friday and heard it. When I asked about it, I was told, "This is Akbar." He died in the year 1605! That's how long this continues to have an effect.

For termites, too, such a life-giving force radiates from their queen, and when she dies, the community perishes (at least in certain species of termites). Is there also something in the unconscious of the individual that we could compare to this archetype of the king?

Participant: The Self as the center of the unconscious.

Professor Jung: Yes, when the *Self*[11] emerges from the unconscious, for example, in dreams, it is always pictured as a *center*. Occasionally it is directly identified with the king, as in the Messiah legend, for instance.

---

[10] Built during the second half of the sixteenth century by the Emperor Akbar, Fatehpur Sikri (the City of Victory) was the capital of the Mughal Empire for only some ten years. The complex of monuments and temples, all in a uniform architectural style, includes one of the largest mosques in India, the Jama Masjid.

[11] As a transcendent, if empirical, term, the *Self* designates the whole scope of all psychic phenomena in man. It stands for the unity and wholeness of the personality. It is the quantity that is superordinate to the ego complex (the center of consciousness), and therefore comprises not only the conscious but also the unconscious psyche. In dreams, myths, and folktales it appears as the "superordinate personality" (king, hero, prophet, child, savior, etc.), as a symbol of wholeness (circle, square, cross, quaternity, etc.), or also in the form of a unification of opposites, as tao (yin and yang) or mandala. The empirical symbols of the self often possess remarkable numinosity, and thus a high feeling value. The Self proves to be the central archetype. Cf. the glossary in *Memories, Dreams, Reflections*; C. G. Jung, CW 6, para. 891; CW 7 (index), etc. (G).

At first, the Self is always something simple, something little, or cheap. It turns out, however, that it's the king or even the savior. It is the crown, the phoenix, the saint, the savior, even the deity. It is the center toward which everything is oriented. That's also how the *idea of the deity* came into being, as an expression of this orientation of man toward his center. It is the smallest of all things, the most hidden, the innermost one, and at the same time the greatest of all. Analogously, the termite queen is actually like the deity of the community: just as God is everywhere, in every single human being, in every single heart, and also everywhere around us, the queen too is everywhere, exercising her biological function. One could almost say that the community of termites is an archetype made real!

The soldier sentry of the termite queen also makes an archaic impression. It's like a primitive court, in which soldiers walk around the queen in an apparently ecstatic state. They have no independent existence, but merely "function." They dance around the queen as in a veritable *circumambulatio*.[12] This is a very common custom of worship. In the Apocryphal Acts of St. John it is reported that Christ steps into the middle of his disciples who form a circle around him; then they have to circumambulate him. Circumambulation was also practiced around the statues of gods. In the Buddhist stupas or Shiva sanctuaries, people circumambulate clockwise. This is exactly the activity of the soldiers that form the court of the termite queen.

Participant: In the kingdom of Darius, the messengers sent to the satraps[13] were called "the King's eyes and ears."

Professor Jung: Yes, they were simply seen as the king's functions.

Participant: Can the blind termites be seen as the less differentiated side of the termite community?

[12] "Circumambulation is the movement around a holy object, or of a holy object. The completion of a circle of protection, or of community, creates an integrity that is otherwise difficult to obtain in this world. The application of this in religions is diverse: examples include the Hajj (the Muslim circumambulation of the Ka'ba); the Prayer Wheel in Tibet; the stupa and Bo tree in Buddhism; the respect shown to the Adi Granth on entering a gurdwara; Lavan; the Hindu 'following the sun' around the sacred fire and, in the temple (and in *pradaksina*) to go around any sacred object, person, or place, including the whole of India; the seven circuits (hakkafot) around a cemetery before a burial by Sephardi and Hasidic Jews. In Witchcraft the magic circle would be a circumambulation" (John Bowker, *The Oxford Dictionary of World Religions* [New York: Oxford University Press, 1997], 224). Cf. chapter 13, 213n138.

[13] Provincial governor. King Darius I of Persia is best known for his defeat at the Battle of Marathon (490 BC).

Professor Jung: Not at all. They are equipped with the organs they need, and they don't need eyes. If we want to understand their role in the whole system, we could say that they represent the unconscious building blocks of a function. The function as such is differentiated, but not the function's elements. In a human being, for example, a thought is not conscious as such, it is like a blind being crawling in the darkness; only when light is thrown on it by consciousness will it be able to differentiate itself. The same is true for the other functions. They are composed of single elements that are still unconscious. These elements make up the psyche. They correspond to the workers or soldier termites in the termite community, which go unnoticed as individuals but exercise a differentiated function as a group.

Participant: You are saying that the archetypal ideas are connected to the sympathetic nervous system. What does that mean?

Professor Jung: I don't know either! We'd have to know about the secret of life. In the sympathetic nervous system the regulation of life takes place. It regulates the functional forms of life, such as the movement of the visceral muscles; it innervates the glands and blood vessels. We have to assume that *the life forms are contained in the sympathetic nervous systems in the form of images*, so to speak. You have to picture this like a crystal lattice, which also has to be present in a solution, although no shape can yet be seen. The crystal lattice is the functional form of the salt, which, however, is not visible. As soon as the solution crystallizes, for example, when a dust particle falls into it, the ions immediately dart to the intersection points of this crystal lattice and the crystal develops. This is the *qualitas occulta*[14] of salt. You can observe the same thing when water freezes: as soon as it freezes, hexagonal crystals develop. We must also assume that functional systems are present and invisibly residing in the unknown life of the cells in the sympathetic nervous system, just as archetypal structures are contained in the unconscious. If you were able to have a look at the unconscious *tel quel*,[15] you naturally wouldn't notice any of the images, ideas, etc. It's exactly as if you cut open a butterfly pupa at a certain stage; only a milky liquid will flow, with hardly a form discernible. But if you do not cut it open, you'll have a butterfly after a fortnight. The whole

[14] Latin: the hidden, occult quality.
[15] French: as such, as it is.

gestalt of the butterfly is already functionally contained in the liquid; it possesses a *qualitas occulta*, just like salt.[16] We simply cannot do without this assumption. On the other hand, we also know exactly which caterpillar corresponds to which butterfly. Perhaps you know the story by Erskine, *Adam and Eve*.[17] Eve gets into a very strange state, and Adam can't comprehend it at all. Then a child is there. He's very surprised that it's human, because it also might have been a calf. He simply didn't know that there is a *qualitas occulta*, and that there is the proposition, "*Ex homo nihil nisi homo*."[18]

To conclude, I'd like to touch on another important point made in the paper: in more highly developed animals instinct can be repressed. In exchange, they are capable of living out of an individual experience; one can make them get accustomed to an unnatural life. Primitive animals, on the other hand, can live only out of their instinct. They live as they are, or they croak. *Sic ut est, aut non sit*.[19]

Now termite life is so wonderfully regulated that we ask ourselves where this order actually comes from. After all, the word "instinct" doesn't explain anything. And it's just an analogy when we say that the queen is the life center, or that the life center of the community is in her. Life radiates from her, but she is not life. As a matter of fact, we are forced to assume that there is some guiding being there, or above, that can in no way be identified with the queen. If we reapply all this to man, we come up against the unconscious, which always surrounds us, and which guides us to a large, perhaps decisive, extent. Our life center lies in the unconscious. Certain structural images have their roots in the unconscious, images that apparently are not peculiar to man alone, but perhaps, or even probably, also belong to the animal soul. But only man is capable of becoming consciously aware of these contents. One of these contents is the Self, or rather its symbols. These symbols have always belonged to the images, or at least the attributes, of God. Their becoming conscious has always meant *gnosis*, that is, knowledge of God as the center of human soul life, of which we already are somehow aware; it already coincides with the image of God and, furthermore,

---

[16] These are Jung's favorite examples for explaining the notion of the archetype (G).

[17] John Erskine, *Adam and Eve: Though He Knew Better* (1927; Whitefish, MT: Kessinger Publishing, 2003).

[18] Latin: nothing but a human being [comes] out of a human being (G).

[19] Latin: it is as it is, and cannot be otherwise (G).

the experience of such contents is usually regarded as an experience of God. Such a judgment is not arbitrary, but is naturally based on the numinous character of the experience. Insofar as "something totally different" cannot be recognized, it is deduced that God and man, or rather, the human ego and the Self, have something common in their natures (therefore, in Catholic dogma, *homousie* necessarily gained victory over the *homoiusie*[20] of the son, that is, the Self). Insofar as nature is unconscious, it can only follow the law. To the extent that there is consciousness, however, the possibility of freedom exists. Thus the development of consciousness out of the darkness of the unconscious results in exemption from the law, or rather in relative independence of, and relative otherness than, original nature. Consciousness emerges out of the creature and becomes creator. In this manner the "relationship with God" develops through consciousness, that is, the relationship with the Self, which as a super-ordinate entity is the creator and guide of our life. The creator is the Lord and the lawgiver. All freedom lies in God, therefore, and in man only insofar as he has consciousness, that is, as he was able to save his light from nature's darkness. Consciousness is related to God, because it has the possibility of freedom. It can also disobey, whereas nature cannot. The only one who can disobey God completely and absolutely, however, is God Himself. Absolutely speaking, God proves His freedom only by his capability of being in complete contrast to Himself. Humans can do this only in a very imperfect way, because they are too much of an animal and, as such, obedient and pious, that is, they blindly fulfill the will of God. The condition for divine freedom is the absolutely antithetical nature of God. Freedom cannot be had without limitation, just as consciousness cannot be had without unconsciousness. Anything we say about God stems from our experience of the Self, thus also the statement of its antithetical nature. The Self is not only the light but also the darkness, the good as well as the evil, freedom as well as restriction. God's true God nature, however, lies in the *unio oppositorum*,[21] an unimaginable paradox and, as such, the symbol of an existence transcending consciousness, which we can only postulate. We must postulate it, however, because we cannot let phenomenal qualities emanate from nothingness.

---

[20] Greek: *homousie* = identical in nature; *homoiusie* = similar in nature (with God) (G).
[21] Latin: union of opposites (G).

D. Visions and Dreams

CHAPTER 12

Discussion of the Visions of St. Perpetua[1]

Paper by Marie-Louise von Franz[2]

Professor Jung: You have gotten an excellent impression of the strange mentality of those early Christians, or Montanists[3]—namely, the strange mixture of Christian ideas with purely pagan ideas. It's of secondary importance to which of these two groups Perpetua belonged. When we've received a Christian education, we've generally been raised with the idea that Christianity came directly down from heaven, that it has no history, so to speak. But nothing exists that hasn't been around for a long time. In reality, all essential ideas can be found much earlier. The figure of the shepherd, for example, already existed long before in paganism. In Perpetua's third vision in particular, you find a

---

[1] Perpetua (ca. AD 181–203), born into the Carthaginian nobility, and a nursing mother at her death.

[2] The paper appeared under the title *Die Passio Perpetuae*, in C. G. Jung, *Aion, Untersuchungen zur Symbolgeschichte*, II. Teil (Zurich, 1951). Von Franz reprinted it as *Die Passion der Perpetua. Eine Frau zwischen zwei Gottesbildern* (Einsiedeln: Daimon Verlag, 1982) (*The Passion of Perpetua*, trans. 1949, Elizabeth Welsh [Dallas: Spring, 1980]). In the visions of Perpetua, the transition from antiquity to Christianity becomes visible (G).

For a thorough textual study, see Peter Dronke, *Women Writers of the Middle Ages: A Critical Study of Texts from Perpetua to Marguerete of Porete* (Cambridge: Cambridge University Press, 1984). See also Joyce Salisbury, *Perpetua's Passion: The Death and Memory of a Young Roman Woman* (New York: Routledge, 1997), which cites Jung but not von Franz.

[3] Schismatics of the second century. The sect was founded in Phrygia by a prophet, Montanus, and two prophetesses, Maximilla and Prisca. The Montanists had an immediate expectation of Judgment Day, and they encouraged ecstatic prophesying and strict asceticism. They believed that a Christian fallen from grace could never be redeemed. Montanism antagonized the church because it claimed a superior authority arising from divine inspiration. Tertullian was a notable member of the movement (see below, this chapter).

superb example of such a *Poimen* figure, *Poimen*, *Poimandres*, or whatever he is called. In that sense we can only affirm the importance of
the fencing master;[4] the "spirit of authenticity" in general, by the way,
pervades Ms. von Franz's work.

So I can list only a few more details. For example, the colored shoes
of Pomponius. What shall we make of these? Why does he wear colored shoes? It's quite correct that he wears a special garment. But why
colored shoes? Such a priestly gentleman! He's the confessor of the
imprisoned saints. So we'd hardly expect to find colored shoes there,
but extreme modesty instead.

Participant: He actually comes from paradise, and there one is in a
joyous mood, just like children.

Professor Jung: What's to be expected in the pagan paradise?

Participant: Festivities.

Professor Jung: Those colored shoes are a sign of joyfulness, like a
party gift. Pomponius is actually an *angelos*, who has been sent from
paradise expressly for this particular occasion. Let's not forget that these
visions of Perpetua are most likely authentic. We have no reason at all
to assume that they were written for edifying purposes. If that were the
case, many details would have turned out quite differently. One would
smell the missionary character in it. The *Poimen* figure, for instance,
would not be a gladiator trainer and an Egyptian, but quite simply the
devil. There would have been no need for any finesse to further explain
the details. In any case, it's absolutely necessary to examine the contemporary background carefully.

Pomponius has been interpreted as an animus figure. I'd like to em-
phasize that he has the character of the *angelos*, the messenger sent
from beyond. Isn't that a remarkable detail? Usually the animus doesn't
appear as an *angelos*, but at first makes himself felt in a highly unpleas-

---

[4] Jung actually refers to the fourth vision, in which Pomponius as Perpetua's inner guide is
soon transformed into a titanic *lanista* or gladiator trainer—thus *Fechtmeister* (fencing master,
swordsmanship trainer) in von Franz, (1982, 95, and 1980, 62)—who also embodies what Jung
paraphrases here as the "spirit of authenticity"—in von Franz's text, the attitude that emboldens
a martyr's walk into death. "Er ist in diesem Sinne wirklich 'der Geist der Wahrheit,' der 'in euch
sein wird'" (1982, 96)—"In this sense, he is truly the 'spirit of truth' which 'shall be with you'"
(1980, 63). Again, on the *Poimen* as a *lanista*: he is "the personification of a guiding principle
which will settle the conflict and be the absolute judge of the life and death of the soul" (1980,
62–63). Although Jung's usage in this seminar is the mildly euphemistic *Fechtmeister* or "fencing
master," this translation employs the straightforward rendering of *lanista* as "gladiator trainer."

ant way. But this story—which is very probably a true story—is about a supreme moment—namely, death and martyrdom. And when we investigate such a vision psychologically, we must not forget that the tragic end is pending. So Perpetua is *in aspectu mortis*, facing death, a situation in which certain things happen naturally that usually do not occur in our ordinary existence.

In this respect, I remember the vision of a dying woman. She died a few days later. She was a former patient of mine; she was down with a fatal illness, was completely in her right mind, and reported that a messenger had come at night, and had come, strangely enough, through the window. At first she thought he was a thief or some other intruder. It was summer, the window was open, and he floated into the room. He was an Indian,[5] dressed in white. He sat down on her bed and just looked at her. Then she knew: this is a messenger announcing death. So that was an apparition from the other side. And he wore the white garment, which stands for the incorruptible body, for the immaculate, pure, and unsoiled. So this is probably also the reason for these colored shoes.

You've heard that in the fourth vision Pomponius leads Perpetua by the hand, and that they follow tortuous paths. In that case I would rather assume that she passes through bleak country.[6] That suggests obstacles, that is, resistances, because the way leads to the amphitheater where a cruel death awaits her. So it is understandable that obstacles and difficulties arise. We can answer the question raised by Ms. von Franz: Does the unconscious have the tendency to drive her to her death, or does it simply state a fact? I don't have the impression that the unconscious drives her toward death, for the unconscious only goes along, in a very sensible way, with an absolutely fateful and inescapable situation. In my view, there are no signs that would indicate that the unconscious plays an instrumental role in driving her to her death against her will. On the contrary, it actually seems that Perpetua was in perfectly conscious agreement with going voluntarily to her death. This is all the more likely in that the bishop of Carthage just then was Tertullian, who in one of his works recommended to catechumens

---

[5] I.e., from India, as opposed to Native American.

[6] "And he took my hand, and we began to walk through a rough and pathless country" (fourth vision, von Franz, 1980, 13).

that they voluntarily die a martyr's death. At that time Tertullian had just converted to Montanism, and Montanism was characterized by a special, voluntary devotion to martyrdom. So we may suppose that Perpetua, too, was in that situation. That era was a bit like the era of the French Revolution, when everybody found it natural to be carted off to the guillotine on a wheelbarrow the next day. When many people die, dying is easy. It's an everyday occurrence. Perhaps that's the case again today. At least it happens to very many people these days.

Well, it's highly probable, or even certain, that Perpetua had become convinced, out of a development and also, naturally under environmental influences, that martyrdom was inevitable. So the unconscious had nothing more to contribute in this respect, but gave her the necessary support in that state of consciousness, so that she might be fairly ready to enter into this tragic process. In a way, it also made the meaning of the whole process clear to her, with a quite pedagogical intention from the outset, starting with Dinokrates, her little brother, who was not baptized and had facial cancer. He represents a certain spiritual attitude of hers. So he is actually an animus figure, and a pagan one at that, who therefore also dies from facial cancer. If that detail is not literary fiction but factual, then it's a cancer of the face, that is, of vision; because he was not baptized and had not received the living water, he thirsts for it. She must still redeem this pagan residue in her, so that she can be sent to martyrdom without being plagued by any doubt—for doubt indeed threatens her. She has to be shown that when she steps on the ladder, she'll be able to crush the head of the serpent, the adversary, and place her foot on the dragon's head.

In the second vision she goes up and there finds the good shepherd. In part this is a consolation. The unconscious says: You will find the good shepherd. And in the fourth vision she is given the palm, so to speak, as well as the golden apples (the *cibus immortalitatis*, the food of immortality) or the passport that lets her pass unharmed through the gates of Hades. You see, this structure is elucidative. It comes about through a stage in which she also becomes her father. By prayer she can redeem her spirit from *agnosia*, lack of knowledge. She partakes of the *communio* with the shepherd, with *Poimandres*. Spirit also changes, so that the boy turns into a man and even into the father; the little boy becomes the old man. And this is Pomponius, who assists, consoles, and helps her in her extreme distress, who leads her through danger-ous, bleak country, and who also therefore is a preliminary stage of the gladiator trainer, who attends the *agon*[7] and decides it, and who pres-ents the trophy. This master trainer is the cosmic shepherd who brings order into the world and performs the *diakosmesis*,[8] that is, he unfolds spirit throughout the whole cosmos in an organizing way, and thus also forms her destiny accordingly. The keenest and most perilous conflict, however, awaits her in the amphitheater. It was diagnosed absolutely correctly. It is a conflict with pagan spirit, that is, with everything that was experienced as most fascinating and that blossomed with paganism.

Well, this ancient spirit, the pagan spirit, is really rolling in the dust, to put it in Christian terms; it's utterly drenched with earth, identical with nature, a nature spirit as creator, the divine Demiurge who rules this world and is constantly present to our eyes in natural phenomena. The evidence for this in antiquity was shown in its nature cult, which was extremely threatening to Christians. I have often quoted the pas-sage in Augustine: "And men go to admire the high mountains, and thereby lose themselves."[9] They go on losing themselves in the gor-geous divinity of things, of the world and nature. For us, this is actually no longer so, and we probably regret it. True, the sea is beautiful, and so are the Alps. But we're in no danger of having the deity manifest to us in such beauty. For antiquity, however, it meant taking a look, being touched, and immediately losing themselves.

One of Augustine's friends went to a gladiator fight. He shut his eyes to avoid seeing horrors, but then opened them nevertheless. His soul was struck by a deeper wound than that of the defeated gladiator, says

---

[7] Greek: struggle. A combat or competitive encounter, which in later usage became the Olym-pic Games (G).

[8] Organization of the world.

[9] "And men go to admire the high mountains, the vast floods of the sea, the huge streams of the river, the circumference of the ocean, and the revolutions of the stars—and desert them-selves" (Augustine, *Confessions* X.8.15). The regret that Jung indicates has its pious inaugural in a famous passage of introspection. When Petrarch climbed Mount Ventoux with his brother and drank in the vistas, the latter asked him to use his dog-eared copy of *The Confessions* as an instru-ment of divination, just as Augustine had been moved to open Paul's epistles at random when he was converted, and as Romans often used the *Aeneid* (in the *sortes Vergilianae*). Petrarch opened to this same passage and was stunned into prolonged silence. The upshot: "What I used to love, I love no longer. But I lie: I love it still, but less passionately. Again have I lied: I love it, but more timidly, more sadly." See "The Ascent of Mount Ventoux," in *The Renaissance Philosophy of Man*, ed. E. Cassirer et al. (Chicago: University of Chicago Press, 1948), 36–46.

Augustine. What Christianity really struggled against was that cling-
ing to the object, to natural reality. Christianity has brought about a
higher level of consciousness by stressing the autonomy of the idea.
There was mind independent of matter, but it had taken hundreds of
years for that idea to become common knowledge; in that era it indeed
became common knowledge, taking hold of the individual. One came
to understand that God is different from the world, that He is neither
the storm nor the fire; that *logos* is not an object, but autonomous; that
he is different from concrete phenomenality; that a thought can exist
by itself and does not necessarily depend on physical life—that was the
decisive achievement of Christianity. It was a new level of consciousness, and it was so evident that it had to be maintained at all costs.
The subsequent martyrdom was a fate taken for granted, just like the
realization that two times two is four, not five. Once one comes to this
realization, one can never go on saying that it's five. Once we know, we
can no longer *not* know. There is no way back. This even moved people
toward martyrdom. Perpetua, too, was mutinous, with her contemporary animus. So the authorities told her: Well, what the devil, if you really want to be thrown to the animals, just go ahead! Like many saints,
Perpetua unconsciously died for the fact that mankind had advanced
in knowledge, that spirit exists in and for itself. She laid her stone in
that great edifice of the human mind that would rule the world for the
next two thousand years. At that time, a transition took place, from
deep darkness into a first dawning. We might also say, into the light.
One might suppose that today, once again, the temperature of human
consciousness is about to rise a few degrees. And two thousand years
from now one will say that higher consciousness arose again out of this
so-called newer luminosity, which was actually a dawning. Of course,
it's easy to philosophize about these things, but one must pay a very
high price to live them. One's head may roll, as we can see.

At a Later Meeting of the Seminar

Professor Jung: Last time we began with the interpretation of Perpetua's
visions. There are cases in which the unconscious aims at death *against*

consciousness. Not often, thank God. For there are cases when people actually would like to go on living, but for unconscious reasons are not able to, and are simply induced by the unconscious to die. Thank God, I have not encountered many such cases. But I've seen two or three, and they were very impressive. The unconscious prepared the ground for death, and there was no escape. Such is not the case, however, in these visions, as they simply present a picture of the spiritual situation. They lend meaning, as it were, to what Perpetua would doubtless do anyhow. Let's not forget that in the meantime this is the age of Tertullian, and we read that he recommends to his catechumens that they seek martyrdom. Perpetua probably came to adopt this attitude through the influence of the Montanists. They were particularly famous for their extremely ascetic ethics. Under these circumstances, her consciousness was completely convinced that she wanted martyrdom. In that case there is no need for an unconscious attitude or arrangement to make her meet her death; more likely, it would be the unconscious that doesn't want to. When, for example, the confessor (deacon Pomponius) takes her by the hand and leads her through wayward and bleak back country, the obstacles in her nature show themselves. Her natural humanity, or what is left of it, struggles against this terrible procedure. And before being ready to die, it is of course still her task on this earth to deal with the fate of her brother, who obviously suffers pain in his unredeemed state in the beyond. What we can see from these visions is simply that they grant meaning to what obviously happens without the consent of consciousness.

Participant: Isn't this conscious attitude, this readiness for martyrdom, already a special constellation of the unconscious?

Ms. von Franz: Christian faith, which is her actual conscious attitude, is represented in the dream by an unconscious figure, a symbol of her Christian faithful attitude. Seen in this way, it seems as if in fact it came out of the unconscious.

Professor Jung: Wait a minute. It's not that simple. You're only partly right. First of all, we have to answer the philosophical question: Isn't the unconscious also to be held responsible for the fact that such readiness existed? And we must say that this is surely the case. Because it's not some commonplace human invention, as if now it's fashionable to go to the amphitheater and get killed. The ground for that whole attitude had unconsciously been prepared in the populace, which then came to the fore with tremendous force. That was already expressed in the symbol of Christ's voluntary sacrifice of dying on the cross. He said that he would die. The imprinting of that symbol caused this attitude in his successors. That wouldn't have been possible if this had been Christ's individual problem. People are not so dumb as simply to mimic such a thing; for there were many in those days who already maintained this attitude unconsciously, and that explains the explosive emergence of Christianity, which all of a sudden was just there, having risen from the cloacae of Rome. Within three centuries it flooded the whole of the Roman world empire. That can't be explained by merely arbitrary or personal imitation, but only by an unconscious disposition. In this sense one can of course say that Perpetua's unconscious produced the idea of martyrdom. Otherwise this fate of Christ could not have become a symbol for her. The unconscious said, Death is necessary! One must accept death. This unconscious discovery was one that existed in general. Otherwise one couldn't explain it at all.

Now to the question of the gladiator trainer. It was maintained that he actually represents the Christian faith. To this I must say, by qualification, that he does so in our individual analysis. But when you do not analyze him, and only read the visions, you won't exactly get that kind of idea. He's a very unusual figure. That precisely a gladiator trainer is the one fighting for the Christian faith—that is uncommon. This is also indicated by his attributes: the branch with the golden apples and the shepherd's crook—these are all objects that Frau von Franz correctly brought up in connection with the *Poimen*, a pre-Christian figure. It appears, for example, in *Poimandres*, the work of certain Hermetic writers,[10] and there is also a [Christian] work that competes with *Poimandres*, *The Shepherd of Hermas*.[11] In addition, we must take account of those symbols, those allegories of Christ, in which he is represented, for instance, as Hermes, shepherd, or Orpheus. These too are already pagan intruders into Christian symbolism. In this way Christ

---

[10] Cf. *Corpus Hermeticum* (G).

[11] *The Shepherd of Hermas* (sometimes called simply *The Shepherd*) is an influential Christian work of the second century, sometimes considered canonical by some of the early Church fathers. It consists of five visions, twelve mandates or commandments, and ten similitudes or parables. Cf. the discussion below in chapter 13 and the closing mention in chapter 14.

was assimilated into contemporary mythology. As far as the figure of that gladiator trainer is concerned,[12] I'd like to say that although inwardly it personifies Christian faith, in its whole structure the figure is a successful achievement by the unconscious in adapting Christian faith to existing pagan material. Why?

Participant: Because, after all, Perpetua is not Christian through and through.

Professor Jung: Yes, that's it. Until shortly before, Perpetua had been a pagan imbued with the contemporary pagan atmosphere. Her upper story was Christian; everything else was pagan. The same is true for us, by the way. Perhaps Christianity reaches a few floors deeper down. "For everything below is hideous, man should never test the gods."[13] So she was still full of paganism, which was quite naturally averse to martyrdom. She probably would have stumbled over the surviving pagan in her at the last minute, if the unconscious had not adapted her to the pagan conception of the world by merging the pagan ideational world with the figure of Christian faith. That is how Christianity developed in general. Take early Hebrew Christianity—there is a world of difference between that and what Christianity became later on. Already in Paul, gnosis and philosophy were added to suit the Greek mind. To a great extent Christianity was formed by assimilation. When we compare what had come in at first, the Gnostic gospels, with John's gospel, we notice an enormous difference. Renan[14] quite correctly states that the synoptic gospels[15] are still idyllic; they are still set in the countryside, in

[12] In Jung's lifetime, the extant early Christian literature supplied no evidence of the actual assimilation of Christ to this figure. In fact, however, evidence of that assimilation has come to light since then. Christ as gladiator trainer stars in a dream vision attributed to the martyr Dorotheus, son of the poet Quintus of Smyrna and an émigré intellectual at the court of Diocletian. He was martyred in the last persecution, under Diocletian, after conspiring to convert the emperor. See the text, discovered near Nag Hammadi, with translations in A.H.M. Kessels and P. W. Van der Horst, eds. and trans., "The Vision of Dorotheus," *Vigiliae Christianae* 41 (1987), and also John Peck, "*The Visio Dorothei*: . . . Studies in the Dreams and Visions of St. Pachomius and Dorotheus, Son of Quintus" (C. G. Jung Institute diploma thesis, Zurich, 1992).

[13] From Friedrich Schiller's ballad "The Diver," stanza 16: "Long live the king! Happy are those / who take their breath in the light of day! / For everything below is hideous, / man should never test the gods, / and never wish to look upon / what they mercifully drape with night and terror." ("Da unten aber ist's fürchterlich, / Und der Mensch versuche die Götter nicht.")

[14] Ernest Renan (1823–1892), *Dialogues et fragments philosophiques* (Paris: Calmann-Lévy, 1876).

[15] The gospels according to Matthew, Mark, and Luke (whose texts by and large correspond to each other).

a lovely atmosphere, the Sermon on the Mount has a certain charm. In Paul a different, somehow sanguinary spirit is added from the Eleusinian Mysteries.[16] This spirit formed something that we now call Christianity. The Christianity of John is also of Greek provenance, but was assimilated by the Jewish people, by the lowest *vulgus*,[17] and has acquired a certain rural charm. The Greek influence can be seen nowhere very clearly. The whole Gnostic theory is veiled by the synoptic evangelists. When you read the synoptic gospels, for example Mark, you will see that, although he is far removed from philosophy, he writes on the basis of philosophical *sous-entendus*.[18] After all, a certain atmosphere from the past was present, and what they made of it is all very personal, very human. I would say that it is essentially ethical, whereas in the gospel according to John a philosophical layer is added, a philosophical atmosphere, and this is still more distinct in Paul. These are phenomena of assimilation. The great Greek culture of mind assimilated these first germs, and eventually led to the development of the Catholic Church as we see it. The Catholic Church and the synoptic evangelists are on completely different planets. There is a world of difference between them. The first Greek Christians were actually pagan up to here. They had an enormous amount of paganism within them, which cried out for adaptation. If Christian ideas were to take root, they had to affect those depths, and those same depths swallowed them in the end. St. Perpetua is by no means the only one. Justin Martyr says, for instance, "Our philosophy, which already blossomed at the times of Augustus." "Our philosophy"—that's not what Mark or Matthew would say. Or Synesius of Cyrene,[19] who was simply a Neoplatonist accidentally made into a bishop; he was pagan to the tip of his nose, and on top there was a little spark of Christian philosophy, which went perfectly well with his Neoplatonism. You see, these are characters who still clearly show us how strong paganism was, and how much Christianity was infected

---

[16] The Eleusinian Mysteries were annual initiation ceremonies for the cult of Demeter and Persephone, based at Eleusis in ancient Greece.

[17] Latin: the people (G).

[18] French: hints, allusions.

[19] Synesius of Cyrene (ca. 370–ca. 413), Greek philosopher and poet, and bishop of Ptolemais (410). Cf. chapter 3, the report by Rivkah Schärf. As a representative Neoplatonist, he took on board certain aspects of Christian dogma while dissenting on questions of the soul's creation, literal resurrection, and the final destruction of the world.

by it. Thus, if Perpetua hadn't had these visions, one would have to assume that she would have failed, because although the Egyptian in the vision would have appeared all of a sudden, there would have been no moral support for confronting him. Perhaps she would have lost courage at the last moment, simply because the unconscious would not have been ready. That is precisely what is interesting in these visions. They show how the unconscious mentally prepares her, for example, by situating this figure of the gladiator trainer, who naturally was known to her and is, so to speak, for her a Christian. But actually he is no Christian at all. He is the senior gladiator in the combats with animals. He commands the fighters in the arena. And now in the vision he is precisely a Christian. That is what convinces her, what gives her the courage to have for herself such a helper at the place of her martyrdom. This figure is actually pagan, as mentioned above, but Christianity was already present *in nuce* in that paganism. It was like a core wrapped in a philosophical mantle. It was already at hand all over the place. So it needed only that external impulse, and the flame flared up through the wrapping, and there was Christianity.

Participant: That would be a case in which the meaning of martyrdom is lived, so to speak, or is represented dramatically, by the animus figure, that is, the figure of the gladiator trainer.

Professor Jung: One Gnostic school taught that men enter paradise directly; women, however, become men, and only then enter the *pleroma*[20] in the form of male angels. There is a medieval master who painted the *Madonna with the Weasel*. This weasel is found in popular Greek superstitious belief. Subsequently the weasel exists only as a female, as far as I know, and conceives through the ear. And so it stands as an analogy for the Virgin. Well, such analogies were made, and in such a way paganism and the whole animism of nature were integrated into Christianity at the same time.

Participant: Are there criteria in a dream for discerning whether physical death or an inner change is meant?

Professor Jung: Yes, that does exist, and one must look very carefully to see whether it points toward the body or the soul.

---

[20] In Gnostic cosmology, *pleroma* is the realm of divine spiritual fullness, the dwelling place of spirit, the nonmaterial world; in contrast to *kenoma*, material emptiness.

Participant: In Tunis a cameo was found that portrays a praying virgin, a gladiator with the palm of victory, a gladiator trainer, and Nike.[21] It is assumed that Nike is a personification of femininity. Others held that the praying virgin is the soul, and the gladiator the victor. Nike signifies that the soul struggle went well.

Professor Jung: That's difficult to say. It could also be the winged soul beginning her flight after death. In that case it would be the figure of the Self.

Participant: Couldn't we say, from the viewpoint of individuation, that martyrdom is only a preliminary stage of individuation here? That is, the question is whether the martyrs wouldn't have transcended it [martyrdom] if they had reached a more advanced inner stage.

Professor Jung: Of course. Two thousand years have passed since then. Many things have changed. Our psychic development, too, occurs in stages. And I have no idea what will be said about us in another two thousand years.

Participant: Why is Perpetua's sex changed? Is she a hermaphrodite, so to speak?

Professor Jung: The idea was there. Alchemy was the first to seriously address the question. Before that, in classical mythology, the hermaphrodite was rather obscene, only the archaic Aphrodites were bearded. They were hermaphrodites, male-female figures. In addition, primitive prehistoric beings were, in general, hermaphroditic. This is part of the oldest philosophy of humanity. Therefore the idea of the *hermaphroditus* suddenly reappears in the Middle Ages. The first traces can be found in the Arabs; they had already referred to the hermaphrodite, whereas the term "*hermaphroditos*" does not appear in ancient Greek alchemy; this idea played no role in it at all. It came up only with the Arabs. Only from about the fifteenth century onward does it play a substantial role in alchemy, chiefly in its later stages, until the notion, seeming absurd, vanished with the demise of alchemy.

Participant: A late painting of Leonardo da Vinci, *John the Baptist*, with a smile like that of Mona Lisa, was regarded as shocking by art historians.

Professor Jung: In the Reichenau Codex, Christ is even portrayed with breasts. He is female beyond any doubt.

---

[21] The Greek goddess of victory.

Participant: Can the Christian concept of priestly celibacy be traced back to that?

Professor Jung: The clothes of priests are female. This is connected with the worship of Cybele,[22] in which the priests castrated themselves as a matter of principle, for the sake of the realm of God. Where were the Christians at that time? This would be a very strange Hebrew scriptural passage. It is based on primitive ideas.

A chief, an Indian, had a dream at the age of forty, in which he was told: "You have to sit among the women, eat their food, and wear their dresses." And he accepted it and subsequently enjoyed an even higher reputation. He had been addressed by the Holy Spirit and turned into a woman.[23] This is uncanny and full of meaning. One becomes a *mana* personality, that hermaphroditic primordial being. Winthuis went to the Australian Negroes and made a terrible mess out of that hermaphroditic being. Now he thinks that it can be found behind everything. He let himself be taken in, because primitives feel what others wish them to feel and then they produce it. But in essence Winthuis nonetheless came up with a very real thing, because it is a primordial idea, extremely primitive and thus obviously a fundamental truth.

Participant: Can one still experience such preparation for death today, for example, in today's soldiers?

[22] A manifestation of the Earth Mother goddess, worshipped in Anatolia since the Neolithic. A goddess of caverns and mountains, walls and fortresses, nature, and wild animals, she embodies the fertile earth and presides over life-death-rebirth. Her most ecstatic followers were males who ritually castrated themselves, after which they were given women's clothing and assumed female identities.

[23] While no apparent identification of the dreamer lies at hand, it may pertain to Jung's connection with Jaime de Angulo, the outriding ethnographer and linguist affiliated with Alfred Kroeber, Franz Boas, Robert Lowie, and Paul Radin. Born in Paris to Spanish parents, a salvage ethnologist in Boas's vein, he began sending ethnographic material to Jung from tribal informants in California and New Mexico as early as 1922. Jung paid de Angulo at that time for fieldwork on the Achumawi. Cary Fink (later de Angulo, then Baynes) mediated the contact. De Angulo's tie to Tony Luhan, a Taos Pueblo Indian (a.k.a. Mountain Lake, a ceremonial officiant) who married Mabel Dodge Luhan to the amazement of the tribe, prompted Jung's visit to interview Luhan and others in 1925. If the dream is not Luhan's, still his singular path and his prominence among Jung's informants insert him into the larger picture. See Wendy Leeds-Hurwitz, *Rolling in Ditches with Shamans: Jaime de Angulo and the Professionalization of American Anthropology* (Lincoln: University of Nebraska Press, 2004), 45ff., and Gui de Angulo, ed., *Jaime in Taos: The Taos Papers of Jaime de Angulo* (San Francisco: City Lights, 1985), 18f., 36f., 87. Comparable allusions to Native American informants, as yet to be identified, also occurred in Jung's 1933 seminar on yoga and dreams; see Giovanni Sorge, ed., *The Berlin Seminar*, Philemon/Princeton University Press (forthcoming).

Professor Jung: I wasn't in it. But such stories are told, and there is some evidence for them that is not so bad. People are so ready [to die] that they go with the certainty that it's all over now. It was dreamed in advance, and then it was confirmed.

Participant: Hans Carossa[24] told such a dream.

Professor Jung: There is a whole collection of such stories from the last world war. For example, there's that incredible English collection: *Phantasms of the Living*,[25] a collection of extremely well authenticated visions, removed in both time and space. There is hardly an important experience in human life that hasn't been announced by some dream. When a man enters on an important stage of his fate, one can expect with certainty that he will have dreams about it. So when we check dreams continually, for instance, one will see how certain things emerge. Naturally we cannot always interpret them; our means are insufficient. It's too difficult, perhaps one doesn't have the courage, but still one might possibly have a feeling like, "Something's coming up now, something is up now, this is uncanny," or, "What the devil does that mean? And, whoops, it's here already!" Sometimes the interpretation is extremely difficult, because in most cases the dreams do not tell the whole story, but only what happens unconsciously, for example, what this particular fact means in the unconscious. It's nearly impossible to say from a given unconscious constellation what it will be for the dreamer in reality. Sometimes it can be seen; we can make it out in the case of illness and such, but, as I said, the most difficult thing of all is to interpret dreams with regard to the future. One really must be clairvoyant. But when we go through the dreams of a deceased person retrospectively, we can see all kinds of things.

Participant: I know the example of a mountain guide. He predicted that he would have an accident.

Professor Jung: I published such a case:[26] a colleague, a great mountaineer, told me such a dream. I told him that he was finished. He

[24] Hans Carossa (1878–1956), German poet and writer.

[25] Edmund Gurney, F.W.H. Myers, and Frank Podmore, *Phantasms of the Living*, 2 vols. (London: Society for Psychical Research and Truebner, 1886; reprints 1918, 2010).

[26] See CW 17 paras. 117–23 ("Child Development and Education," 1923), and also CW 16, paras. 323–24 ("The Practical Use of Dream Analysis," 1934). Jung also mentions it briefly in the long letter to A. D. Cornell on Psi-activity, of February 9, 1960, *Letters*, vol. 2, 542.

should no longer climb any mountains, except with two guides. He went on a mountain nevertheless, took a young man with him, and was without a guide. He took the young man with him when he fell to his death.

Participant: Others have such dreams about specific persons.

Professor Jung: It also happens very frequently that relatives have the dreams. Often the dreams are not *within* someone, but *around* someone. I know a physician who has a secluded house somewhere in southern Germany. From time to time he accommodates patients, and he keeps a daily account of the dreams of his wife, his children, the servants, and the patients who come to him. He said that from the first moment on, dream fragments appeared in the dreams of the household that stemmed from the unconscious of those patients; so it could well be true. In my opinion, it's not only probable but also something that I claim; it's my postulate that this would have to be so.

·· CHAPTER 13 ··

Discussion of the Dreams[1] of the Renaissance
Scholar Girolamo Cardano[2]

Paper by Dr. E. Levy[3]

[1] Girolamo Cardano (also Jerome Cardan) (1501–1576) died at seventy-five. The dreams selected span thirty-seven years, from ages twenty to fifty-seven. In this longest section of his course, Jung evidently intends to show how a long dream process naturally subsides or slackens unless the dreamer manages to engage with it. A schematic outline of the dreams and seminar sessions has been added below; Jung twice breaks chronology, first by giving a later dream priority as #3, grouping it with others on death, and then by advancing the *peripeteia**(the ninth dream) heuristically from chronological seventh place into pedagogic ninth position. See the introduction for reflections on this aspect of Jung's treatment of such a dream series.

Dreams, by date, in the sequence taught and Cardanus's age		*page*
1. ca. 1521	[dream paraphrase] An ape, prophet of death 19–20	123, 135
2. 3 Oct. 1537	The dead Prosper Marinonus 36	123, 139
3. 15 Aug. 1547	The dead judge J. B. Specianus, & mule—**4 6**—	124, 146
4. Spring, 1538	The red-robed angry mother 37	156
5. 5 May 1538	A shooting star 37	159, 165
6. 15 Nov. 1538	Two constellations 38	162
7. 1 Feb. 1544	The lion combat of Alexander—**4 4**—	175
8. n.d.	Two wolves at the Papal court [_]	180
9. <u>9 Feb. 1540</u>	The black sun ["That is the peripeteia," 195] <u>40</u>*	181
10. 5 Jan. 1544	Marinonus & son, Death, corpse, & dog 45	183
11. 5 Jan. 1558	From Milan to Bacchetta/Naples, & mule 59	195
12. n.d.	A large snake & a narrow escape [_]	214

Session	*Dreams by number and date*	*page*
A. 1, 2, 3	ca. 1521, 1537, -**1547**-	123
B. 1 & 2, cont.	ca. 1521, 1537	135
C. 3, 4, 5, 6,	1537, 1538	146
D. 5 & 6 cont.	7 ,8, 1537–8, -**1544**-, n.d., <u>**1540**</u>*	164
E. 10, & summary	1544	183
F. 11	1558	195
G. 11, cont. & 12	1558	202

[2] Meeting on November 12, 1940 (G).

[3] The paper is missing; instead, a short biography and the dream texts have been added (translated directly from the Latin) (G).

A. Initial Session of the Seminar

The doctor and philosopher Girolamo (Hieronimus) Cardanus (Cardano) was born on September 21, 1501, in Pavia. He was a typical *"uomo universale"* of the Renaissance: doctor, mathematician, astrologer, physicist, musician, politician, and philosopher. His mathematical formulas for solving quadratic equations and his invention of the Cardan shaft[4] are known to this day. In philosophy his stance was in part still committed to medieval Aristotelianism, but in part already adhered to a more modern naturalism. In his medical theory he favored Epicurean principles. He was dealt a heavy blow in life by the execution of his son, whom he often mentions in his autobiography.[5] The son was accused of having poisoned his wife. Cardanus himself died in Rome on September 21, 1576. In his autobiography as well as in his commentary on the dream book by Synesius, Cardanus mentions several of his own dreams.[6] In one class of dreams that recur repeatedly, Cardanus is preoccupied with the length of his life, death, and various fears. In these dreams[7] animals or dead people give him relevant answers to these questions.

In the first dream Cardanus sees an ape that can speak with a human voice:

1. This being a miracle, Cardanus decides to ask him how long he still has to live. The ape answers: "Four years" (quatuor annis). Cardanus: "Not more?" The ape: "No."[8]

In a further dream appears a dead man somewhat as the ape did:

2. On October 3, 1537, two hours before sunrise, I saw my particular friend Prosper Marinonus before me, who had died the previous year. He was in a joyful mood, and dressed in a scarlet coat. He approached

[4] The universal joint between driveshaft segments.

[5] *De propria vita: The Book of My Life*, trans. Jean Stoner (Toronto: J. M. Dent and Sons, 1931).

[6] Cf. *Synesiorum somniorum omnis generis insomnia explicantes libri quattuor* (Opera Lugduni, 1633), vol. 5 (G).

[7] Another psychological study of Cardanus's life and dreams is by Enrico Rivari, *La Mente di Girolamo Cardano* (Bologna: Zanichelli, 1906).

[8] This and the following dreams have been translated directly from the Latin. For this dream, cf. *Synesiorum somniorum, omnis generis insomnia explicantes libri IV* (1562); *Opera Omnia V* (1663, repr. 1967), 5: 720, and Cardanus's autobiography, *Des Girolamo Cardano von Mailand eigene Lebensbeschreibung*, trans. Hermann Hefele (Jena: Diederichs, 1914), 179 (G).

me and wanted to kiss me, and I asked him if he knew that he was dead. When he answered in the affirmative, I took the liberty of embracing him, and he kissed me on the mouth. I asked if he remembered who he was. He said, "Yes." "Does one suffer pain at death?" "When it has been endured, one does not yet die," he answered—so that I should apply this to the anguish of the soul. "How?" (I asked) "As in a high fever." "Do you want to live again?" "Absolutely not." "So death is much like sleep?" "No." When I wanted to learn and ask more, he left me, so that I was left behind in a sad mood.

Cardanus also adds that Prosper Marinonus meant the city of Pavia, because he was a citizen of that city. That he appeared as a dead man would indicate a change in his (Cardanus's) life. That he was a friend and kissed him would promise honors.[9]

Again in a third dream a dead man appears whom Cardanus questions about death:[10]

3. On August 15, 1547 I saw Johannes Baptista Specianus seize my hand, the former judge for capital crimes, who at the time had died only shortly before. But I thought that he was dead and withdrew my hand. I asked him, however, "Now that you are dead, and I am sleeping, do tell me something about the life where you are now." To this he replied, "Nothing is left of which you believe the opposite" (*Nihil superest cuius oppositum tu credis*). After that he vanished, and a thin, pale-faced young man with a long face appeared in his place, in a scholar's long gown whose fur was turned outside in; on the outside it was ashen. He too was dead and unknown to me. I asked him, "What lies ahead of me?" He answered, "I won't tell you, because it would sadden you too much." I said, "What, will I die?" "No," he answered, "you will be wounded by a male or female mule, but will then make a great profit without much work." "What's your name?" "Hieronymus Frige, the son whose name corresponds to Johannes Baptista (or so I believe), who will not outlive me."

Professor Jung: Well, Cardanus has a very philosophical temperament. And so we must very carefully take apart the sentence in the third dream here, "*Nihil superest cuius oppositium tu credis.*" First, he be-

___

[9] *Synesiorum somniorum, op. cit.,* 5: 715.
[10] Ibid., 5: 720.

lieves something with his consciousness, and what is believed stands in contrast to something of which nothing remains. Thus, "*oppositum tu credis*," and this *oppositum* refers to *nihil superest*, something of which nothing remains: "nothing is left of which you believe the opposite." This is an incredible involution. And therefore he consciously believes the opposite of what probably has stayed in the unconscious or in the other world. And what is that? Can you solve this riddle? This sentence resembles the famous story of the nun who receives a young man in the visitors' room. The abbess watches through the keyhole and sees the nun kissing the young man farewell. Afterward the abbess takes the nun to task and asks how that could have happened. The nun says, "Why shouldn't I kiss him, whose mother was my mother's only dear daughter [her son]?" Let's assume that there is an X, and this X stands in opposition to that of which nothing remains—to what no longer exists. So that can only mean that there is nothing in the unconscious. And you believe the opposite of that nothingness. Nothing has been left in the unconscious; nothing, of which he believes the opposite, exists any longer.

Participant: He no longer stands in opposition to the unconscious.

Professor Jung: That's right, because the opposite of that, which is nothing, is something. Thus he believes something, and this something he believes does not oppose what there is in the unconscious, because there is nothing like it in the unconscious. There is nothing that actually doesn't correspond to these conscious beliefs.

Participant: But this is about the question of the afterlife.

Professor Jung: Not necessarily. It could also refer to beliefs that are not conscious.

Participant: Could it be that these are paradoxical beliefs, so that there is no opposition to the unconscious?

Professor Jung: Yes, that's a question in its own right: how come Cardanus formulated it in antinomies? That's completely paradoxical; so he must have a strange attitude. He probably thinks in mathematical terms. In mathematics such paradoxes are common, such as: two parallels intersect in infinity. That's the way it is formulated, extremely confusing; but the real meaning is that his conscious belief is not in opposition to the unconscious. So whatever this is—perhaps one would have to take an even closer look at the dream—it has got to refer to existence after death, with which he is preoccupied anyway, as we can already see from the following dream. And he has certain ideas about which, however, we learn nothing here. These ideas or beliefs do not stand in opposition to the unconscious.

Participant: But then he does dream this. It answers some anxious question of his.

Professor Jung: Which is in the dream, however. He asks the dead man in the dream, doesn't he, and on that occasion hears that the unconscious has nothing to contribute, because there'd be nothing there that would oppose his belief.

Participant: Isn't that a reassuring answer to a question?

Professor Jung: Surely, yes, we'd have to assume for the interpretation of the whole dream that he is anxiously preoccupied with death, and with existence after death. And the unconscious assures him that his thinking is actually accurate. That's how we have to see it. But the dream goes further still, for when the spirit disappears, another figure appears, a thin and pale-faced young man with a long scholar's gown, lined with fur on the inside and ashen on the outside. "He too was dead and unknown to me. But I asked him, 'What lies ahead of me?' He answered, 'I won't tell you, because it would sadden you too much.' Then Cardanus said, 'What, will I die?' 'No,' the young man answered. 'You will be wounded by a male or female mule, but will then make a great profit without much work.'"

Regarding the paradox, I'd like to remark first of all that the unconscious is in a paradoxical situation toward consciousness. It is sometimes in complete antinomy toward consciousness, down to the last detail, in the following way: white is black, black is white; what is above is below; what is good is evil, etc. This can be seen above all in those cases in which a strong conflict exists, for instance, in persons whose consciousness takes a very one-sided position. Then the unconscious develops the counterposition, and we'd have to suppose in such a case that Cardanus had gone through a phase in which he, at least as a mental exercise, had put himself in opposition to the unconscious. This characterizes the age of humanism, in which thinking suddenly took a very strange upward trend and freed itself of dogmatic beliefs, and in which people went for trends in free thinking—they enjoyed being able to think so freely. They also entertained immoral, blasphemous thoughts, in order to put themselves in blatant opposition to dogma, to challenge the gods, so to speak. There are several examples, a very good one being Agrippa von Nettesheim, who in certain respects already thought along lines similar to Nietzsche, a shatterer of existing values. He tore down everything, just like Nietzsche. I have just read his work, *Vanitates scientiarium*, in which he criticized and tore to pieces anything and everything in which the world had believed—a remarkably negative spirit. On the other hand, apart from this strikingly negative and critical work he also wrote a *philosophia occulta*. This is part of humanism, also of the age of Reformation, in which all values began to falter, in which every edifice crumbled and a whole new world emerged. You know, the sublime Gothic ideal collapses at that time, but, on the other hand, scope is broadened immensely by the discovery of America and the upswing of the natural sciences. Well, Cardanus is such a natural scientist, and these men have put themselves—at least mentally—in very strong opposition to prevailing traditional views. Another example is Theophrastus Paracelsus. On the one side he is a strict Catholic; when he dies, he receives extreme unction and is buried as a good Christian. On the other side, however, he has a completely Gnostic worldview, with strange mythical ideas. His philosophy is actually completely materialistic, which at the same time, however, is not materialistic in our sense, but would actually have to be called Gnostic. And he is also someone who, for instance, tore Galen and the ancient doctors to pieces, burned their books in the market square in Basel, no longer taught in Latin, and no longer walked around in a doctor's gown but in a laboratory coat, to the supreme annoyance of the Baselers. He then had to leave again and go off on his travels. So he too was not only negative but also very stimulating; he set a revolution in motion. You see, Cardanus belongs to a series of such people. And precisely the fact that his dream expresses itself so paradoxically actually accords with the paradoxical nature of the unconscious. It harmonizes with the unconscious to a great extent, something we have to presuppose in a man who had begun so early to observe dreams and visions. He is probably completely imbued with it, and therefore his dream expresses itself in the way the unconscious talks.

Participant: Doesn't the second dream about the spirit of the dead man also indicate this? He lets himself be kissed and embraced by the dead man. In that way one becomes a living being oneself. In that case it would also mean the collapse of the reigning worldview.

Professor Jung: That's absolutely correct. We have to see the dead man as a figure representing the unconscious. You see, when we read those ancient masters, in the first place we naturally always must bear in mind that the dead are absolutely real figures. These are real spirits, and that's also how they saw them. It is quite authentic that Cardanus immediately thinks in the dream, "Now this is someone we've got to interrogate about what it's like after death." You can see how literally he takes this. From a higher, scientific viewpoint, however, we have to say that, first and foremost, these dead represent certain unconscious processes and also must be interpreted on the basis of Cardanus's psychology. So we'd have to say, for instance, that in Cardanus there exist autonomous contents of the unconscious that occasionally make use of a deceased friend to cloak and thus personify themselves. Instead of "I think," somebody else says what *he* thinks. That is how this thought appears to me; it is projected onto such a figure. So if I say, for example, that I'm sad, a figure dressed in black will come and say that *he* is sad. In that way, then, we could view this dead man in the dream as the personification of a thought that approaches Cardanus and expresses itself to him somewhat indirectly. This peculiar relation with the unconscious is found very frequently. For instance, if we still lived in a culture in which it would be usual to have spirits in mind—so that we close the windows at nightfall, for example, so that nobody can get in, or that, God forbid, the broom isn't put down the wrong way, so that something could get into the house—in such a culture our dreams, too, would naturally express themselves in this language. In the case of Cardanus, who comes closer to the unconscious, the relation with the unconscious is expressed in his ideational world as a relation with those who come from the realm of the dead. There are also many ancient texts, for example, the Apocalypse of St. Peter, in which two dead persons come from the beyond to bring Peter the revelation—two ambassadors from Hades, so to speak.

Participant: It also says so in the *Somnium Scipionis*.

Professor Jung: Yes, that's an excellent example. There too it is a dead man who is the guide on the great journey to heaven. That is still the old style. What is strange, however, is that these people are really Renaissance free thinkers and nonetheless are more superstitious than primitives.[11] Paracelsus, for instance, who was a heretic of the greatest magnitude and who believed in no authority, did indeed believe in sylphs,[12] salamanders,[13] incubi, and succubi.[14] He wrote to the emperor at the time of a surge in endemic syphilis that all brothels had to be banned because they would breed succubi, which then caused syphilis.

Participant: If we see these figures as personifications of the unconscious, the unconscious of good Catholics, for example, would still be the beyond. I know of educated Catholics who as it were speak with the dead, and this is something completely natural.

Professor Jung: By all means, the Catholic mentality is still a medieval mentality. It corresponds to what was thought and believed in the Middle Ages, which itself of course is continuous with a still much more primitive mentality in which these things were more alive than ever, very much so. The interesting thing is that the more successful an attempt to realize a primitive mentality, the more such unconscious contents will come alive, so that it gets really spooky. We can see this in primitives. It's really very strange. It's as if the world were a function of our consciousness, so that were we to alter consciousness, then quite different things would happen. The laws of nature are apparently shifted a bit—at least that's how it seems to us. Then all kinds of things

---

[11] Jung's discussion here, through his comments on the *I Ching*, pertains to Anthony Grafton's survey of Cardano's working hypotheses as an interpreter of dreams, astrology, and other methods of divination. Caspar Peucer, Melanchthon, Jean Bodin, Pomponazzi, Guarico, and later John Dee convened around the acceptance of certain methods, including confidings by their tutelary spirits or personal demons. More to the point, Jung's comment on the Chinese perception that "everything is a part of the whole" is similar to certain Renaissance cross-readings of the stream of events. "They inserted numerous accounts of visions and encounters with spirits into their astrological diaries, and looked as eagerly as Cardano for every predictive art that could complement astrology. Dee, for example, eagerly underlined Synesius' statement, in his work on dreams, that 'everything is signified by everything, since all things in the one great animal of the world are related, and these are like letters of every shape, signed in the universe as in a book. . . . This is my Cabala of being.'" See Grafton, *Cardano's Cosmos: The Worlds and Works of a Renaissance Astrologer* (Cambridge, MA: Harvard University Press, 1999), 171–72.

[12] Paracelsus describes sylphs as invisible beings of the air, his elementals of air (an elemental is a creature, usually a spirit, that is attuned with, or composed of, one of the classical elements: air, earth, fire, and water).

[13] In medieval alchemy the salamander was regarded as the Spirit of Fire. The spirit Salamander was believed to live in the flames and feed on the fire.

[14] An incubus is a demonic entity capable of sexually arousing and sometimes assaulting human females. A succubus is the "female" counterpart of the incubus, a demonic entity said to inspire inconvenient lust in men, sometimes capable of physically attacking and inflicting injuries.

happen that shouldn't happen at all, and primitives are always infected by it. Then something completely absurd emerges, and it seems absolutely possible that it be so. One is actually silly if one doesn't adapt to it. Because that's how it actually *is*, it is in the air. A Dutchman said, "Magic is the Science of the Jungle."[15] I was asked why the Chinese, who are so highly intelligent, had no science. I answered that they do indeed have one, but a different one. Just read the *I Ching*. It is so sophisticated, however, that we actually don't understand it. We'd have to make a *salto mortale* to be able to grasp it (it's about the principle of synchronicity, in a word). When such a synchronicity occurs, we ask, Why? What's the reason? How come? Say we find an old hat on the beach. Why? How come? A ship passed, and the hat was blown away. That satisfies us. But the thinking of a Chinese is completely different, because he notices that an old bottle is lying beside the hat, as well as a piece of wood, and a jellyfish, and somewhere nearby a little cask was also washed ashore. And so now for him the question is not simply, "Where does this hat come from, why the piece of wood, why the bottle?" But rather, that all of these things are here together, at the very moment when he himself is there—that's what interests him. What does it mean, he there together with an old hat, a bottle, and a piece of wood on the beach. That's his scientific problem, that's what he wants to know. For him it's completely irrelevant where that hat comes from, that's completely unessential. Naturally it comes from somewhere, but that doesn't interest him. But the fact that all this is here together, at this moment, and that he is there too, that's the great world problem. If only someone knew! Therefore, the ancient King Wen and the Duke of Chou together had already devised this method for interpreting such coincidences—or what we call coincidences—as constellations. You can see how unscientific we are. We simply attribute it to coincidence. The Chinese say, "This causality, now that's coincidence, but the fact that all this happens together, that's no coincidence." Whereas we say, "By sheer coincidence there's an old bottle there, too"—or all people initially say, "It's by mere coincidence that I have this dream." And then I say, "You are completely unscientific." If someone is a conscientious European, he will eventually come around. But if I confronted him

[15] This quote in English in the original.

with the old hat and the piece of wood on the beach, he'd think that I was completely nuts. A well-known philosopher told the story that he had a Chinese pupil, a cultured philosopher, whom he wanted to quiz, and asked him to explain what Tao is. The Chinese said, "This is Tao." He tried really hard, but the other didn't understand. So the Chinese took him to the window and said, "What do you see outside?" "Houses, windows, streets, and it's raining." "And what else?" "The wind is blowing and the trees are rustling." "Well, this is Tao!" You see, he simply didn't know it, just as we don't know that we view everything causally. We don't know that we speak prose.[16] And of course the Chinese doesn't know that either. He is at such pains, therefore, to explain what he means. He should have explained it to the European with the help of principles, but he simply didn't know that; all he could do was hand over the ensemble of what was there at the moment. But the ancients are not aware of this. I had a talk with the best-known contemporary philosopher in China. It was terrible. I asked him little bits of information about the *I Ching*. It was unbelievable; he put a whole garden in front of me. After two hours the good man was completely finished. He had to set everything in motion to hand me a leaf, a single flower. He is unable to take anything out of context. Everything is a part of the whole. He has to unhinge the whole world to explain something. And pray, consider, that's a thinker!

To return to the dreams of Cardanus and the interpretation adequate for his times: you will find such interpretations in ancient writers time and again, even already in the Romans. It's the kind of interpretation that we generally encounter in the natural sciences over and over again. But it is extremely alien to us, because long ago we forgot to think in this way, which we do only when we must deal with something completely unknown. Then we regress again to these habits of thought. Formerly, nature was seen exclusively from the human perspective. There were useful animals and vermin, edible and inedible plants. The inedible plants were of no interest whatsoever, but the edible ones very much so—when they were good, that is. The useful animals were the interesting animals, while the rest were treated with indifference

---

[16] Allusion to Molière's play, *Le Bourgeois Gentilhomme* (*The Middle-Class Gentleman*), in which Monsieur Jourdain realizes: "By my faith! For more than forty years I have been speaking prose without knowing anything about it."

or seen as outright evil; they became interesting only with regard to fighting. So, long ago nature was generally a matter of utility for us. Take precious stones, for example, utterly indifferent as such, whereas in reading Pliny you will find they possess the most wonderful qualities: amethyst is a remedy for drunkenness, another stone for epilepsy. Botany was nothing but books on the classification of herbs, where one could look up what influence each herb has, and against which illnesses they are effective. Paracelsus's whole botany is based on this principle; sulphur cinquefoil,[17] for instance, was good for diseases of the hand. He even classified diseases according to remedies. Thus he calls one group of ailments tartaric diseases because they were cured by tartar.

Insofar as nature reflects divine secrets, the unicorn is good and beautiful, because it represents the Holy Spirit, the God who has only one son, a horn growing out of his head. God is a unicorn, therefore, in the terminology of the Church fathers. The dove also represents the Holy Spirit. Under certain conditions the snake represents either the devil or medicine, which to us is Christ. The serpent set upon a pole by Moses[18] became a remedy for snake poisoning. So the greater part of the flora and fauna was tested for its correspondences, that is, if plants and animals somehow divulged divine secrets. St. John's Wort,[19] for instance, symbolizes the blood drops of Christ; the blue passion flower[20] allegedly contains all the implements of torture in its form, etc. And naturally dreams, too, were explained this way, that is, to what extent they were good for someone, how useful they were for him. One asked oneself: what can this dream show me? Apart from that, dreams were completely uninteresting. For us there is something intrinsic in dreams, however, and we must investigate them, not only pay attention to them because of their analogy to what is already known.

Participant: Wasn't there a connection with our attitude toward the Church? The utilitarian side could be understood because everything else was in the possession of the Church.

Professor Jung: That's correct insofar as the dogma was seen in the stones and the stars. But the other standpoint, the utilitarian one, is

[17] *Potentilla recta.*
[18] Numbers 21:8ff.
[19] *Hypericum perforatum.*
[20] *Passiflora caerulea.*

simply the standpoint of primitives. Their only relation to nature is to ask what can be eaten. When I walked around with the Negroes, one of them said, "That is edible"—it could be eaten like straw out of a mattress. Everything has been tested by man with regard to its edibility or usability. From that comes his knowledge of nature, but not of nature as such, only with reference to man.

Later the dogma was added to this—that nature is an expression of the spirit, a viewpoint that was also applied to dreams. Thus they were examined for what they were good for, what they showed me, and how they functioned with regard to myself. First and foremost, therefore, dreams were mainly examined with respect to their relevance for the future, which can actually be found in certain dreams. That's why there are some quite surprisingly correct interpretations. Quite a number of such dreams can be found in the older literature. In the history of the Jewish war by Flavius Josephus, the dream of a slave is mentioned. Or think of the dreams in the Old Testament. Naturally, we don't know to what extent they are authentic; but those in particular might well be authentic. And as far as methodology goes, we can't do better. There existed a school of *therapists*, as they called themselves; they lived in the Jordan valley in monastic communities, in pre-Christian monasteries. They are probably identical with those described by Philo Judaeus. And these *therapists* concerned themselves with dream interpretation, working in a way not unlike ours, and their approach was not bad at all. What is still known in the Orient today also corresponds to this. I have talked with Egyptian Somalis about their views on dreams. They've got a veritable flair, also for the psychological meaning of dreams. Naturally, the utilitarian element was not missing either; the dream as such was not that important, only insofar as it was of practical use to the dreamer.

To some extent Cardanus is far ahead of his time;[21] but he is completely oblivious of the fact that the dream could also have a subjective psychical meaning. In fact, nobody was aware of that.

However, there was indeed a category of dreams that were accorded objective validity. Which one?

[21] Jung twice cites "Cardan's rule that the object of the work of interpretation is to reduce the dream material to its most general principles" (as quoted here from "The Psychology of the Transference," 1946, CW 16, para. 486, and earlier in the supplement to "The Phenomenology of the Spirit in Fairytales," 1948, CW 9.1, para. 436).

Participant: The so-called public dreams.

Professor Jung: Yes, dreams of public interest. Do you know examples?

Participant: In the case of early Christian bishops it could happen that someone dreamed he would have to become a bishop, and at the same time someone else dreamed that a successor would replace him. It was then generally acknowledged that one followed the other. The dreams refer to public institutions.

Professor Jung: There are also examples in the Roman Republic. For example, a senator's daughter had a dream in which Minerva complains that her temple is in a deplorable state. So she goes to the senate and demands to speak, declaring that she's had a dream that she must report to the senate. She is allowed to speak, and then the senate approves a sum for restoration of the temple. We already find such examples in primitives. I was told by the natives near Mount Elgon, "When someone has such a dream, he will gather all the men, and then we sit together in a circle, and he tells his dream, everybody listens, and then we go home again." This will then sink into the unconscious. You see, that kind of listening means, "We have accepted it, we have shown our reverence." No one asks if it is understood; what is received is the message as such. These dreams have the quality of *"somnia a deo missa."*[22]

Participant: They are like oracles.

Professor Jung: Among the incubation dreams in the old clinics, however, certain dreams were also interpreted in a quite utilitarian manner. But those dreams were of great importance for the whole community, for the fate of the sovereign, etc. In Greek literature there is the dream that came to a dramatist. He dreamed the same dream three times, that a golden cup of great value had been stolen from the temple of Hermes. And then he also dreamed who the thief was and where the cup was hidden. After the third time, he thought that something had to be done. So he went to the Aeropagus[23] and reported it. The cup was found and the thief hanged. This was a public dream. Such dreams constitute a certain exception, however. But as far as the dreams presented by Dr. Levy are concerned, we have to take into account the fact that of course a great deal more was thoroughly known at that time. So what

---

[22] Latin: dreams sent by God (G).
[23] The Athenian high court.

we need in connection with these dreams is to know about Cardanus's biography, and then acquire the ability to interpret the dreams in their contemporary context. Some of them are great dreams, for example the dream of Mercurius.[24] There is something to it; these are contemporary problems. Cardanus was on quite good terms with alchemy and the whole matter of black magic. In the latter the black sun is the *sol niger* of alchemy. There are alchemical problems implied in all of this; the reaction of the objects expressed his psychological situation. It would be possible to find out a great deal about the unconscious psychology of the Renaissance from such dreams. But that would be a very exacting work in its own right. For there is a great deal of data, including literary productions, that pertain to it. I am thinking of the *Poliphil*,[25] a work that in a way is also a dream. It gives us valuable insights into the psychology and the spiritual problems of the Renaissance, which of course it was not aware of, just as we are never aware of our own spiritual problem. It is unconscious; it is precisely what we do not know, just as we do not know, for example, that what we are speaking is prose, not until someone tells us; then we know it, but not before.

B. At a Later Meeting of the Seminar

Professor Jung: Now we must return to Cardanus's first dream, in which the ape appears. Cardanus is surprised that the ape can speak. And it is a kind of miracle. If he can speak, then he should also be able to predict all kinds of things, in a magical way. So that's obviously the reason why Cardanus asked him how long he would still live. And the ape answers, Four years. The dreamer asks, Not more? The ape, No. Four years. The association Cardanus gives is a very popular explanation—namely, that four years is unthinkable as well as undesirable. It's obviously very disagreeable that he has only four more years to live. He was about nineteen or twenty years old at that time. He figured that it had to be four

---

[24] See below, the dream of November 15, 1538.
[25] Francesco Colonna, *Hypnerotomachia Poliphili* (1499). *Le songe de Poliphile ou hypnerotomachie de frère F. C.* (1883).

Jupiter years, because then the result would be forty-eight[26] years, so that he would reach the age of sixty-four or even a bit more, as he says. You see, it would be nice if it were a bit longer. Then there follows some very strange arithmetic, a calculation of the letters of the word "Quatuor": QVATVOR (U = V). When we leave out the V, because it is not pronounced, the result is seventy-seven years. You see from this precious example how "scientifically" Cardanus proceeds. Somewhat similar to the biorhythm theory of Fließ, values of twenty-eight can be reached in arbitrary numerical terms. But this is outrageously unscientific. In Fließ's book you'll find a long table in which each number represents a function of twenty-eight, so that everybody can calculate his period more easily. Sometimes the number one is added or subtracted. And why not also plus two?[27] Well, naturally such an explanation is good for nothing, but the dream belongs to a series of interrogation dreams, as Dr. Levy has quite correctly understood. In the first dream, however, not a spirit but an ape is being questioned. What does this mean? We've seen that he puts this question about life to spirits in the other two dreams, while here he asks an ape. Apparently the ape takes the place of spirits, or spirits take the place of the ape. But how do these two come together? What does the ape mean?

Participant: They come together in the primitive, instinctual, and the human. The ape is actually an animal man, and when he appears as a spirit he has less consciousness than a primitive man.

Professor Jung: What does "less" mean?

Participant: Half animal, half human.

Participant: He is the *simia dei*,[28] the antagonist of God.

Professor Jung: That's going too far.

Participant: He represents the most ancient human form.

[26] In the original: "28"—obviously an error or typo, the Jupiter year being circa twelve of our years.
[27] Dr. Wilhelm Fliess (otolaryngologist, Berlin, 1858–1928) pioneered the study of biorhythms, which Freud followed enthusiastically. Dr. Hermann Swoboda of Vienna extended both of Fliess's twenty-three- and twenty-eight-day cycles to periodicity in illnesses as well as dreaming. Recent studies of suicide rates among American VA hospital patients have claimed significant correlations with relevant cycles; see *Journal of Nervous and Mental Diseases* 172 (August 1984). It is of interest here that Fliess's theory unknowingly elaborated Cardanus's games with the life cycle, attempting to ground what the wily mathematician had juggled with. Jung's dismissal is of course unfriendly to the statistics used in this field.
[28] Latin, God's ape = the devil.

Professor Jung: Yes, that's what is hidden deep in the animal soul. That's the soul that's already disowned by human beings, and which no longer reaches consciousness. But it lies just beneath the threshold, and has just about found a voice here. We do not know what the ape said, but we can say that the whole lower consciousness, actually a part of the unconscious, has found a voice. It reaches the region of speech and starts to speak. The ape represents the animal instinctual soul, which extends far into consciousness. We've got many affective facial expressions that are directly borrowed from the apes, for example, the way some primitive tribes speak—I nearly said, how *one* speaks! Imagine you go to a party, and are standing outside; suddenly a door opens, and you are able to listen, but without understanding what's being said—that's like an ape community sitting in the treetops making a racket. They simply address each other, and it's either amusing or an expression of hate, rage, or jealousy. I once had the following experience, for instance. Professor Claparède kept a female ape in order to do research on apes. His daughter was four years old at the time. He took the daughter in his arms and went into the ape cage together with her. The ape became extremely jealous, because usually it was she whom he took into his arms. She then assumed a regal mien that immediately reminded me of the painting, *La Rivale*, in which a man goes up the stairs with his lover, and the wife comes downstairs and gives her the same look as the ape gave the child—as feminine as it can get, so human and so animal-like, if you will. Many of our affects are of a purely animal nature; we only think they are nobly human. Well, here the instinctual soul finds a verbal expression. But Cardanus, so to speak, intervenes in the dream already, by asking how long he still has to live. But why is this so important? Why is it a matter of such concern to him?

Participant: Four years are like the symbol of a transformation. But in his consciousness he equates it with real death. It means a transformation that is connected to some quaternity.

Professor Jung: Well, that goes a bit too far.

Participant: He himself says that because of his fear of death he had always lived provisionally.

Professor Jung: Yes, well, you see that's true if we take the dream completely out of its context. Let us assume that one of us had had this dream—then we'd have to presume the existence of a heartfelt hope

to go on living for a very long time, because of a secret fear of not living long—thus the question. To whom does such a question occur? I
for one would much more be interested in asking, "Who taught you to
speak? Do you have a soul?" The purpose of the ape is to instill fear in
him. He says precisely what Cardanus is afraid of, and intimidates him
all the more. That's the reason why he has to make the long calculation
afterward. So we can be pretty sure that Cardanus, as he himself says,
leads something like a provisional life, a life, that is, in which there is
one thing that it does not reckon with. And what kind of life is that?

Participant: Life without a belief in God. He lived at the beginning of
the Renaissance, so he no longer has the medieval belief in a continued
existence after death.

Professor Jung: We don't know that, but we can assume that he is living in the Church outside of which there is no salvation.[29]

Participant: His attitude is something like saying, one will live *sometime*.

Professor Jung: Yes, one lives with a certain promise, with a guarantee, without taking the whole of life into account. If somebody builds
a provisional house, for instance, he builds this house with the promise
that it would be like that for the time being, but *sometime*, when etc.
For example, some people live this provisional life without knowing it;
their life is built on the secret promise that lies behind it and makes
such life possible. I remember the case of a very ambitious man, who had
ambitious plans and constantly failed because of that. Because secretly
he believed that some day it would be revealed that he was the great
genius, the Messiah, maybe. I barely managed to make him adapt to
an active professional life. But then he again made up his mind that
surely he would be promoted to a certain influential position. That
didn't happen, however. He had a complete breakdown. It was only
on this occasion that it turned out that he'd gotten the idea from his
mother of being the Messiah. He had built his existence, his life and
work, on that promise. A complete unreality. Something like that must
have been present in Cardanus, because in any case he focused his attention on unimportant things, thereby overlooking certain especially

---

[29] I.e., the Catholic Church. Jung refers to the Roman Catholic doctrine *Extra Ecclesiam Nulla
Salus* (outside the church there is no salvation; often abbreviated EENS).

important necessities of his soul. What is real is the instinctual soul; this is the reason why he dreams of an ape, but we don't learn what the ape really would have to say. Cardanus also uses the belief in immortality to assure himself of a long life, if possible. The guarantee has to cover the beyond. He cannot access reality, but is driven by an ambition. In the case I told you about, the mother set all her ambition on the goal that the boy would become a Messiah child. He let himself get infected by all that. In the case of a real vocation there would be no such symptoms. Then one lives along one's line; then the instinctual soul cannot be split off.

In the second dream a real spirit appears, who comes near him and wants to kiss him. But he is afraid of that. What does the dead man mean? What do you think?

Participant: He's afraid of getting infected by the kiss.

Professor Jung: Yes, the dead man invades his private sphere; something of the breath of death could enter into him. For primitives, but also far into differentiated culture, mourning is a contamination. In the primitive's mind, he is impure when a relative dies. Nobody may touch him. One must not enter the charnel houses, because contamination by the dead is a nefast[30] omen. The dead person is bad luck,[31] uncanny; he who is struck by disaster is always impure. He is always contagious. As Napoleon once said, a general who isn't in luck is not a good general. He can be very good, but he is of no use, he is ill starred. For primitives, as an unlucky person he is a man to be avoided. They avoid anyone who suffers. All those who suffer are unsavory and bring bad luck on the house. As soon as someone is ill, he loses his prestige, he is avoided, and no one any longer comes near him. He has lost his authority. To give you an example, there was an Englishman who had a hunting accident; the lock of his gun had exploded. He suffered severe hand injuries. He anxiously had to conceal it, because he knew that if his boys[32] discovered it, he'd lose all authority. It can happen to anyone, of course—it happened to me too. I traveled the desert with

---

[30] Jung's term, modern English: wicked, contrary to divine law.

[31] This expression in English in the original, followed by the German equivalent that is left out here.

[32] This word in English in the original. This term, especially in the context of the following example, points to an incident in Africa.

an Arab as a guide, south of Tunis. I had inhaled some desert sand and simply had to cough. So he quizzed me, who I was, where I lived, about my wife and children, my profession, and then said: "*Médecin, mais comment tu tousse?*"[33] That was it; I'd had it as far as he was concerned. A doctor who coughs is completely out of the question. So if the dead man touches you, you are infected by death. Therefore Cardanus is afraid of this dead man. And how does he protect himself? He asks him if he knows that he is dead.

Participant: Isn't that a differentiation—that is, if the other knows that he is dead, he himself will be alive?

Participant: That's also an important issue in the *Tibetan Book of the Dead*. If a spirit knows itself to be dead, it will no longer affect the living.

Professor Jung: Exactly. The dead person only wants to get into the living as long as he doesn't know that he's dead. Then he wants to have the body of the living person. All spirits of the dead who possess the living are convinced that they haven't died yet. Even a few years ago there was a doctor in California who practiced a strange kind of psychotherapy.[34] These were partly psychotic cases, all of which he thought were possessed. His wife was a medium, and he brought the patient and his wife together, put the latter into trance, and she was then taken over by the spirit in the patient. She took the spirit out of the patient and incarnated him, speaking out of this spirit. Usually, the result was that, for example, a man's voice spoke through her and announced who he was. So he was asked, "But haven't you long been dead?" He said, "Not at all! I haven't died. Here, that's my body," and he moved the hand of the medium. Then the doctor said, "But look at this hand, just look at it!" At first the spirit said, "That's my hand." Then, "Oh my God, it's a woman's hand!" Again the doctor said, "Well, you see, you're in a woman's body." The spirit replied, "I'm sorry, I didn't know

---

[33] French: Doctor, how come you're coughing? (trans.).

[34] "The greater number, after passing out of the physical are not aware that the transition has been made. . . . Lacking physical bodies through which to carry out earthly propensities many discarnate intelligences are attracted to the magnetic light which emanates from mortals, and, consciously or unconsciously, attach themselves to these magnetic auras, finding an avenue of expression through influencing, obsessing or possessing human beings" (Carl A. Wickland, *Thirty Years among the Dead* [Los Angeles: National Psychological Institute, 1924; reprints 1974, 1990, Newcastle Publishing Company], chap. 1). About the prevailing lack of awareness that death has occurred, Emanuel Swedenborg attested to the same finding, from his visions.

that." Then he was persuaded finally to accept that he was dead and had to take a completely different path, the opposite path. Normally he then left the patient and went over to the other side, to his own fate as a dead person. Case after case was treated along these lines by this doctor, as described in his book, *Thirty Years among the Dead*. He is simply a primitive medicine man, a totally naive American, unclouded by any psychological ideas. He again takes up the old theories that neuroses and psychoses are actually cases of possession, which is indeed correct. But what possesses us is an autonomous complex, which has seized power over the whole or a great part of the psyche, and causes these phenomena of splitting, because the psyche cannot tolerate this [attempt at total possession].

When the dead man in Cardanus's dream knows that he is dead, the question put to him is an apotropaic[35] one. For if the dead man said yes, then he'd go. In the *Tibetan Book of the Dead*, the priest says to the dead person, "You are dead." He proves it to him. He tells him, "Go through the wall," which the dead person does. So the priest says, "Gotcha! You can walk through the wall, so you have no body." This is still practiced today. A lama told me that the *Bardo Thödol* is sung at the bed of the dying person before death, and beside the dead body after death. Making the person aware of the fact that he has died belongs to a series of apotropaic measures. Another one is the dead person's departure from the body. During this procedure, the priest produces a high piercing tone, which is supposed to reopen the dead person's fontanelle, through which the soul leaves. Accordingly, the members of the Ainu sect[36] make a hole in the top of their saints' heads; because the saints are those who already have an open fontanelle when they are living, where the spirit may go in or out as he pleases. There are many more such customs, also in Switzerland. In the canton of Aargau, for example, it is customary to open all the windows and doors when somebody dies, and they always say to the soul that wafts away from the dead body, "Go and flutter!," an invitation to the dead person to leave. In Polynesia this ceremony is very elaborate: the ship of the spirits comes from the island of the dead, and the dead person is sent away with compliments. He is

---

[35] Averting or combating evil.
[36] A pre-Buddhist sect, approximately 60–600 years before Buddha (G).

laid into the spirit boat, full of fruits and food, and then they wish him a good journey, push off the boat and say, "Farewell, we hope never to see you again." To this end the dead were also nailed down in the grave. They also use a slab or heap up stones on the grave, so as to prevent the dead from coming out again, which would make them "*les revenants*," those who come back again. The whole spiritual life of many primitives revolves exclusively around this question. Several times I discovered little spirit houses on the narrow bush paths near Mount Elgon, a kind of mousetrap for the spirits, very well built and roofed with grass. Inside they were fully furnished: bed, water, Negro sorghum, corn, and food. At night, when the spirits come out of the bush, where they live, they are bored because they always have to stay in the bush. On the way to their relatives in the village, they come past these spirit traps. A Negro demonstrated to me what the spirit then does; because he has "no sense of proportion,"[37] he thinks this is a house, looks into it, and says, "Fine house, good bed," goes in, and lies down on the bed. Next morning the sun rises and he has to leave at once. They build these spirit houses for the protection of the village, or the kraal. When a kraal develops, the spirit houses are built first. There the spirits are intercepted. A little clay figure, a simulacrum of the dead or ill person, is put into it. Then the spirit goes into the clay figure. During the day, however, the Elgonyi have a different philosophy, being enlightened by the sun and the light.

Well, the dead person in Cardanus's dream now knows that he is dead. Therefore, he'll no longer harm one. So Cardanus might as well let himself be kissed, he won't be infected by death. But then the question arises, whether he knew who he had been, that is, the question of identity, and how souls would fare in the beyond, whether it would be painful or not. What does the dead man stand for here?

Participant: Perhaps again for the split-off primitive soul, which seeks to establish contact with him?

Professor Jung: Yes, this is the transformed ape. Cardanus is now thirty-six years old.[38] The dead man is again the split-off complex, the autonomous complex, the instinctual soul. Why is it a dead man?

Participant: Perhaps he has actually died now?

---

[37] This expression in English in the original.
[38] In dream 2, of October 3, 1537, featuring the dead Prosper Marinonus.

Professor Jung: No. What is the bridge?

Participant: What is split off is death. If a complex is split off completely from consciousness, this will be its death, because it is no longer linked to the living personality.

Professor Jung: But he isn't dead.

Participant: But still in the beyond.

Professor Jung: That's it. The notion of the unconscious doesn't exist in primitives, or in the Middle Ages. Even today this notion doesn't exist; only some eccentrics like myself talk about the unconscious. There *is* a beyond—then one is mystical and has convictions.

Participant: The dead man is like the shadow soul in Hades.

Professor Jung: Yes, the split-off soul can take the form of an ape or of a dead person. Why? Where does Cardanus meet this figure?

Participant: The dreamland can be compared to death.

Professor Jung: Of course. The ape does exist in dreamland. For the primitive man, and also in the Middle Ages, that is an absolute reality. Just pay attention to how a primitive speaks: "I slept in my bed, and I saw how this and that happened." That's how he tells a dream, for it is another reality. Dream and spirit world are absolutely identical. When someone says, "I've dreamed," he either means, "I've been in the spirit world," or that representatives of the spirit world have visited him. When he dreams of an ape, it is a doctor ape, a spiritual ape, an inhabitant of the spirit world. Magical, spiritual beings live there, and so do the dead, and therefore the appearance of the ape is the same as the deceased friend. Now this friend wants to come near Cardanus. What does that mean?

Participant: The split-off complex is going to unite with the conscious personality.

Professor Jung: Yes, and that's exactly what is disagreeable and frightening, and what is feared in a neurosis. Something that I don't want, not for the life of me, snakes toward me and wants to sneak into me. In this case the dead man wants to get into the living Cardanus. What does that mean? Why does he want to approach him, to infect him? To what purpose?

Participant: He wants to be lived.

Professor Jung: That's it. He's looking for a body. That's what the dead strive for. They look for a body. They want to live and be real.

So this spirit wants to be lived, he doesn't want to be dead. In a way he wants to become identical with Cardanus, and this has the same meaning as the ape that comes to him; the ape, too, wants to become identical with him. We'd say that he ought to, or would have to, unite with the instinctual soul and bridge the split; in any case, the situation is such that this is advisable. What would then stop?

Participant: Provisional life.

Professor Jung: Yes, he would be confronted with his own reality.

Participant: The name Prosper Marinonus could mean, "something favorable from the sea."[39]

Professor Jung: That's not inconceivable, but we have no evidence for it. Now, the answer he gives is that the situation over there is not quite so rosy. Cardanus asks the spirit what pains him. The spirit says: A high fever. Cardanus then asks him if he'd prefer to be still alive, whereupon the spirit says, Absolutely not. Then Cardanus, So death is like sleep. The spirit, By no means. When he wants to ask more questions, the spirit departs, leaving him all alone. So the spirit does not give him a favorable image of the beyond. What's the effect? Can we deduce something *ex effectu*[40]?

Participant: He's afraid of it.

Professor Jung: Yes, it gives him the creeps. Here one simply is and lives, and then somehow one finds oneself in a mess. Why does this have to happen? What effect does it have? As a matter of fact, he wants to exist provisionally, in an unreal way. And now he is told, in effect, the situation you are aiming at is very unpleasant, and is definitely not a goal one should set oneself. Why the fever?

Participant: This is purgatory.

Professor Jung: The fire, the heat, that awaits us after death.

Participant: Emotions, affects, which he hasn't lived.

Professor Jung: Why do we live provisionally at all?

Participant: If one hasn't lived the primitive soul in this world, it will be projected onto the other world. Then there will be a unification, but a forcible and painful one.

---

[39] Latin: prosper = favorable, fortunate, propitious; mare = sea.
[40] Latin: (a conclusion drawn) from the effect.

Professor Jung: The instinctual soul is evaded, if possible, because it has the unpleasant characteristic of causing affects in us. Why does it give rise to affects? What will happen if we evade it?

Participant: They [the affects] will act out of control.

Professor Jung: Yes, that's some pretty awkward situation, isn't it? There one is, a bit possessed; one can't draw one's life line with a ruler. One depends on the wind a bit, because there's a bit too much turbulence. Most people shun the instinctual, therefore, because it interferes with adaptation. It can also tarnish one's reputation. It's very embarrassing. So if one can at all save oneself from it, one will. But then one has already arrived at the provisional; one is already outside. When the instinctual soul affects a person, it fills him with all kinds of strivings that interfere with his life. One would have to set up a termite community against it. One would no longer have any complexes. Nothing could plague one any more. One could set off like a machine, on a beautiful straight line; but all that is screwed up by the instincts. Affects are caused by collisions. An affect is always a failed adaptation. We have an affect where we are not adjusted. This upsets us, however. We must hate, and we must love, and we don't know which is worse. So if one draws a straight line in the air during life, one will come into the fire afterward. One comes into the fire after death, because one has not lived it.

In the nineteenth century a nun, a modern saint,[41] was admitted into a monastery when she was a poor girl. She was so terribly pious that she wore only the clothes discarded by the other sisters. She earned a reputation as a saint and later became an abbess. She was a paragon of humility, self-denial, of absolutely truthful saintliness. Then she died, as even saints must do, eventually. After her death two young sisters were occupied in the laundry room folding bed sheets. All of a sudden

---

[41] The saint who matches Jung's description eludes a preliminary search. However, similar episodes of scorch marks from a burning hand are on record in the seventeenth century at the convent of Santa Clara di Todi, and at the Franciscan convent of Santa Anna di Foligno in 1853, where "the spirit left an imprint as if by an iron hand heated red-hot on the door" (a grave was reopened to match the hand, which was found to fit: Lewis Spence, *Encyclopedia of Occultism and Parapsychology*, part 2, Kessinger reprint, 2003, 938). In the case of the Spanish Saint Josefa Menendez, who like Jung's nun practiced extreme humility, her habit was often seen smoldering in the choir during the morning office.

the dead abbess is standing in the doorway with a terribly sorrowful face, and says that she suffers terribly because of her humility. As proof of her manifestation to them she puts her hand on the door, and afterward the hand was branded in the wood of the door. This was shown as evidence of a miracle. It was thought that she had reached a state of special saintliness, and so one did not figure that she was standing in the fire suffering terrible pain. Why?

Participant: She was dragged into affects.

Professor Jung: Of course. She was dragged into that which she hadn't lived. She had always lived *above* herself. She had lived provisionally, and not in her affective and instinctual world.

C. At a Later Meeting of the Seminar

Professor Jung: Let us come back to the third dream, the one from 1547, which we haven't finished discussing yet. You'll remember that it's also about a dead man who appears to him, one Johann Baptist Specianus. "He seized me by the hand, but I thought that he was dead." Typically, Cardanus interrogates him, because as a dead man he might perhaps be able to tell him something about life in the other world. The other answers in that cryptic language, "*nihil super est cuius oppositum tu credis,*" "nothing is left of which you believe the opposite."

We agreed that this is a highly abstracted reversal. What it really means is that his conscious thinking is in accord with what he thinks about the beyond. The question is thus left *in suspenso*.[42] There is no positive answer, and that's also why the formulation is so strangely negative. Right after this figure of Johann Baptist Specianus there appears another young man, thin, pale, and with a long face, in the long gown of a scholar, lined with fur on the inside and ashen on the outside. The young man is neither related to nor known to the dreamer; he is just some dead person. Naturally Cardanus repeats the question about how he will fare in the future. Again this curiosity, therefore, about the future or the afterworld. Now the question is this: why does a dream recur? Why does this particular dream recur again and again?

[42] Latin: undecided.

Participant: This is an important problem for him.

Professor Jung: Which important problem?

Participant: Perhaps the answer is insufficient, because it's too negative.

Professor Jung: Yes, the answer is strangely negative and twisted; so when we find such a sentence in a dream, what could the reason be?

Participant: Perhaps the attitude is not right.

Professor Jung: Yes. Ask a stupid question and you'll get a stupid answer. That's an old joke. A fool asks much, to which a wise man replies little, or he says something foolish because he lets himself be tempted into foolishness. This ridiculous, childish curiosity could really be a wrong attitude. And so the reaction of the unconscious is contorted. In most cases of such monstrous or hybrid formations in dreams, things that don't belong together get thrown together, and there are incoherent motifs that do not belong in the context. It's highly likely that that kind of question actually provoked that silly answer, with the result that the situation matches up, that is, the vision of the dead man is repeated. We know, moreover, that the dead *do* appear in dreams. After all, Cardanus did not make these dreams, so there must be something in them about the dead themselves. They must mean something special. Imagine having a dream in which a dead person appears to you. In former times dreams of the dead were much more frequent than nowadays. In our case they are very veiled; rarely do we have real dreams of the dead like these. In modern times these dreams are highly unusual; earlier and among primitives they were much more frequent.

Participant: For Cardanus, the dead person is not really dead.

Participant: The realm of the dead is approaching him.

Professor Jung: Yes, the dead person is a kind of *angelos*, a messenger, who approaches him. He is the *oneiros*, the dream that simultaneously represents the realm of the dead, the *aljira*. This is the land of the dead, the land of the ancestors, for the ancestors are all dead.[43] In the majority of cases it is also the land beneath the earth, or the land in

---

[43] Jung treats the *aljira* or *altjiranamitjinas*, or the first heroes of "the *altjiranga* time before the grandfather," "the *Urzeit*, the *alcheringa*," when discussing Nietzsche's prophetic sense of the popular modern dictators, whose ideas "go back just to the grandfather" just short of such primordial foretime, in the February 8, 1939, session of *Nietzsche's Zarathustra: Notes of the Seminar Given in 1934–1939* (James L. Jarrett, ed. [London: Routledge], vol. 2, 1522–23). Jung's source, as noted by Jarrett, is Lévy-Bruhl's *Primitive Mythology*. The *aljira* ancestors of the central Australian Aranda are treated by Alexander Goldenwieser, *Early Civilization: An Introduction to Anthropology* (New York: Knopf, 1922), 211–12, and later by Claude Lévi-Strauss in *The Savage Mind* (1962; Chicago:

the West, the Westland, the island out in the sea, the Green Isle. In the Epic of Gilgamesh it is the Westland, the land of the netherworld,[44] and that is represented by a messenger coming from there. Well, how would you translate such a dead person into modern psychological language? What is this land of the dead?

Participant: The unconscious.

Professor Jung: The unconscious is the land of the dead. It is the other side; that which is unconscious to us, which is not seen but affects us. So for primitives these are spirits, representatives of the land of the dead, the netherworld, and the only thing we can determine is that they represent an unknown psychic region. What else they might be, *if* such a land of the dead exists, where spirits of the dead are found or where such spirits come from, cannot be proved. We can only be subjectively convinced of this, to a greater or lesser degree. It does frequently happen that such apparitions appear after death.

Participant: Could one say that some part has been split off when the unconscious appears in the form of dead persons?

Professor Jung: Yes, the distance is very great when the appearance of the unconscious is so palpable, so substantial, so to speak—so active, spontaneous, and plastic. In those cases a great distance always separates consciousness from the unconscious. What does that mean?

Participant: Consciousness has distanced itself from nature and is laboring under apprehensions that do not correspond to natural life.

Participants: In abstractions.

Professor Jung: Yes. What else, for example?

Participant: The conscious attitude is always somewhat artificial.

Professor Jung: Yes, abstractions are always artificial—not always artistic, but in any case artificial. What else?

Participant: Something conventional.

Professor Jung: Now that's a dirty word! Let's rather say, rational: rational views or ideas that are basically rational formations. You know that reason is one of the most glorified human characteristics. I don't

University of Chicago Press, 1966), chap. 3, "Systems of Transformations," 85–86. See p. 152n48 below with respect to Jung's further comment on the totem-hero aspect of the central figure.

[44] More recently the two places are distinct, the Westland being Uta-napishtim's homeland and site of the divine Cedar Forest guarded by Humbaba. See Willem Zitman paraphrasing F. de Liagre Bohl, in *Egypt: Image of Heaven*, trans. Peter Rijpkema (Amsterdam: Frontier Publishing, 2006), 204.

want to debase it. It's one of the highest achievements, but it can also be abused. Humans always do that. When they have invented something, the first thing they do is to horribly abuse it. One has dreamed for centuries that peace would come once man could fly. Well, just look at the mess we've gotten into! And people pretend that reason is the absolute criterion for everything. Reason is a valuable tool in known areas, but reason can't be applied at all to what is unknown and new. We psychologists are accused of having an irrational attitude, but we can't do without it, otherwise we wouldn't be able to do research. After all, we don't have a proper knowledge of the human soul, and still want to be rational about it. To begin with, however, we have to open our eyes and ears to collect perceptions, until we know what is going on. But until then we can do without reason. We can't say that anything is irrational, except when it's illogical. Is it rational or irrational that elephants and lice exist? How could I prove on rational grounds that elephants can't possibly exist? Elephants *do* exist. Afterward, we may be rational. Well, if we have only a rational attitude toward phenomena that occur, that is, if we abstract in order in order to generate ideas and views, and then go on to assume that this now represents the world or reality—then we'll be one-sided, and also will be separated to a great extent from real perceptions of the world, of the world as it really exists. The distance between consciousness and the unconscious will become very great, because the unconscious somehow coincides, so to speak, with objects. The unconscious is a *mens dissoluta*, a spirit that, per se, contains only objects, only existence. So we might also say that the unconscious is not within us, but right here around us; not within ourselves because it coincides with the world—not with the rational world, however, but the world as such, the one we don't know, beyond any perceptions and definitions. That's why what is unconscious is also what is not known about the world.

It is so easy, therefore, to immediately project the unconscious into some unknown thing we come across in the world. We don't project it ourselves, but find it in the world in projected form. The hole is filled with marvelous ideas, which then emerge as mythological ones. You see, as long as we don't know how light travels through space, we fill this hole in the world order with ether. We then say "ether," and that suits us just fine. One doesn't know why, but this ether has always been in people's minds. The ancient Greeks already knew of it. The concept is that there is extremely fine air; this is the fire air. Primitives also know that man's soul is fire air. This is ether. But we think that's unscientific. When I did my studies, I said to my physics teacher that ether as matter or substance simply doesn't exist. I made a hole in his mythologem. He simply filled that hole with ether without noticing it. That's how it goes. If the unconscious actually fills all the holes in our worldview and we don't notice it, but think that we live in a rational, well-ordered world, we will be cut off from the unconscious, because we will locate an essential content, an archetypal content of the unconscious, out there in the world order, and will not feel it to be a projection. Ancient physics did not conceive of ether as a projection. And when you go back to ancient natural science or alchemy, for instance, the wildest projections abound. The ancients were unaware of this. Nor were the ancient Christians aware, for example, who believed they were cleansed from sin by the blood of the lamb—aware of the fact that exactly the same was done in the taurobolias[45] of Mithraism, during which the mystic sat in a hole, a bull was killed above him, and he washed himself in its blood. Such taurobolias also took place, for instance, on the site where St. Peter's Basilica is situated today. This was a pagan practice. But they did not realize that their idea about the lamb's blood was exactly the same as the pagan one. It was totally unconscious. Well, anyway, whenever one has filled up all the holes in one's system with mythological ideas, one is separated from one's unconscious. One no longer lives in the unknown world but in a kind of darkened room where the only film running is the one you have produced yourself. Consequently, one is separated from the unknown world. In just such cases dreams like these may occur.

Participant: But if the projected contents are full of life, it's not a box.

Professor Jung: Well, we always assume that this period was critical, in which consciousness supposedly made progress. I don't begrudge the ancient physicists their ether when they are happy with it, but then they shouldn't call it science. But if they think it is science nonetheless, then let their peace be disturbed. If someone declares that he's got a scientific conscience, then he is also saying that he never wants to have a quiet time of it, that he wants to be continuously disturbed.

---

[45] A cultic ritual in which bulls were killed.

Science has ethics. I readily concede that it's certainly nice to live in a world where paths and meadows are still populated by Oreads,[46] Hamadryads,[47] nymphs, and gods. That's how it's always been, and that's OK, but once science comes into play the fun is over.

We have to assume something similar in Cardanus. In his way, he was a scientific man. He was undoubtedly driven by a tremendous thirst for action. He lived at a time when the undetermined extension of the earth was realized, in which the Gothic outlook was about to collapse, and in which one began to think rationally about the universe, in which physics and chemistry were just about to come into being. That's the atmosphere from which Cardanus comes. So naturally he was not one to turn his attention to the inside and criticize his inner preconditions; he opened his eyes and ears to absorb the totality. He was completely split off from the unconscious; he simply was no psychologist, thus these dreams of the dead. They come as messengers from that unseen unconscious, they want to announce themselves and sort of tell him, "Here I am. We bring you something. We're warning you of something." And in his rational consciousness he can't think of anything else except to make it useful, by telling himself, "These animals or plants are not harmful, they're good for something." In the same way that natural science has made such classifications, he interpreted and classified what the unconscious brought him according to its personal use value. He simply remains stuck in that attitude.

The dead man in the dream is obviously a scholar; he wears a scholastic gown. Why is the gown lined with fur on the inside?

Participant: It goes inside.

Professor Jung: What goes inside? What does a fur mean, whose hairs are turned inside?

Participant: The animal is an interior one.

Professor Jung: Yes, the fur coat is a compensatory animal. That's why the ladies are so fond of wearing furs—in order to compensate themselves. They greatly value animal psychology; they wear the skinned animal on themselves but are not identical with it. That's a subtle hint—that's why fashion changes so often, because the ladies express their psychology through it. Just pay attention to the hats! The general

---

[46] In Greek mythology, nymphs of grottoes and mountains. One of the most famous Oreads was Echo.

[47] Tree nymphs, embodied by the tree that houses them.

view a woman has of herself is expressed by the hat. Now I've divulged a little secret. The gladiators in Rome wore animal skins. In a way, they represented animals to be slaughtered. Quite often, the hide of wild animals is used in the dances of primitives for this purpose. The magician likes to dress up as some kind of animal. In our dream the scholar wears the fur outside in. So that would be a kind of werewolf, a disguised animal, an animal that actually seems to be a human being, but which can also turn into an animal. What has this to do with a figure that represents the unconscious?

Participant: Doesn't this also point toward the ape?

Professor Jung: Yes, this pertains to that figure of the ape. In that dream a representative of the unconscious appeared to him in the form of a talking ape. Then the figure develops. The fur is turned outside in: a kind of were-ape, a werewolf, a humanized ape. This goes back to the original animal nature of the unconscious. Therefore, the ancestors are usually half animals.

Participant: In Greek mythology we find the centaurs, the lion skin of Heracles, or semi-snakelike humans such as Kekrops and Erechtheus.

Professor Jung: Yes, those are excellent examples of *aljira* ancestors.[48]

Participant: Does the she-wolf of Romulus and Remus have the same meaning?

Professor Jung: Yes, the motifs of the animal mother belong here. Vishnu is half man, half lion. And all the heroes and gods who were raised and fed by animal parents, all that also belongs here, of course. The hero in the Nordic saga has snake eyes, because he is also the snake or dragon that he fights. Thus the image of the fur turned inward means that in actual fact only the outer appearance is that of a human being. In reality the creature is an animal and therefore belongs in that dark animal sphere, where the ancestors come from.

Now Cardanus quizzes the scholar, too. The scholar tells him that he would become sad if he answered him. Then Cardanus asks if he will die. The scholar says, no, he will be wounded by a female mule, but will eventually make a great profit with little effort. What could this mean?

[48] Page 147 above. Cf. footnote 43, this chapter. In the *Nietzsche Seminar* passage cited there, Jung cites Kekrops and Erechtheus. For the Australian Aranda, *Aljira* proper names an axial ancestor like these same Greek examples: a large red man with light hair and emu-like legs, who stands as the great Father in the beyond, though not a creator. See Goldenwieser, *Early Civilization: An Introduction to Anthropology*, 211–12.

Participant: It's reminiscent of Balaam and the ass, only there it is the other way around. The ass leads Balaam to truth.[49]

Professor Jung: It frequently happens that animals talk, and it means precisely what the talking ape is, the intelligent manifestation of the unconscious appearing in the animal. You see, we know little about the psychology of the animal. We don't know what kind of souls animals have—therefore the assumption that animals might perhaps even know much more than man, for example, about the future. Therefore, too, the common folklore assumption that horses have a special ability to smell out the future or death. The same is true of the ass. Balaam's ass is a good example. The Middle Ages were very much occupied with it; in the history of the heretics, for instance, Balaam became a swear word to designate heretics, whereas this good ass or donkey also became a sacred animal, so to speak, in early Christian legend: there is a sacred donkey that was so pious that it always went to church with the parishioners. It was buried beside the church because it was so pious. Under these circumstances one might also have assumed that Cardanus would rather have dreamed of a donkey than a mule.

Participant: It could also refer to the donkey that carried Jesus.[50]

Professor Jung: But it's a mule.

Participant: The mule is a hybrid of horse and donkey and cannot procreate.

Participants: Mules are characterized by infertility and stubbornness. They are good pack animals, however.

Professor Jung: I have looked up some old, contemporary sources for the symbolism of *mulus* and *mula*.[51] In the Middle Ages animal figures were viewed moralistically, so to speak, that is, as examples of moral behavior. What is said about animals shows how those animals were viewed. Regarding the mule, the saying, "*Ex fecundis infecunda*," was stressed, from the fertile comes the infertile. And "*Genitus non generat*," it is generated, born, but does not generate itself. Also "*Ingrassatus—inoboediens*," when it has grown fat, it is disobedient. So ingratitude and the feature of stubbornness were assigned to the *mulus*. It is further said, "*mulum imitatur homo*," man imitates the *mulus*. If he does, he is

[49] Cf. Numbers 22:1–41.
[50] Matthew 21.
[51] Latin: male and female mule.

ungrateful, because he is infertile and emptied of good deeds to his core. Thus a person who performs no good deeds is empty and infertile like a mule. You can see that there was a particular focus on the infertility and stubbornness of the mule. Thus we must assume that, provided there aren't very special, individual motives in this case, we have to make do with these contemporary views. So it would mean that Cardanus was wounded by the pack animal. And he was wounded because this animal is a stubborn and ungrateful animal, which is also infertile. What could that mean?

Participant: Because his conscious attitude is so far removed from the unconscious, his unconscious is infertile.

Professor Jung: Yes, he is condemned to infertility. This is typical dream psychology. The unconscious introduces him to this figure—to the very figure that he is. He hurts himself, so to speak, by being a *mulus*, by condemning the unconscious to existence as a *mulus*. How?

Participant: He doesn't assimilate it.

Professor Jung: Yes, just as the *mulus* is not created naturally, but is a product of humans—*muli* are bred by humans, after all—man has also created this aspect of the unconscious. He has turned the unconscious into a sterile being, which then gives him a swift kick like a *mulus*. As we know, *muli* are quite malicious. The soldiers serving in the *Saumkolonnen*[52] can tell us a thing or two about what *muli* are able to do. So in our dream this is meant to indicate that the unconscious will eventually give him a kick. But he will certainly make an easy profit without having to work hard. What does that mean?

Participant: The kick is a fertilization.

Professor Jung: Where did you learn that?

Professor Jung: But what is actually written there?[53] You know perhaps the phrase, "*pulsatur terra*," the earth is being beaten.[54] Natu-

[52] A column of pack animals (mules, horses) to transport goods in the mountains on *Saumwegen* (mule tracks). Cf. 195n130, this chapter.

[53] "It is not only the feet themselves that have a fertility significance, it also seems to extend to their activity, treading. I observed that the dance-step of the Pueblo Indians consisted in a '*calcare terram*'—a persistent, vigorous pounding of the earth with the heels ('*nunc pede libero pulsanda tellus*': 'with unfettered foot now we are to beat on the ground,' Horace, *Odes* I.xxxii). Kaineus, as we saw, descended into the depths, 'splitting the earth with a straight foot.' Faust reached the Mothers by stamping on the ground: 'Stamping descend, and stamping rise up again!'" *Symbols of Transformation*, CW 5 para. 480.

[54] In the original, the translation is mistakenly given in the active, not the passive voice: *die Erde klopft* = the earth knocks (or beats).

rally, today we no longer understand this. We think it's a metaphor for "dancing." But, as we can very clearly see in primitives, the old dance consists of "laboring" the earth; libido gets worked into the earth. For hours, the earth is being trodden on in order to fertilize it. The gesture of kicking has become a symbol of fertilizing the earth, therefore, or of fertilization in general—hence also the hoof instead of the phallus. The horse's hoof is also a flash of lightning, which, as we know, splits and fertilizes the earth. Anything that strikes, hits, opens the earth, is a phallic symbol; thus the kick can assume that meaning of fertilization. That would explain why Cardanus is supposed to be blessed in his work later on, that is, it will be fertile without much labor.

Participant: But this is the kick of a sterile creature.

Professor Jung: That's the paradox. Infertility causes fertility. Exactly like that passage in the legend of Samson: "Out of the eater came forth meat, and out of the strong came forth sweetness."[55] This reversal is very typical. Sterility will be fertile. A virgin, not a married woman, gives birth to the Savior.

So Cardanus is pursued by an animal, pursued by robbers. This is all very negative. He is beset by an evil being, and so one assumes that this can only lead to something evil, to destruction. Strangely enough, the result is something good, because the split (that which is infertile), or the reason the two cannot come together, eventually has the effect that one must join the two (the opposites) together.

There is a beautiful alchemical legend about this, the *Visio Arislei*. The philosophers come into the realm of the sea king and find beautiful but infertile trees there. The women have no children, the animals no offspring. They ask, "Don't you have philosophers?" "No," they are answered. The philosophers find that the king does not rule his people properly, for otherwise there would be fertility. After all, it makes no sense to pair beings of the same kind. So they ask the king if he doesn't have someone male and someone female. The king tells them that he has two children whom he has carried in his head, the famous Gabricus and Beia. The philosophers recommend incest, which in fact is carried out. But then Gabricus dies; this is something bad and damaging, and the king is appalled and revolted. The philosophers placate him only with great difficulty. He wants to lock them up, but they manage

[55] Judges 14:14.

to persuade him to give them Beia, too. At first he is reluctant, but eventually they succeed in bringing both children back to life, at first reviving Gabricus, then finally the fertile royal couple. That is one such story, which begins with something evil and destructive happening; infertility had resulted from the fact that philosophical principles, the unification of *This* and *The Other*, had not been applied. *This* is consciousness, *The Other* is the unconscious. We exclude the latter because it is different, because we always procreate by resorting to consciousness. We constantly breed horse with donkey, constantly create *muli*, and the result is sterility. That is precisely what the dream criticizes.

Now we'll have to check the correctness of this view by having a look at subsequent dreams. At first Cardanus narrates a dream about his deceased mother:[56]

> 4. In the early spring of 1538 I saw my mother stand at the foot of my bed and, almost towering above, sit on the bedstead, dressed in a laced-up scarlet dress, like a robe, as she wore it when she did her housework. Her eyes sparkled and she called to me that I should come with her. I said, "Why so? Aren't you dead?" She answered, "Certainly." "So why do you want me to come with you, which I can only do if I myself die?" She said, "It is better for you and you will live more peacefully." When I refused, and she kept on insisting more heatedly, she finally seemed to go off in an angry mood.

Professor Jung: What does it mean that it's the mother?
Participant: It's a figure for the whole unconscious.
Professor Jung: In which form?
Participant: In a related form.
Professor Jung: So the unconscious comes near, very near actually. Why does the mother wear a scarlet dress?
Participant: She possesses the feeling that he lacks.
Professor Jung: Why should that represent feeling?
Participant: The red color.
Professor Jung: That's very abstract.
Participant: Honor is associated with it, because it's a royal robe.

[56] *Synesiorum somniorum, op. cit.,* 5: 722.

Professor Jung: But why the red?

Participant: It's the color of blood.

Professor Jung: Yes, in a previous dream a blood-red chief justice appeared, the *"praefectus criminalium capitis,"*[57] and Marinonus was also dressed in red, hence the color of blood. What sources are there for the scarlet color in this respect?

Participant: It's also the language of the Bible: "When your gown is as red as blood, I will wash it."

Professor Jung: Where does the scarlet color appear?

Participant: In the book of Revelation.

Professor Jung: Yes, the Son of Man appears there in a scarlet gown; He is the One who treads the winepress.[58] The gown is spattered with blood. This is the powerful blood vision in which He treads on the peoples in the winepress, with blood flowing from the temple. It comes up to the horses' teeth. Now how is the color of blood linked to the mother?

Participant: The mother represents instinct.

Professor Jung: That's too abstract.

Participant: Blood is lifeblood.

Professor Jung: Yes, the stream of life. Ancient embryology taught that the withheld menstrual blood that fills the uterus coagulates and gradually solidifies. That's the ancient theory about the creation of children.

Participant: In the Gnostic version it says that the child lives on vessels of blood and air.

Professor Jung: Yes, that's how the veins and arteries were interpreted. This is ancient philosophy. Blood is absolutely identical with the mother. The blood of the mother, or the mother as blood, is the nourishing medium of the child. It's actually the truth, the child is

[57] *Chief criminal magistrate*: the German term here, *Blutvogt* ("blood reeve"), in lower jurisdictions indicates a sheriff or bailiff, but among nobility carries the old Roman prefect's compound rank of military protector and chief justice. Jung is harking back to both the second and third dreams in the series about Cardanus's two dead friends, conflating one with the other: Prosper Marinonus in the "scarlet coat" and Johann Specianus "the former judge for capital crimes." *Blutvogt* in fact parallels the medieval German term for a high court, or *Blutgericht*. The participant's subsequent allusion is probably to Isaiah 1:18.

[58] Revelation 14:20.

nothing but withheld menstrual blood, but blood also has a psychological meaning.

Participant: Blood contains the soul.

Professor Jung: Blood *is* the soul. There are blood rituals, for example to wash something with blood. The prayer of Anima-Christi says: "*Sanguis Christi inebria me*."[59]

Participant: It also plays a role in the taurobolias.

Professor Jung: Yes, blood is licked directly off the flesh of the lacerated animal. Hence the strange cults, for example, the fact that Cabirus,[60] a chthonic god, is worshiped with bloody mouth and bloody hands. Naturally, this is also known from the Dionysian orgies, because in them the soul substance is drunk. The *anima Christi*[61] is drunk with the wine, the blood, as a *pharmakon*, a remedy, so that our soul is healed of the damage it suffered from the world, because the soul is corrupted and hence loses its divinity. This disease gets cured by the consumption of the *anima Christi*. So, when the mother appears to Cardanus, it is unconscious life itself that appears, the mother medium, the blood medium, the soul substance, out of which consciousness is born; that is the anima, the primeval notion of the anima, and she wants him to go with her, to the other side of course, into the land of the dead. He thinks he would have to die, and she is of the opinion that he will feel better. What does that mean?

Participant: His consciousness is darkened.

Participant: He will then be acting out of his unconscious.

Professor Jung: He unites with the unconscious; he goes into the unconscious with his consciousness. This results in a synthesis between consciousness and the unconscious, because the one is united with the other, the same with the disparate, the male with the female. This further results in a fruit, that is, the outcome is a fertilization of consciousness and the correction of conscious one-sidedness. Naturally, this would lead to a compensation for leading too much of an outer life, that is, for the fact that he is not reconnected to himself.

---

[59] Latin: *Blut Christi, berausche mich, mache mich freudetrunken* (G). Blood of Christ, inebriate me.

[60] This Macedonian and Thracian god, a patron of Thessaloniki when Paul preached there, had been murdered by his two brothers and was slated to return to aid the poor.

[61] Latin: soul of Christ.

Participant: It felt like death to him.

Participant: If he had understood it in concrete terms and had said he would have to die soon, he might have joined a monastery. This could have had that effect.

Professor Jung: Yes, he certainly could have joined a monastery *in concreto*, just as Kaiser Heinrich [Henry] V did.[62]

Participant: He also could have occupied himself with alchemy, for example; that would have been possible at the time.

Professor Jung: It's not certain that this would have happened. What would he have busied himself with? With philosophy as a preparation for death. He could have occupied himself with philosophy in the ancient sense. He would have had to say, "I must prepare for death so that I can live a better life." That would amount to the realization that one must undergo the regime of compensation. "Right in the middle of life we are surrounded by death."[63]

Participant: But doesn't it mean that he *cannot* do it?

Professor Jung: Yes, for the dream continues. The mother angrily leaves him. He has assumed a completely unphilosophical attitude.

The next dream goes as follows:

5. "In the year 1538, on May 5th, in a dream I saw a glowing star that fell into my farmyard. There it was instantly extinguished.

This dream is from the same year. The two dreams probably closely followed each other, so that we may relate them to each other. What is the *missing link*[64]?

Participant: The star and the mother are representations of the unconscious.

Professor Jung: That's going too far. We have to have the bridge to the mother. Where is the bridge between the mother and the star?

---

[62] Unless ironic, this allusion remains enigmatic. The German Emperor Henry V continued the fierce squabbles with the papacy over rights of investiture waged by Henry IV, which featured a papal kidnapping and the appointment, and then abandonment, of an antipope, but neither father nor son relinquished the crown to take the tonsure. Pope Gregory VII, witnessing Henry IV's famous three-day penance standing in the snow before his castle at Canossa, later taunted the emperor for being "a false monk."

[63] From the Latin *media vita in morte sumus*, the first line of an eighth-century antiphon later adapted by both Luther and Cranmer.

[64] This expression in English in the original.

Participant: The mother would be the earth into which the star falls.

Professor Jung: That's too abstract. The shooting star is a birth. A soul has fallen into creation. That's an ancient belief. Each time a shooting star falls, a soul has plummeted into space. The yard is the earth; the star has fallen into existence; and the mother means birth. This is about birth. The sentence simply goes on, as it were. Here is the mother. She is the personification of blood, of the soul. And so the whole thing means, "I have fallen from the skies like a star, from eternity into time." He himself is this star.

Why does he dream this? It's as if he has driven away the mother. He didn't want to obey; he didn't want to be taken back by the mother. So in a way he overlooked the fact that he is a meteor that fell from the sky, out of eternity. And when the mother says, "Come with me, back to eternity," he refused. And therefore comes the dream that tells him, "You'll have to remember that you are a star that has fallen into time." Surely you remember other cases in which something falls from eternity into time.

Participant: The star that falls into the well in the book of Revelation.[65]

Participant: The star of Bethlehem.[66] A great soul has come to the earth.

Professor Jung: And another wonderful dream in antiquity, in which someone dreams that a star had fallen down: *Gilgamesh*. You know, Gilgamesh dreams, and then goes to his mother to tell her the dream, to discuss with her what the dream might mean. He dreamed that a star had fallen on his back and weighed him down, but he managed to carry it and bring it to his mother. He struggled with that star. It's as if he laid his masculinity on it, like a man on a woman, and had united with that star. And what happened afterward, how did his mother interpret the dream? The very friend he had won, the gods would have created as an enemy. More precisely, this friend, the shadow, the animal man with fur growing inward, lived at the watering hole with the gazelles. He came from the beyond to hurt him, to kill Gilgamesh and break his power. That's why the gods had made him. It's exactly this same

---

[65] "And the fifth angel sounded, and I saw a star fall from heaven unto the earth: and to him was given the key of the bottomless pit" (Revelation 9:1).

[66] Cf. Matthew 2.

story. And Gilgamesh managed to make the enemy his friend and to unite with him, that is, to assimilate the star into himself. And by assimilating the star into himself, what did he become? What did he do afterward?

Participant: He became the divine hero.

Participant: He made the journey into the land of the dead.

Professor Jung: Yes, it is part of the hero's destiny to reopen the access to the unconscious, to harness rivers and springs, so that everything can live. That's what the hero does. He opens the heavenly waters, because man is moving away from the sources. That's the psychological difficulty that crops up again and again, that one moves away, separating oneself from instinctual preconditions, and consequently becomes sterile. This is expressed in the Epic of Gilgamesh or in the dragon myths. Countries are devastated; fruits and crops no longer appear. The dragon has to be killed, and then everything is put right again. The hero takes the dragon's blood, which makes him invulnerable. So these are the motifs you find in the hero myth. And therefore we may say about this dream of Cardanus, that if Cardanus realizes he is actually a star that has fallen from the sky, then this will relate to the past, to his own birth from his mother, but also that this star is falling from the sky *right now*. What does that mean?

Participant: A rebirth.

Professor Jung: He is being created now and reborn as a star. Because if the mother appears in that symbolic form, then that form will indicate that now is the moment at which one is reborn, when a star is born.

Participant: It means fate.

Professor Jung: Yes, Gilgamesh attains his supreme fate because the star becomes his friend. Now what about Cardanus? What effect does the star have on him? What does it mean psychologically?

Participant: It's an enlightenment; he is illumined.

Professor Jung: Yes, I have to draw your attention to a primitive custom. When the king has to sneeze, the whole royal household bows for five minutes, because a new soul has gone into the king; that's why he had to sneeze. Why does sneezing have this meaning? What happens after birth? The child's first action is to sneeze. The sneezing is the moment at which the soul enters the child. It's an ancestral soul, which has to be greeted with low bows. Therefore we still say, "*Gesundheit!*,"[67] because a soul has entered someone, for which we must wish him good luck. After all, it could also be a harmful soul, to which we must attribute an apotropaic meaning. Today, of course, we think of influenza bacteria![68] Meteors are called shooting stars. In America they are called "the urine of the stars."[69] A heavenly being has urinated. This is *mana*-liquid. By this means the medical power of the chief is transferred onto his successor. A shooting star is also something very unappetizing.[70] Likewise, many terms for natural places are often obscene or indecent. A waterfall is called *voile de la vièrge*,[71] in the Valais it is called *Pissevache*.[72] Someone blew his nose but, mind you, without a handkerchief. That was no *voile de la vièrge*. You see, when such a star falls into one, a new soul has flown in. The fate that had already been written in the stars has entered into him. That would have the effects we have seen in Gilgamesh.

Now comes the next dream:[73]

6. In the same year (1538), on November 15, I saw the starry sky, but Mercury seemed to be missing. Shortly afterward, I saw it shine among many other stars, which were much bigger, but not in any order. Next, on the left side, I saw about fifteen stars, definitely not fewer, touch each other, as if they were strung together on a string. There also were very bright stars, which formed the image of a wonderful rose. I rejoiced in their sight and heard a voice say, "Expect the coming together of moon and Mercury."

---

[67] Literally, health.

[68] *Sic*; actually, influenza is caused by viruses.

[69] While several western Native American tribes saw meteors as souls passing to the afterlife, or fire from heaven, or refugees fleeing danger, or omens of illness and death, other tribes entertained "less polite explanations. . . . The Nunamiut Eskimos, the Koasati Indians of Louisiana (formerly living in Tennessee), and most southern California tribes saw meteors as the falling feces of stars. The Kiliwa Indians of Mexico's Baja peninsula believed that meteors were the fiery urine of the constellation Xsmii." Mark Littmann, *The Heavens on Fire: The Great Leonid Meteor Storms* (Cambridge: Cambridge University Press, 1998), 45.

[70] The German *Sternschnuppe* is derived from medieval expressions for sneezing, blowing one's nose, etc. (Duden, *Das Herkunftswörterbuch*).

[71] French: the virgin's veil.

[72] French: pissing cow.

[73] *Synesiorum somniorum, op. cit.*, 5: 716.

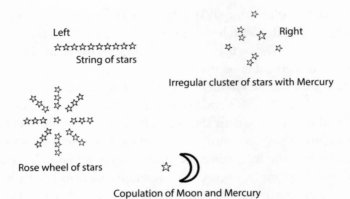

Left
☆☆☆☆☆☆☆☆☆☆☆
String of stars

Right
Irregular cluster of stars with Mercury

Rose wheel of stars

Copulation of Moon and Mercury

Professor Jung: The Latin term here is *congressus*, not *coniunctio*. In alchemical and astrological terms he'd have had to say *coniunctio*.[74] *Congressus* means *congressus feminae*, sexual intercourse. That's what is meant here. The fifteen stars form a half moon. This is so because the moon comes into play, so these fifteen probably represent a half moon. What could that star cluster on the right side possibly represent? What is usually on the right side?

Participant: Consciousness.

Professor Jung: Yes, because the right side is the one with which we act consciously. The left side is the superstitious side, the unconscious, also the feminine side. The right side is the side of the sun, the left one that of the moon. These are very ancient beliefs, which can be traced back to the mists of remote antiquity, and which, of course, are all the more valid for Cardanus. So what would you expect to find on the right side, when you see stars there?

Participant: The sun.

Professor Jung: And if it's expressed in the language of the dream?

Participant: Order.

Professor Jung: Yes, order, of course. The cosmos is a conscious arrangement. One would assume order to be on the conscious side. Cardanus sees Mercury, but he is placed within the disorder. What does this mean?

---

[74] As in the English "conjunction," a term used in positional astronomy and astrology.

Participant: Couldn't one say that he is the guiding principle among the disordered stars? Afterward he has to move to the moon on the left side.

Professor Jung: Yes, he is the male principle on the right side, and the moon would then come on the left side.

Participant: Because Hermes[75] is the shepherd of the stars.

Professor Jung: Yes, as herald of the gods he is always linked to the sun. He always travels with the sun. Therefore he is the shepherd of the stars, and thus may easily appear among the herd of stars. Now Mercury is also the intellectual God. Hermes is actually the *nous*, the divine mind, divine reason. Or he is simply identical with *pneuma*. Well, he's on the right side, and given this fact, that Cardanus has Mercury on the right side, what will inevitably happen to him? What conclusion do we inevitably come to? He is identical with Mercury, the *nous*. That's precisely why he is so far removed from the unconscious.

D. At a Later Meeting of the Seminar

Professor Jung: Last time we ended with a discussion of Mercury. We found that the stars Cardanus sees are arranged unsystematically on the right side, whereas on the left side they are strung together as on a thread. And there are also very bright stars among them, which look like a beautiful rose.

Well, here we naturally have to deal a bit more with the meaning of Mercury at that time. We have to bring to mind that Cardanus is someone well versed in the natural sciences and philosophy of his age, and thus quite knowledgeable about astrology and alchemy, in which Mercury definitely plays a great role. As you know, in astrology he stands for the planet that is nearest to the sun, and, because he is never distant from the sun, wanders through all the houses of the planets with him. The ancients call him Stilbon, the shining one; as his name shows, he naturally stands in connection to the well-known herald of the gods.

[75] Mercury/Mercurius was the Roman name for the Greek god Hermes.

He is, as it were, the prime minister of the sun, of *sol* or *helios*. So what we find here is, in a way, the image of the highest god, the sun, and his vizier, his closest minister. In astrology Mercury takes on a further meaning, that of an intellectual celestial body. He actually means *nous*, also *mens* or *mind*, because of his agility and lucidity. He is a shining little celestial body. He is nearest to the light. Therefore he is always illuminated by the divine rays of the sun—as is also the *nous*, according to certain views. The nous is a sort of a sphere around the deity, or is even identified with the deity as such. So it says, among other things: God creates the *nous*, which takes the form of circular or global fire. This *nous* is like a global mantle around God, or even God himself. And in this sphere, or perhaps outside of this sphere, moves Mercury, or Hermes, who embodies the *sapientia dei*.[76] In later antiquity, in the age of syncretistic Hellenism, he therefore became the God of revelation par excellence, the revelatory soul guide. He's been that for a long time already, of course, already in Homer. And so later in antiquity he becomes above all a soul guide through the darkness of the mysteries and plays a particularly great role in magic. He is identified with the Egyptian god Thoth, the grandfather of all sciences. In Hellenistic interpretation he becomes Hermes Trismegistos, the arch-father of all hidden sciences. The role that Mercury—whose name is simply the Latin equivalent for Hermes—plays in Latin alchemy corresponds to this meaning. There he is identified with mercury, or quicksilver, which is identified with the planet Mercury because of its extraordinary versatility. In alchemy he plays the role of the divine spirit that entered into the darkening of matter.

For instance, let's remember the dream in which the star fell down into Cardanus's farmyard and was extinguished in the dark earth. This is a spark of the divine fire that had fallen into the earth, into the body, into Cardanus's own darkness, into his unconscious—a kind of spiritual fertilization. Well, this Mercury, who had fallen into earthly captivity, is a central motif in all Gnostic systems. It is a main task to save this *nous* from grasping bondage, from being held captive by the earth. Alchemy also has this same goal, as you heard in my public lecture. The

[76] Latin: knowledge of God.

masters of the art endeavor once again, by the *opus contra naturam*,[77] to free the spiritual powers of the deity that are captured in the elements and matter. Cardanus, too, was knowledgeable about these things, like all learned men of that time, insofar as they occupied themselves with natural philosophy at all. So we have to assume that ideas of that kind are also discernible in Cardanus's dreams.

The star that fell into his farmyard marks the moment, so to speak, at which a *calling*, one is nearly inclined to say, happened in Cardanus. It is a star of annunciation, and it falls into his farmyard, of all things. It's as if he were marked by the gods, he has a direct connection to the divine stars, and, therefore, he himself is a star, or has become a star, in some way without knowing it, because at that time as well as in antiquity a star always stood in a direct relation to man—namely, to an important personality. There was the star of Caesar, for instance. The ancient view was that we are linked to the cosmos by the force of the stars, by Heimarmene.[78] This Stoic notion expressed the fated relatedness of man with the stars, and the salvation was precisely to free oneself, or to be saved, from the coercion of this Heimarmene, the force of the stars. That lay on the negative side. On the positive side it meant that when the star appears, it announces the birth of the important personality, as we can see in the story of the star of Bethlehem. The stars are always brought into connection with important personalities. From ecclesiastical literature, for example, I can cite the following: "Just as the stars differ in brightness, so the differences between the righteous are due to the differences in their merits."[79] So the righteous are compared to the stars. This corresponds to the comparison between holy or important men and star constellations in Dante's *Paradiso*. They form constellations in the other world, that is, star constellations, or for instance, it's said that a star represents the bright, shining, and continu-

---

[77] The work against nature.

[78] One of the three Fates referred to by the ancient Greeks, also known as immutable fate.

[79] Paul's first letter to the Corinthians, 15:41–42, prior to the hymn on the resurrection body, supplies a cousin to this passage: "There is one glory of the sun, and another glory of the moon, and anther glory of the stars: for one star differeth from another star in glory. So also is the resurrection of the dead." Both Origen and Augustine take up this passage, one in his Commentary on Matthew's Gospel (Book X.3, "The Shining of the Righteous") and the other in his tractates on John's gospel (tractate 67).

ous spirit of the hero. I have mentioned that Gilgamesh's real experience of his calling was that dream in which a star falls on him. The dream is interpreted by his mother as referring to Enkidu, the appearance of Gilgamesh's natural brother, a savage who lives with the gazelles, and whose arrival now makes Gilgamesh begin to pursue his divine path of life.

So this dream of Cardanus is actually a sequel to the appearance of that star; what happens now is that in consciousness the ewes are on the right side and the rams on the left. So consciousness is on the right side, there is Mercury, whatever he may mean to Cardanus. On the left side, in contrast to the right, the stars are brought into an order, strung together as on a thread and constellated in the form of a rose. Well, this is actually rather astonishing, because we would expect order in consciousness and disorder in the unconscious, whereas it's exactly the other way around. Concerning the left side we also informed that there are fifteen stars, and this comes up in relation to the moon. We'll see later on that the moon, too, will come into play, because Mercury will appear with the moon in this *congressus*. The 15 can probably be interpreted as "justice,"[80] and the rose is a symbol of totality. In Dante, too, it is a symbol of hierarchy, of the legion of the saints and angels in the great, final vision. In addition, the rose as a mandala is world order; thus, for example, a human figure is placed in it, and then a line goes from the bodily organs to the zodiacal signs. This is the *melothesia*,[81] as can still be found in modern astrological works. The single bodily regions and organs are linked to the different signs of the zodiac. Sometimes you don't find a human figure at the center, but, for example, *Rex Gloriae*,[82] the cosmic appearance of the Almighty Christ, who appears at the Last Judgment in an apotheosis.[83] There he is flanked by the four evangelists in the four corners of the mandala. Or we find a *coniunctio Christi* with the virgin Church, an image as we also know it from the

[80] The interpretation of 15 in contemporary numerology (G).

[81] Harmonious order; the idea that the planets and the signs of the zodiac each rule over specific parts of the body. The usual version assigns one part of the body to one sign: Aries rules the head, Taurus rules the neck, Pisces rules the feet, etc. This is the origin of the picture of the "zodiac man" still seen in modern almanacs.

[82] Latin: the King of Glory (trans.).

[83] Matthew 25:31–46 (trans.).

East, of Shiva and Shakti, the creator of the world and his female counterpart.

On the left side we have order, and disorder on the right side. What do you think—what should the dreamer be told by this?

Participant: It indicates that the previous attitude of consciousness is no longer valid, and that a new order is about to rise from the unconscious, one based on the natural, earthy, lunar principle, on the ape and the instinctual soul!

Professor Jung: Yes, we must conclude that there is actually disorder on the right side, the conscious side. Now, from which standpoint does one arrive at this conclusion? Who says this? Who makes this statement?

Participant: The unconscious.

Professor Jung: Yes, the unconscious finds that what Cardanus calls conscious order is actually disorder, and that there is order in the unconscious. It's one against the other. Now, what do we have to know about the meaning that Mercury has for Cardanus? What do you think?

Participant: His consciousness overvalues the intellect.

Professor Jung: Is this correct in the light of what I previously said about Mercury? One can hardly value *nous* higher than I did.

Participant: He is identified with Mercury.

Professor Jung: Yes, and what meaning does Mercury then get? What is he then for Cardanus?

Participant: He's equivalent to his ego.

Professor Jung: What kind of evaluation would that be?

Participant: A negative one.

Professor Jung: Yes, for him, it's simply a term for the intellect.

Participant: It's simply an instrument for him.

Professor Jung: Yes, as it is for us, too. Mercury is simply an instrument for us.

Participant: Couldn't it be, if he is the *psychopompos*,[84] that he has a completely different function in that star constellation?

Professor Jung: We must realize that in astrology he is not the *psychopompos*, but simply an element of reason, by no means something especially divine or magical.

---

[84] Greek: guide of souls. Hermes is the *psychopompos*; he leads souls from the bodies of the dead to the banks of the Styx where he hands them over to Charon.

Participant: *He* thinks; he does not let it be thought in himself.

Professor Jung: Yes, there is simply the intellect, an instrument, which Cardanus then uses. Evidently this is never a revelation from God; for then one has done everything oneself, one becomes Mercury. We think that we actually make our thoughts ourselves, but in truth I don't make my thoughts at all. If somebody says for example: *it suddenly occurs to me that. . .* and I nail him down to it, he will say, "Well, that's what I *thought.*" In French one says, *J'ai fait un rêve.*[85] That's most definitely not what we do, yet it happens to us. We say, "It came to me"[86]—yes, it came to us: through the fontanella. If we were precise we'd have to say, "It has come to me, it has fallen to me." Here you must be very careful. You must recognize if something was thought, or if it came to someone. We are still very naive in these matters. Only when we horribly fool ourselves with these thoughts do we say, "I really have no idea how the hell I came upon this idea! I just don't know!" We are perplexed. But if it's something good, we think, "What a swell guy I am, that's *me* thinking!" It's a hubris of consciousness. In this dream we see that Mercury does not play the ancient, divine role for Cardanus, but that he is simply an element of reason. Cardanus did not achieve a decent order in this way, however. The opinion his unconscious has of this is very low. On the other hand, everything runs just like clockwork. The precious *gemmae*, the gemstones, form a necklace, or some other form, even a rose. As far as these symbols are concerned, however, we may assume with some certainty that they did not mean anything special to Cardanus, that he would by no means have come up with the association of the *rosa mystica*.

Participant: Hasn't it got something to do with the rosary when it is unstrung?

Professor Jung: No, it is a setting in order. Thoughts are strung together for him.

Participant: Don't we have to suppose that he read Dante?

Professor Jung: Why yes, of course, but in any case nothing in his view of the dream indicates that he had thought in the least of such connections. That's not the way he thinks. For him the unconscious is the same thought stuff as conscious contents are. *He* thinks, and he also

---

[85] Literally, I made a dream.

[86] In the original: *es ist mir eingefallen*, literally, it fell into me.

thinks with the unconscious. The unconscious has no independent value for him, although he uses it to fulfill his wishes. All he thinks is that this refers to him—namely, as far as pleasant and unpleasant events in the future are concerned. This he arranges as he pleases, as vulgar dream psychology has always done it. Even in our own time it's outrageous for me to say that the unconscious might have autonomy. This can get people really steamed up. For them the unconscious is a cesspit, in which there's nothing that hadn't been in consciousness before. According to Freud, too, there is only old junk in the unconscious, which had been lost and worn out: an old hat, a couple of shoe heels, a newspaper—that's the unconscious. But that it might have an existence of its own, and could be effective on its own, that's not accepted. And why not?

Participant: One is afraid of it.

Professor Jung: One is naturally scared stiff by the possibility that the unconscious could do something on its own.

I remember a colleague, a psychotherapist, who likewise couldn't believe that the unconscious is not a manure pile. Well, I told him, "It moves. It is alive!" He couldn't grasp this. I told him to try and have a look at his fantasy images. He didn't know what that meant. I said to him, "Take a look at such an image before falling asleep. Concentrate on it." This he did, and an image appeared to him, a rock face and an ibex, which stood there completely stock-still. He concentrated on this image. At first nothing happened, and he thought that that was it. He wanted to avert his head. At that moment the ibex turned its head. He was so terribly frightened that he was more perplexed than ever. Then he said, "I don't know how it happened, but it did move!"

I once treated an artist, a very amusing personality, a stage director, but not from here. He lived in the same boardinghouse as some of the patients. He soon found out that people are frightened when something they hadn't expected happens. So then he would always ask, "Was it black? Did it move?"[87] Here again you find that terrible fear of the autonomous unconscious. Hence we don't want it to be alive. Such persons get into an anxiety state with a pulse rate of 120, or they stage hysterical vomiting.

---

[87] The quote in English in the original.

Then they say that it came out of the unconscious, but the unconscious is not allowed to do anything, one has to think there's nothing to it. After all, one has already done away with the spook, hasn't one? It's not spooky any longer. Haven't we cleared up the matter? And still Tegel is haunted![88]

Let us get back to Cardanus: it doesn't occur to him that the unconscious could be something on its own. He nevertheless assumes that it's able to make prophecies, and he addresses the spirits. In reality, however, he simply treats it as if it were material for his thoughts. The unconscious tells him that there is a very beautiful order in the unconscious; in addition, this order forms the meaningful symbol of the rose, which actually he completely overlooks. His interpretation is totally inadequate. He also identifies quite directly with Mercury on the right side. This gives us an insight into this man's state of consciousness. It was the time, the beginning, of the great hubris of consciousness, in which even the Christian gods were doomed; it was the age of the Reformation, of the great voyages of discovery, of the revival of antiquity, etc. I once quoted to you from the confession of Agrippa von Nettesheim, who calls himself *"daemon et deus et omnia."*[89]

Well, what appears here in the mandala, in the symbol of the rose, is a very significant symbol; however, it is also said in a very abstract manner that it is a totality, a circle. In alchemy it is simply called *rotundum*,[90] the round element, and this is the epitome of the microcosm, the roundness of the deity. In Empedocles, too, *sphairos*, the globe, is the highest god. The globe is a perfect shape.[91] And so is the star that had fallen into Cardanus's yard, and which is found here in the unconscious, indeed where the fifteen stars and the moon are.

Now at the end of the dream there comes the hint that he'd have to wait until Mercury had a *congressus*[92] with the moon. The moon always

[88] Goethe visited the castle of Tegel (Berlin) on May 20, 1778, and was told the story that something spooky had happened in the forester's house. He alluded to this in *Faust*, when the Proctophantasmist scolds Faust and the two witches: "Still there? You are very impertinent! / Vanish, will you! This is the Enlightenment! / The race of devils will not play by the book, / Clever as we are, in Tegel there's still a spook" (Constantine, *Faust Part II*, vv. 4158–61).

[89] Latin: demon (or evil spirit) and God and everything (G).

[90] Latin: the round one.

[91] Cf. vol. 1, chap. 2/A/1, 32–40.

[92] I.e., sexual intercourse (see above).

means the female, the shadow side, the dark side or the night side. In a man it is a symbol of the unconscious, the anima, whereas the sun represents male consciousness. And the goal of the development in the dream, the goal of the individuation process, is that "*coniunctio solis et lunae*,"[93] to bring consciousness into connection with the unconscious. Why is he supposed to get in connection with the unconscious? What might be the reason? And what happens afterward?

Participant: Then order will be established in the totality.

Professor Jung: Male, mercurial consciousness will unite with the lunar unconscious, and Mercury will thus enter into that symbol of the rose, into the cosmic order of the unconscious. What will develop in the lunar world if Mercury enters into it?

Participant: There will be consciousness.

Professor Jung: Yes, at first there is no consciousness, but when Mercury enters into it, consciousness will develop. After all, that's the purpose of the *coniunctio*, that the unconscious be filled by consciousness. And what should fill consciousness from the unconscious? What does the unconscious bring into consciousness?

Participant: Life.

Professor Jung: Yes, the unconscious, the dark, simply lives and simply goes on functioning. It *is*. But nobody knows it. Nobody is present; nobody takes part in this. We only fear it, keep it at a distance, so that we make certain that we are not going to be lived, so that we can go on cherishing illusions. Man, however, is both someone who thinks *and* is thought.

Participant: The dark is chaotic.

Professor Jung: That's what we think. One would think that the cosmos is what is conscious, but this is not so at all. Sometimes it is ordered, sometimes not. Sometimes there is simply disorder, disorientation, in the unconscious. We have no order in consciousness. Therefore we find order in the unconscious, not in consciousness. That's the remarkable discovery: there is order in the unconscious, not in consciousness. At what time was there order in consciousness?

Participant: In the Gothic, for example.

Professor Jung: Yes, at that time the world was a theocracy; one had a feeling of orderliness. There was no doubt at all about it. Or take

[93] Latin: conjunction of sun and moon (G).

the ancient Egyptian world, for example, in which there was a natural order of things; there was no problem. Just as in antiquity, when barbaric chaos lay outside while inside ruled the *Pax Romana*,[94] we have to assume that the same was true for consciousness at such times. Consciousness had an order; it was embedded in an order. Hence that extremely secure feeling of being in the world that those people had. There was simply a kind of calm and security. You have only to read the confessions of the early Christians; there you see how wonderful a release it was for them to be situated within a divine order. Today all this is different. By devaluing the unconscious through rational thinking, we have destroyed these old orders and are disoriented. And that's why we need to have a psychology, that is, to discover order, because we no longer have an ordering principle in consciousness.

And the dream ends with the important thought that a *congressus* will take place.

The next dream goes as follows:

7. On February 1 of the year 1544 [. . .], at the crack of dawn, I had a dream in which I saw Alexander the Great go hunting to kill a lion without weapons. Hephaestion[95] wanted to stop him. Finally they agreed that Alexander should deal with the lion, but that Hephaestion ought to carry a club. At once a giant lion appeared, who seized Alexander with his maw and tried to tear him apart. At first he[96] seemed to succeed, but soon afterward the lion gripped Alexander's hands in its maw. When Hephaestion saw this, he clubbed the lion on the head, was able to kill him with one stroke, and freed Alexander.

Cardanus goes on to say that in his view Alexander seems to point to a due process that seemed to have been lost long ago, and also to the authority of the sovereign, of the senate, while Hephaestion would probably stand for a certain Lucas, etc.

Well, what does Alexander represent? How come Cardanus had this dream?

---

[94] Latin for "the Roman peace," the long period of relative peace experienced by the Roman Empire. Roman rule and its legal system pacified regions, sometimes forcefully, that had suffered from quarrels between rival leaders.

[95] Macedonian nobleman, closest friend and alleged lover of Alexander the Great.

[96] The transcript reads "it," where "he" is obviously intended.

Participant: At first we had the spectacle of the *coniunctio*, the drama in the sky, and now the problem is transferred into antiquity and portrayed as a contrast between Alexander and Hephaestion.

Professor Jung: This relocation to antiquity, what does that mean? How does this usually happen? Usually something is not "transferred into antiquity," but something else happens. What?

Participant: The conflict is expressed archetypally.

Professor Jung: When consciousness is united with the unconscious, an archetypal moment occurs. Because this has happened countless times. It's an archetypal situation. It is a great event, that unification, a mighty, a memorable shock, a memorable experience. Can you tell me historical instances of such archetypal experiences? In literature or in world history?

Participant: Nietzsche said, "At once then, my friend! One turned into Two—/—and Zarathustra strode into my view."[97]

Professor Jung: Yes, just think of it! Nietzsche is in Sils Maria.[98] And there Zarathustra, of all persons, walked past him. Here his most intimate experience is transferred into the distant past. And what does he know about Zarathustra? He is the oldest known founder of a religion, that is, a shepherd and guide of people, a *Poimander*,[99] the Revealer par excellence. He gives the first decent religion to mankind. And Nietzsche meets him. Can you imagine anything more archetypal? And just when does he meet him? This takes us to Nietzsche's more secret side.

Participant: When he discovered his soul.

Professor Jung: In what form did it happen? What did he himself call it? He gave the experience a name. He called it the *Dionysian experience*. He wrote some remarkable things about it in the letter to his sister quoted in the complete edition of his works. So this Dionysian experience is the encounter with Dionysus. The history of this experience goes back to his adolescence, when this Dionysus appeared to him. In what form? What was he called then?

---

[97] "There sit I, waiting, waiting—yet for nought, / transcending good and evil, sometimes caught / in light, sometimes in shadow, all game, / all sea, all midday, all time without aim. // At once then, my friend! One turned into Two—/—and Zarathustra strode into my view." Nietzsche's "Sils-Maria," in *Songs of Prince Vogelfrei*, appendix to *The Gay Science* (poems translated by Adrian del Caro), ed. Bernard Williams (Cambridge: Cambridge University Press, 2001), 258.

[98] A village in the Engadine in the Swiss Alps.

[99] Greek: shepherd. Also, a section of the *Corpus Hermeticum*.

Participant: Wotan.

Professor Jung: Yes, that was when he had the famous dream of Wotan, which is memorable in every respect, because it has very much to do with our time.[100] Nietzsche's biography is a wonderful anticipation of our time. This, too, was already an archetypal experience, which was reflected in him again and again in various forms. He called it Dionysus, because "Wotan" didn't mean anything to him as a professor of philosophy. That belonged to another faculty; it was the business of specialists in German studies. Dionysus is a very close blood relation, a cousin of Wotan. He's just a bit more colorful, more Mediterranean, more Asian. Do you know of other examples?

Participant: The Classical Walpurgis Night.[101]

Professor Jung: Yes, that's also a fairly good example in which ancient archetypes appear. At what moment?

Participant: When Faust meets Helen.

Professor Jung: Yes, of course, because Faust had been with the Mothers. But why had he been there?

Participant: To fetch Helen.

Participant: The Kaiser had sent him.

Participant: Because he couldn't get over the experience with Gretchen.

Professor Jung: Yes, of course, that whole unfortunate story that he didn't understand. That was a veritable anima story, and he didn't know what it was. By God, he had to descend into deepest hell to find out the secret, which was personified in the figure of Helen. He was confronted by Helen, and then he performed the *coniunctio* with Helen. This is Selene,[102] the moon. He went down into the depths as the sun, the *nous*, consciousness, and united with Helen, which was a bit of a blunder, as it were. It should have been different. He should have left

[100] Jung's assimilation of Nietzsche's dream to both gods is supported by the biographical evidence reviewed by Paul Bishop—material that includes Jung's own dream of Wotan in 1923—in *The Dionysian Self: Jung's Reception of Friedrich Nietzsche* (Berlin and New York: De Gruyter, 1995), 311–14. The translated dream text, from Nietzsche's GW § 382, reads: "At last we reached a valley surrounded on all sides by thick undergrowth. Suddenly our guide put a whistle to his mouth and blew shrilly. Taken aback, we looked at each other; but all at once, everything in the wood came alive. Here and there, torches lit up, and wildly masked people came and surrounded us in a circle. I lost consciousness; I didn't know what was happening to me" (312).

[101] *Faust II*, act 2, scene 3.

[102] The archaic Greek moon goddess.

that to Paris. So their son flew away from him, and was consumed again by the fire.[103] Again, that's an archetypal experience. Perhaps you also know an example from the history of Christianity?

Participant: The conversion of Paul.

Professor Jung: Yes, Paul was not actually a personal disciple of Christ's. What was his Gospel source? How could he call himself an apostle? Jewish Christians held that claim very much against him. He referred his claim to experience—he saw Christ Himself. Therefore to Paul, Christ was not a human being, but simply a God. For Paul, Christ had no biography; He was a divine shepherd. That's also why the whole Pauline movement blended so much with Gnosticism later on. That's an archetypal experience. The motif of the shepherd then underwent a change in ancient literature. What is its pagan form?

Participant: The *Poimandres* of Hermes Trismegistos.

Professor Jung: Yes, in the *Corpus Hermeticum*. Christians also wanted to have their own version of it. A Christian version was *The Shepherd of Hermas*,[104] a work from the time of Pope Pius, around AD 145, also in the form of an archetypal experience. Do you know how it took place?

Participant: Hermas is sitting on his bed praying.

Participant: Then someone comes and sits beside him, saying, "I am the shepherd, to whom you have been given." Then he is transformed, and Hermas says, "Now I have realized to whom I was given."

Professor Jung: What happened before that?

Participant: He was in love with a Christian woman.

Professor Jung: He went for a walk on the banks of the Tiber. Now a certain Madame Rhoda, whom he greatly admired, was bathing in the Tiber; he had to help her out of the water and could not help noticing certain details of her anatomy. He swore that he really wasn't affected in the way one might think, but obviously there was more to it than he was ready to admit. That was the starting point. He couldn't stomach it, and then he had the vision of the old woman. She is the

---

[103] The Icarian death of Euphorion, near the end of *Faust II*, act 3, 9789ff.

[104] A Christian apocalyptic work, composed in Rome ca. AD 139–AD 155. It is a collection of revelations given to Hermas, a devout Christian, by an angel (Shepherd). For the texts available to Jung's seminar, cf. Hermas, *Hermae Pastor* (second century), Graece add. vers. Lat. . . . . e cod Palatino recens; O. de Gebhardt, A. Harnack (Patrum apostolicorum opera, fasc. III), Leipzig (1877); R. Reizenstein, *Poimandres: Studien zur griechisch-ägyptischen und frühchristlichen Literatur* (1904) (G). Compare the mention above in chapter 12, 114. The same holds for the *poimen* below.

Church. And then comes the *poimen*.[105] This experience really shattered his foundations, hence also the archetype. Whenever an experience is earth shaking, these archetypal images will appear, causing the great experience.

We are happily talking away about archetypes, and that leaves us cold, but it is quite different if it really happens. The difference is exactly the same as the difference between talking about the zoology of the lion and being attacked by a lion. When it happens, it leaves a tremendous, lasting impression, which can get people completely derailed and changed.

Participant: Benvenuto Cellini is another beautiful example. He was imprisoned, hungry, nearly dying of thirst, and desperate. Suddenly Christ appeared to him in an immense light, which came in cascades. After this experience he knew with certainty that he had a halo. And no one thought he was crazy.

Professor Jung: Such visions of Christ are also archetypal experiences. They need not take that form, however, because the unconscious is by no means orthodox. It can take the most varied forms. As you have heard, for Ignatius of Loyola it was a snake, covered all over with eyes. There is definitely no mention of this in the New Testament. And so he took it for a deity at first.

Therefore, if this situation occurs in Cardanus—that something shook him to the core, that something was created in him that had to do with the development of the greater and mightier personality that could somehow lead him to his fate—then that's the moment at which everything is translated into the heroic and archetypal. That is the moment at which life can be truly lived heroically, not just as ordinary professional life—the moment at which Cardanus is not simply a doctor but is called upon to face his greatest and mightiest task. This is always translated into archetypal figures: it's the same situation in which the great Alexander, who, like Gilgamesh and Enkidu has to succeed in his adventures, can work wonders. He is the magic figure in antiquity, and still is today in the Islamic tradition. Even old Gilgamesh associated himself with Iskander. There is still a town in India that bears the name of Alexander, Iskanderabad, which has merged with Hyderabad.

[105] Greek: shepherd (G).

There are countless legends of the old Alexander. He even appears in the Koran, where he is called the *dhulkarnein*, the double-horned one. In Cardanus's dream he goes hunting like Samson. This motif stems from the "Samson legend"; Samson, too, is a hero who defeated a lion. What does the lion mean?

Participant: A new force in consciousness, the force of the sun.

Professor Jung: Yes, untamed, animal force. And where does this animal force come from? You mentioned the sun. Well, what does the lion mean?

Participant: He is the *domicilium solis*[106] in the zodiac, at the time of the greatest summer heat.

Professor Jung: What else does he stand for?

Participant: He is the most powerful, strongest animal in the animal kingdom.

Professor Jung: Yes, he is the king of beasts. Historically speaking, however, there are still other symbols. He is a symbolic animal par excellence, a regal animal.

Participant: A heraldic animal.

Professor Jung: He is also portrayed in architecture, for example, in the Alhambra.[107] Then, too, we have the lion as the Sphinx's body in Egypt. There are whole alleys of sphinxes with lion bodies. Where else does the lion appear in architecture in a very typical manner?

Participant: The Basilica of San Marco, on the column.

Professor Jung: At the portals of Romanesque churches. In Italy there are numerous old churches where columns flanking the great doors always rest on the backs of lions. The lions are also bearers of the pulpit lecterns. What does that mean?

Participant: The natural force that is tamed by the spiritual.

Participant: It means overcoming paganism.

Professor Jung: Yes, therefore the column of the church is set on the lion. It subdues the lion. But he also appears in still another form.

Participant: As a symbol of the evangelists.[108]

Professor Jung: Yes, but that is hard to interpret.

[106] Latin: the domicile of the sun.
[107] An Islamic palace-citadel on a hill overlooking Granada, Spain, built in the thirteenth and fourteenth centuries.
[108] Only one, Mark.

Participant: As a guardian of the treasure.

Professor Jung: That is very rare. Usually the dragon guards the treasure —as a rule, a cold-blooded animal. In alchemy it is the *leo viridis*, the green lion, the animal that comes after the dragon, mostly in double form. At first comes the *ouroboros*. Then comes the green lion. The difference between these two animals is that the lion is warm-blooded, the dragon cold-blooded. The lion is already on a higher level. And the greenness means that positive life has already begun there. That's also why they talked about the *benedicta viriditas*,[109] which appears simultaneously with lion power, sun power. What does this mean psychologically? What will happen if I am Alexander? Then the lion will rise.

Participant: Greed for power and prestige.

Professor Jung: Of course! When somebody has an archetypal experience, he gets one hell of an inflation and is inebriated by power. That's also the reason why Nietzsche was a megalomaniac.

Participant: In Cardanus the lion expresses the Renaissance man's greed for glory.

Professor Jung: Yes, the lion is a proud animal, avid for glory and power, filling the world with his roar. So whenever the personality is lifted up by such an archetypal experience, this wild beast that wants to devour everything will be set free. All and everything should serve him, the king. In Nietzsche you can see clearly that a mighty lion was in fact released within him. Now the idea, however, is that this lion is unwelcome. One should overcome this state. He is something dangerous. And the hero actually proves himself only when he can kill the lion, and kill him unarmed. What could that mean? Why must it happen in such a strange way?

Participant: Without artificial means.

Participant: It happens in a close encounter.

Participant: The weapon has been made with the help of the intellect. If someone acts only with the help of the intellect, that's immodest and useless.

---

[109] Latin: blessed greenness. Besides alchemy, there is also the visionary medicine and cosmology of Hildegard von Bingen, in which blessed greenness saturates both physics and the soul from sources both moist and solar; for this "fecund and canny" usage of the term, see *The Letters of Hildegard von Bingen*, vol. 1, ed. and trans. Joseph L. Baird and Radd K. Ehrman (New York: Oxford University Press, 1994), 7–8.

Professor Jung: With a weapon it can't be direct. Why? Without the weapon it is sportsmanlike and fair. He gives the lion a chance, exposes himself defenselessly to the lion, faces his enemy directly, and says to himself, "I've got to do it on my own, if it's to be done at all. If I look for help, it won't really have happened, because this lion—that's me." This realization makes the hero choose to face the lion unarmed. That is, it makes no sense to use weapons against oneself. Am I the master or the lion? This is something the lion must fight out with himself. And because it's not really certain that one will succeed in getting a grip on oneself, one has an insurance policy. Namely?

Participant: The friend.

Professor Jung: Yes, the friend. Doubts are looming. Eventually I might find so much pleasure in being a lion that I won't succeed in doing him in. But I feel that it's got to be done, and hopefully it will succeed. And then it fails. One is between a rock and a hard place, so to speak. So what usually happens in the heroic myth during the final struggle?

Participant: That one is devoured.

Professor Jung: Yes, the typical sun hero is always devoured by the whale dragon. He can just barely find a way out of his predicament; he is already in the belly of the monster. It has already swallowed him completely. Now it is a question of life and death, he barely escapes death, because the opponents are equally strong. So one sets one's hopes on the other, the friend, the helper, who can rescue one at the last minute—who wields, and is allowed to wield, a club. That's how this hero is rescued from the mouth of the lion.

So what we are saying is that this eagerness for power, with its ridiculous demands, has now become the fateful leader. In the language of the Church Fathers, therefore, the lion is also a symbol of what?

Participant: A symbol of the devil?

Professor Jung: Yes, the devil walks around like a roaring lion and looks for whomever he can devour. The *leo* was a symbol of the devil. In overcoming the lion, Cardanus overcomes his private devil, his power devil; this is a psychic process that follows the archetypal experience, going strictly by the rules. Alexander thus would represent for Cardanus what would be called the *mana* personality.

Now let us proceed to the next dream. Cardanus dreamed:

8. that he was at the pope's court, and two wolves came. The little wolf came toward him. Cardanus got hold of its mouth and dealt with it so that it went away. Then the second wolf, too, attacked him, so he stabbed it to death with a little dagger.[110]

What has happened here? Where do these wolves come from?

Participant: In *Zarathustra*, after the ropedancer is killed and Zarathustra carries his dead body on his shoulders, he hears the howling of wolves. As soon as the human is dead, natural greed emerges.

Participant: It reminds one of the Roman wolves.

Professor Jung: The papal court is in Rome, and wolves exist there.

Participant: They could represent greedy priests.

Professor Jung: There are illustrations from the Reformation in which the pope or the clergy are portrayed as wolves. In Cardanus's time, the papal court was the greatest power center. It was *the* ambition of a scholar to get to the papal court. This is also the greatest ambition in Cardanus, the greed that seizes him, the hunger of the wolf, *avaritia*. So this means that now he also must kill another less elegant, less regal form of the lion, and kill it twice. The wolf is a wilder version of the lion and, for Cardanus in particular, stands for professional ambition and influence, etc. And he has succeeded; now he can do it. And here comes another dream:

9. *In the year 1540, on February 9, I dreamed I was in my bed, but the sun above shone completely black, with shining rays, it is true, but blacker than writing ink.*[111]

Cardanus takes this as a sign of an imminent solar eclipse. He also saw the rays shining as though it were night.

Participant: It's a midnight sun.

Participant: It symbolizes the transvaluation of values.

Professor Jung: Yes, quite right. What seems to be shining brightly is black and also shines. What comes to mind here? What would we think if the sun shone black?

Participant: One would be frightened.

Participant: It would be like the end of the world.

---

[110] Quoted in indirect speech in Cardanus's autobiography (G).

[111] *Synesiorum somniorum, op. cit.*, 5: 716.

Professor Jung: Yes, one would think it's the end of the world. And when the stars are falling from the sky, and the moon is like blood, an apocalyptic age begins, with shining rays. Then it will be raining cats and dogs. That's really the end of the world. What does that mean? Think of what we said about consciousness. What had previously been bright as the sun has now infiltrated the unconscious. Now he is in the role of the hero, now he leads the great life of Alexander, now he has killed lions and has thus also overcome himself, so to speak, and then daylight turns black.

Participant: The outer world perishes, and he gets an inner attitude.

Professor Jung: Yes, the outside radiates blackness. Now this world becomes invisible. Now this world perishes, an apocalyptic age begins, and what becomes visible?

Participant: In the dream the stars appear in broad daylight.

Professor Jung: Things appear that shine only at night.

Participant: The unconscious.

Professor Jung: Yes, where no sun is shining, we have our inner darkness. Then the lights of darkness appear. In what form? What are the stars?

Participant: Signposts.

Professor Jung: That's much too embellished. What do stars do? What is visibly written in the stars? There was one well-known amateur astronomer who always wondered how one might know the weight of the stars, even their chemical composition. But the greatest thing of all is that they found out what the stars are called! So what are they called?

Participant: They are the gods.

Professor Jung: Yes, they are called Coma Berenices,[112] for instance, the Great Serpent, the Bear, Heracles, Boötes,[113] etc. Well, if you take into account what these names actually mean, you will find that a grandiose story was projected onto these stars. You can even find the story in the early [Church] Fathers, for example, in Hippolytus, who still refers

---

[112] Latin: hair of Berenice; a constellation located near Leo, and originally considered Leo's tail.

[113] Generally referred to as the Bear Watcher, since it appears to be watching over the constellations Ursa Major and Ursa Minor. The "somebody down on his knees" according to Aratus is Adam, guarding Draco's head while Draco or the Great Serpent guards his heel. See Philip Schaff, ed., *The Ante-Nicene Fathers: Hippolytus, Cyprian, Caius, Novation,* 1885: Appendix, Aratus, *Phaenomena,* v. 70.

to it: there is somebody down on his knees—Engonasis, sinking under his burden, grappling with the serpent. A whole metaphysical interpretation has been read into this story. That is what the ancients projected upward onto the stars. Afterward they thought they had found out how the stars are named—that is, someone simply put labels on them and then we discovered them. So when the stars appear, this story of heroes and heroic fates also crops up. True, these are archetypes, of course. But what appears and what touches us are the stories about the stars told to us by the ancients. And these are precisely the fates of heroes. In Cardanus's dream this daylight world becomes dark, turns black. The contents of the unconscious appear and become very much alive.

E. At a Later Meeting of the Seminar

Now comes another dream:[114]

> 10. On January 5, 1544 [. . .], at the break of dawn, I dreamed I saw Prosper Marinonus. Although I knew very well that he was dead, I asked him to touch my hand, and even added at once, "although you are dead." As soon as I had said this he turned away from me, but then complied nonetheless and touched my hand. Then he left. When I wanted to call him back, my elder son followed him, and when he did not want to agree, I too followed him, together with others, and found him [the son] in the vestibule of a lonely house, but Prosper was nowhere to be seen. Suddenly it seemed to me that I awoke because of some object or other under my pillow. I thought I was awake, thinking about the preceding dream, and believed I was happy that nothing evil had happened to myself or my son from the sight of a dead man. When I lifted my head, it seemed to me as if light came in from the window and reminded me of doing my work. So I hurried up, even more so to shake off the fright I was given by the object under my head. And as I wanted to look out another window to see if the light came from there, all of a sudden the door seemed to be open. Amazed and frightened I grabbed a stick and walked over there: lo and behold, I saw death himself stand before the

[114] *Synesiorum somniorum,* 5: 716ff.

threshold. I wondered if this prophesied the end for me, if I could not chase away death with the stick, and I tried to hit him. But he fled and seemed—chased by me—to flee into another house and to hide in a clo-aca. I imagined that he no longer posed a danger for me. But there was a dead body lying in that place, and I considered how to get it out. Then I thought I woke up for the second time, while in fact I went on dreaming as before. Nothing was left of the previous dream except that I saw the dead body in the cloaca, thought that it had been a dream, and began getting up again. But then I see[115] a shaggy, black dog under the bed that had playfully torn off my trousers. So I said to myself, "Who locked this domestic dog in here?" Because yesterday I did not have a dog. And it was a good thing that I got up before dawn, because I would have been very frightened without seeing and hearing the noise. While I was still contemplating this, I finally woke up for good.

Professor Jung: Let me give you a short summary. Here Marinonus, whom we already met in the first dream, again appears as a dead man. This time Cardanus wants to be touched by him, although he knows that Marinonus is dead. Marinonus touches Cardanus's hand but then vanishes. Then Cardanus sees a light come in from the window. He goes to another window to see if the light is coming in from there, too, and then sees that the door is open. "The door opens, but no one comes in" (*Faust*).[116] He gets frightened, takes a stick, and then death is standing in the doorway. Cardanus chases death away, who goes into another house and hides in a sewer pipe, that is, in a privy. Cardanus thought that a dead body lay there, is impressed by the fact that the body is lying in the toilet, and one more time wants to get up. The dream then ends (Cardanus woke up repeatedly during the dream; his sleep was obviously disturbed) with the dog that had torn off, and torn up, his trousers.

The dream is interesting insofar as it once more takes up the theme that played a great role at the outset—namely, the appearance of the dead,

[115] Present tense in the original.

[116] Goethe's *Faust II*, act 5, section "Tiefe Nacht," 11419–20: "FAUST: Die Pforte knarrt, und niemand kommt herein! / [*Ershüttert.*] Ist jemand hier? SORGE: Die Frage fordert Ja!" *Faust*, He-rausgegeben u. kommentiert von Erich Trunz (Munich: H. Beck Verlag, 1989), 344. ("The door creaks. Who enters? No one. / [*In great alarm:*] Is someone there? CARE: The answer must be yes." Constantine, *Faust II*, 232.)

but this time after the *sol niger*, the black sun, had risen in the preceding dream. Well, what would you generally expect after such a dream in which this black sun appears, which sends out brilliant rays and thus is a positive black sun, a shining black sun? Suppose a modern man, who even had some knowledge of psychology, had such a dream; what would you expect? What do you think? One can't avoid having a fantasy about it.

Participant: The unconscious would have to make itself felt very much in the form of the opposite position of the moon, of the *other* light.

Professor Jung: You'd expect, that is, that he would be facing a very bright moon. Perhaps that could be symbolically correct. I'm not quite sure, however. You should express yourself more psychologically, not mythologically. In the case of psychology one really has to present things very clearly.

Participant: One would have to expect a great conflict to emerge, an amazement at the sun being black, and at what had shone and become dark.

Professor Jung: What had shone until then?

Participant: Consciousness.

Professor Jung: The black sun—this is a blackened consciousness, the antithesis to consciousness. Although it also resembles consciousness, it is black, completely dark. So what conflict would this trigger, put in modern terms?

Participant: Emotion, instinct, moods. The opposite of reason. Couldn't this be what's shining?

Professor Jung: That's correct. Shining is an activity. The sun sends us rays, sends life. Hence the Egyptian sun symbol of Akhenaten. Each sunbeam is a little hand that gives the sign of life. This is the cult of Amenophis IV. Each little sunbeam-hand handed him the sign of *ankh*, that is, life, symbolized by the *ankh* cross.

☥

It probably stems from a loop, a knot, like shoelaces that are tied like so. On top is the loop, and so it is also depicted by ribbons. What it really means we don't know. This positive sun has turned into its positive opposite, which wants to express the fact that what is acting positively, what behaves like consciousness, has been replaced by its complete opposite, so that now—since consciousness has brought us this far (for it knows nothing about the unconscious!)—this opposite is shining in a totally different, opposite way. If we look at such an image quite naively, we will realize that it's a miracle. What had been white is black, what had shone is now black. Good has turned into evil.

Participant: Isn't this his shadow?

Professor Jung: No, not *his* shadow, but the shadow of the sun, the shadow of consciousness, and it's not his consciousness, but consciousness *as such*, as expressed by the sun. Man's conscious spirit is expressed by the sun. You see, the shining sun of reason, of human consciousness, that's the sun, and this sun is now suddenly replaced by a completely opposite principle. This means that anything he had thought until then in consciousness now has the opposite value, has turned into its complete opposite. This is a bit like when a man who believes in his good intentions, his conscience, who has a positive religious conviction, who attributes—not even in an exaggerated way—this and that virtue to himself, who thinks he is decent, reliable, truth-loving, and faithful, is suddenly confronted with the opposite perception: that he is a pig in every respect, and a sad pig to boot, as we can see in which writer, for example?

Participant: Nietzsche.

Professor Jung: Of course. And less so, as far as his life is concerned; his real life actually does not count. It is quite unimportant. What is important is what went on in his mind, and that is the shattering of values. We can see extremely clearly in his case how he saw even the most sacred ideas in a completely different light.

Participant: Aren't these collective views?

Professor Jung: Which he also shared. Those were also his views. After all he was a pastor's son, and actually a very pious man, a truly religious nature. That is why this could turn into its opposite in him. One has to be a religious man for this to happen. Such a thing does not happen in a "wishy-washy"[117] mind, because that kind of fellow is always in semidarkness anyway. If Cardanus had made his dream his problem, if he had had an opinion about his dream, if he had said to himself, "Here I am with my consciousness, but there is another testimony, there is

---

[117] This expression in English in the original.

some other in me who speaks. How come I have this dark brother?"—
then he would have had to tear himself in two, to enter into a confron-
tation, as happened with Nietzsche. This is where the relativity of our
age comes from. As a matter of fact, nobody any longer believes in an
ideal world. And if he does, he will have to defend himself, every day
and every hour, against attacks from the devil of doubt. For we constantly tell ourselves, "Maybe everything is completely different after
all." Well, no trace of this is to be found in Cardanus, because he simply
doesn't relate to that. He doesn't know the real meaning. He can't take
it seriously. That was not a time when one had to be concerned about
the unconscious. The world was still large, still unknown, and it was
still possible that somewhere something existed that one didn't know
yet. Today we know exactly, today nothing happens any more. At most
we could find out whether the Antarctic is separated by a channel or
not. Today we, too, are like the Americans; we, too, are no longer able
to have a pioneering spirit, today agriculture has gone everywhere. So
today we must also reflect on ourselves. Our world is very much confined. The pioneering spirit in us turns toward unknown shores, therefore, and these are precisely the problems of the unconscious. That's
new territory. There we can still apply the pioneering spirit. Otherwise
we could organize things only for the sake of putting them in order.
And that just isn't worth it for people who are able to think; it's really
too silly, isn't it? So what happens now in reality? The dead person reappears in the next dream. So what has happened now?

Participant: Everything has been buried again.

Professor Jung: Obviously, and why?

Participant: Because he didn't face up to it.

Professor Jung: What leads you to think so?

Participant: Because he [Marinonus] is dead again.

Professor Jung: If we integrate something into consciousness, it won't
come back. If it returns, something is still pending in connection with
it. It hasn't been exhaustively dealt with. Then the situation is as it was
before, and anything that had been said, has not been made real.

Participant: It occurs to me that in mental illnesses dreams always
recur in cycles, because something cannot be made real.

Professor Jung: Not only in the insane. Dreams are like meteors, flar-
ing up and going out, passing away. When we don't think of something

as a problem, it naturally sinks down again; therefore the dead man reappears. The unconscious has to become personified again, has to send the dreamer its dead, its *angeloi*, its messengers. This dead man also touches him, precisely because, it seems, he hasn't been touched before. And you also know what this touch feels like for Cardanus?

Participant: He thinks he will have to die, too.

Professor Jung: Yes. So this is very dangerous. One gets infected by death. Thus it should touch him; and because he was not touched by it, the dead man must reappear, and then everything will have to start anew from the beginning. Well, the dead man turns away from him. Cardanus's son wants to follow the dead man. What does that mean? What role does the son play?

Participant: He represents a new attitude.

Professor Jung: No, no! What is a son to a man?

Participant: The new form of the self.

Professor Jung: The son is the complete substitute for the father. I'd like to remind you of a story. You have to remember such things in the form of stories. A Negro has a son, who is grown-up and no longer obeys. The father is enraged and complains, "There he is standing with my body, and doesn't even obey me!" Mind you, with *my* body! The woman who gives the man his son is therefore the favorite woman, for she has given the man immortality. The son is the guarantee of the father's immortality. Usually this younger representative lives longer than the father. When the old man has met his maker, the son carries on somehow, and because he is the father, he will go on living in his son. Thus the son is given the name of the father, to perpetuate him. Now when the son of Cardanus runs after this spirit, what does this show with regard to the son's psychology?

Participant: He is more open to the unconscious.

Professor Jung: Yes, obviously. He is touched. He does not let this messenger leave just like that, but runs after him to maintain a relationship with this dead man, does not let him go, presumably in order to make the dead man give him his message. As soon as the father notices this, he becomes scared. What has happened in the father?

Participant: A split, because the son acts differently than the father would.

Professor Jung: What are these two halves?

Participant: Consciousness and the unconscious.

Professor Jung: What could the son be?

Participant: Regression and progression.

Professor Jung: Yes, it could be regressive, as if one were still infantile. But if it's not regression, then the son in the father is what will live in the father in the future, for consciousness always sides with the past. Consciousness is conscious of what was, but I know that my life will continue after these moments, and this will be the son. The son is what I'll be in the future.

In our age the son will probably have a psychology different from his father's, because this is a transitional age. Therefore the son is as his father would be if the latter had the son's life, that is, if he could add another fifty or sixty years to his life. But in normal times, when there are no such great psychological disturbances as in our age, there is continuity, as it should be. But since we are split off from nature, we fall from one catastrophe into the next. One has no idea when this will stop.

In Cardanus's dream the son is the future man within himself. The son is touched by the dead man. He seems to have gotten the message somehow. So he runs after the dead man, and the father is accordingly scared by this reversion to death, scared for himself, for then it would follow. We may safely assume, however, that this dream of Cardanus, this message of the unconscious, fell into a time in which it could have had a special meaning for him. You see, it often does happen that, as we get older, we can remember times when things happened to us that fascinated us, and only later do we realize *why* they fascinated us.

Participant: So this would have to be understood on the objective plane?

Professor Jung: That's possible, but also only symbolically. That would even support what has just been said.

Now a light appears at the window. The light comes from outside. What do you make of that? What does that mean?

Participant: It comes from someplace other than one's own.

Professor Jung: Yes, because if one is in the house, one is in one's own living space. The outside, that's other people. But it can also be the unconscious, which is outside, as it were, not in consciousness. Now what does it mean that the dream insists that this light comes from outside?

What does it mean, as such? Suppose you live on the fourth floor, and a light appears at the window.

Participant: Somebody else brought a light to the window.

Professor Jung: Something wants to break in from the outside. That's a repetition of what?

Participant: Of the star.

Professor Jung: But originally?

Participant: Of the dead man.

Professor Jung: Yes, the dead man has come to him. Now something similar reappears, but this time it's a light. What does that mean?

Participant: A realization.

Professor Jung: Yes, something enlightening. Something dawns on him. This is due to the fact that the son ran after the dead man. Something uncanny dawns on him, an uncanny premonition. This reaches a climax when death appears in the open doorway. What does it mean that death suddenly appears? No longer the dead man, but death?

Participant: He should realize that it concerns him personally, that the dead man was already his own death.

Professor Jung: Yes, the possibility of fearing death makes its appearance here. Here comes his own fear of death. Which dreams prove this?

Participant: The dream of the ape in the beginning.

Professor Jung: Yes, right; and also still another dream, which expresses something similar?

Participant: When the mother wants to take him with her.

Professor Jung: Yes, the mother advises him to come with her. But then he would have to die. So the thought of death is present and always resonates whenever the talking ape appears. But why must this be linked with the thought of death?

Participant: He experiences this light from the outside as a death in his conscious world.

Professor Jung: This is the end of a living standpoint. You see, for instance, when our belief and the conviction of our values are crushed, we feel we must die. Life is no longer worth it. So when such a deep caesura happens in life, one is always visited by thoughts and fantasies of death, or fear of death. When such a caesura does not happen, what real dangers will there be?

Participant: Physical death.

Participant: Psychosis, for example.

Professor Jung: Yes, that's also possible.

Participant: Illnesses or accidents.

Professor Jung: Yes, that often happens at moments when a fundamental change should occur but does not. When a fundamental change is in order but is assiduously circumvented, accidents often will occur, even deaths or severe illnesses.

Participant: Death and light! Couldn't that also mean, because he had always avoided death, that he really must face up to death consciously?

Professor Jung: That's true, of course. When death appears on the threshold, he would have to confront himself with the idea of death, thus also of his own death. As a matter of fact, the fear of death is linked to psychic change, which is also the reason why people take flight. They do it because they fear dying, because they don't want to risk it. Therefore fear of death has also become the motive for which institution?

Participant: Extreme unction.

Professor Jung: No, no. A very typical institution: the Mystery death. There death is always figurative. "I have stepped on the threshold of *Proserpina*,"[118,119] like dying figuratively. The Mystery death means that the former person dies, the previous person is shed, and the new one is born. Birth is always preceded by death. The former, sinful person has to die, and the new person arises from this through a new birth. That's the meaning of which rite in the Christian Church?

Participant: Baptism. The children to be baptized were immersed in water.

Professor Jung: Yes, a full baptismal bath, over one's head. That means being drowned in water. There are also baptismal dangers, so to speak. That's a dangerous thing, just like the initiations among primitives. Mysteries are dangerous affairs, at which people also often go *kaputt*,

[118] Latin for the Greek Persephoneia, the daughter of Ceres/Demeter who became the goddess of the underworld when Pluto carried her away and made her his wife.

[119] Jung cites the dream-testimony quoted by Apuleius in *The Metamorphoses of Lucius Apuleius of Madaura*, soon thereafter known as *The Golden Ass*, in Book XI.xxiv. In the 1566 translation by Adlington (Harvard, 1915, 581): "I approached near unto hell, even to the gates of Proserpine." Robert Graves's version (Penguin, 1950, 241): "I approached the very gates of death and set one foot on Prosperpine's threshold."

quite literally;[120] these are terrible tortures. It's the narrow gate of death.

Participant: In earlier baptisms (in Russia?), people were thrust into open water. Sometimes even a hole was sawed in the ice.

Professor Jung: That's right. A hole was sawed in the ice and people were immersed under the ice. This is a very unpleasant procedure, from which one could sometimes catch a fatal pneumonia. Baptism is a figurative death as in the taurobolias, etc. There, too, a burial was executed, burial and rebirth. So Cardanus would have to realize the idea of death here. For if he could really and seriously take this thought to heart, he would of course realize—what?

Participant: That new life could start in him.

Professor Jung: But through what?

Participant: Nothingness.

Professor Jung: Yes, the futility, the complete vanity of outer human life, the realization that it's all monkey business, that all of this isn't worth it. It's immaterial if he is a professor here or there; these things don't count "*sub specie aeternitatis*."[121]

Participant: He'd have to realize that he's going to die in a few years.

Professor Jung: Yes, that could have him undergo a spiritual change. One has to see death; otherwise there will be symptoms. I remember a consultation with a gentleman of my age who had dreams to which he paid no attention. He just became terribly irritable. His dreams contained death motifs. I said, "Do you sometimes think about how many years you still have left?" Then he gave me a distraught look. He was completely appalled. I said to him, "When I travel to India, I know it years in advance; and so, what if the trip is to the dark side of the moon?" In any case, he no longer suffered from melancholia after that. He had simply thought he would still be a young dandy, looking after each and every detail in his business.

---

[120] The head, as in baptism, with *kaputt* (Latin *caput* or head), indicates that one can go all the way down (G). In the last century, this word and its history have gone international. The literal sense derives hazily from a plural linguistic background: on one side corresponding to throwing in one's hand of cards, placating others, and starting over from scratch; on the other, to being smashed, broken, or keeled over (capsized). Jung's contextual meaning, as in vigorous baptism, involves the head going under, sinking or capsizing, at times helplessly.

[121] Latin: under the aspect, in the light of, eternity (G).

Participant: Cardanus worried a great deal about death. He was extremely occupied with real death.

Professor Jung: But *how*? Because one can do this in the form of hypochondriacal, frightening imaginings, and not philosophically. Nothing can be learned from a hypochondriac's frightening image. Unfortunately, neurotic symptoms have no merit. You may well have nurtured the most beautiful anxiety neurosis for fifty years. That doesn't help you in the least. Symptoms are the most useless things imaginable.

Participant: You said that it wasn't a personal problem, but a problem of the age.

Professor Jung: That's quite right. It *is* a problem of the age—the not very philosophical attitude, that is. It's the problem of that time, a time of enormous expansion in human consciousness. But then, of course, it's impossible to think of this restriction that death rubs our nose in. Antiquity was much more interested in this. As a matter of fact, it viewed death as very much a part of life, but the Renaissance had a different task. It had to realize, actually come up against, all the boundaries set to human beings, because of the trend toward boundlessness; it was not allowed to trespass them.

Well, Cardanus chases death away. A dead body is lying in the privy. Why?

Participant: This idea goes into the garbage.

Professor Jung: Yes, into the excremental can, from which everything runs out into a sewer, refuse.

Participant: He sees only what is negative, the decay.

Professor Jung: He definitely does. And the dead body, now what's that?

Participant: What has died in him because he did not accept death.

Professor Jung: This is paradoxical, but that's how it is. One accepts death because with that one accepts life on a higher level, because if one doesn't accept it, one has traded it for a [symbolic][122] death. But now comes a young black dog, under the bed. Where does it come from?

Participant: "Transformed."[123]

Professor Jung: Who?

[122] Word in square brackets added by the editors.
[123] "Ever changing shape, I use / any violence I choose" (Constantine, *Faust II*, 11426f.).

Participant: The devil.

Professor Jung: Yes, this is death and the devil. This death turns into an animal, into the black dog. Now the black animal has always been sacrificed to the gods. It is an animal that rises, so to speak, from the sewer. That rises in himself, for it is already lying under his bed, that is, on the lowest floor. Naturally, it refers to his body. It attracts attention to itself and does something very strange. It tears up his trousers.

Participant: The persona is destroyed. The dog represents a negative affect, which also destroys his outer appearance.

Participant: He can no longer go out without trousers.

Professor Jung: No, he really can't. Well, that's bad luck when your pants fall down. That's almost proverbial. A prisoner's trouser buttons are cut off—"Oops, he's caught with his pants down." It makes a dignified appearance impossible for him—for him, the town doctor! In those times people possessed a tremendous dignity. It was held against Paracelsus quite strongly that he walked around dressed in a laboratory coat, and not in the robe of a professor at the University of Basel; it was also resented that he lectured in German. Culture back then consisted of countless ceremonies and costumes. "Fine feathers make fine birds" was hardly ever truer than at that time. After the simplicity of antiquity, it is amazing what kind of persona was established in the Middle Ages. Think of the picture galleries of the sixteenth and seventeenth centuries! Twirled moustaches, curls rubbed with pomade, wigs,[124] caps decorated with feathers, swords, and daggers. That was a wonderful show! Beribboned cocks, all of them, strutting around with a swagger. And in portraits they all adopt the most phenomenal poses. Well, masculinity makes an impression. An unimportant lad really got tremendously puffed up with self-importance. Ruffs wonderfully accentuated the face. We are uninspired proletarians in comparison, thoroughly down at heel.

So, Cardanus really went to the dogs, and now it starts again from the beginning, and that's how this series ends. It begins with the talking ape, meaning that his unconscious starts to talk. Then come the dead. Then the mother, who asks him to come with her, and who ought

---

[124] In 1624, Louis XIII went prematurely bald. He disguised this with a wig and started a fashion that became almost universal for European upper- and middle-class men. After 1740, wigs were worn only by judges, and had gone completely out of fashion.

to touch him in a special way, because the mother always stands for origin, birth, rebirth. Then the meteor falls down. Then that rose appears in the unconscious, the *coniunctio* of moon and Mercury. Then the greater personality makes an appearance, the heroic personality, the *mana* personality of Alexander, and finally the black sun. That is the peripeteia. That's when Cardanus can no longer follow. He stops because it really gets very dark, and then it all goes downhill.

This process—it seems (with some reservation) to be a genuine series —is what we can also find today in a dream series, in which motifs appear but disappear again, so that one gets the impression of a circular process that proceeds on its own, unless it gets interrupted at some point by the intrusion of consciousness. We always try to intrude with consciousness, therefore, to lift out a part of the unconscious and make it a problem for people, so that this process does not remain merely a natural process, so that the person may benefit from it by being included in the process. I'd still like to mention another, completely different case, where you can find this circular flow represented in clear forms, the visions of Zosimos. Actually, he doesn't intervene either, but everything takes place in the unconscious, and he interprets it for the benefit of his conscious psychology. You can find these visions in the Eranos Yearbook of 1933, *Bemerkungen zu den Visionen des Zosimos* (*Remarks on the Visions of Zosimos*).[125]

F. AT A LATER MEETING OF THE SEMINAR

Professor Jung: Now there is still one last dream of Cardanus from the year 1558 to be discussed:[126]

11. On January 8 of the year 1558 it seemed that I was at the Porta Ticinensis[127] at daybreak, and heard one man say to another, "Would you

[125] Also in C. G. Jung, CW 13, paras. 85ff (G), first collected in 1954 as "Die Visionen des Zosimos."

[126] *Synesiorum somniorum, op. cit.*, 5: 721. Also mentioned in *Des Girolamo Cardano . . . Lebensbeschreibung*, 117ff., but without the episode of the dowry (G).

[127] One of the gates in the Roman wall around the older city of Milan, extant in Cardanus's day and which is still visible in fragmentary form.

marry a woman for 6,000 pounds?" When I heard this, I thought this phrase was meant as mockery, because my son had recently married a poor woman—but the other man denied it. Then I seemed to wish, as happens in dreams, that the scene should change from how it had been. And immediately I seemed to go up a broad, steep path with a young servant and a mule, for one and a half hours, and there were many palaces. I wanted to know the name of the city. A woman said, Bacchetta. Given that she spoke in Italian, I was surprised that I had never heard that name (and it really was a magnificent city). And that woman also added that there were only five palaces here, which I denied, because I had seen many more, more than twenty, of great beauty and with golden ornaments. Then the young servant seemed to abscond with the mule. I thought he wanted to abduct the mule, but he answered in the negative, but where he was I could not see him, because a building stood between us. Then I seemed to be awake and was telling the dream to an acquaintance who, however, according to the dream was a stranger: I was wondering what city this was and what it was called. He told me that it was Naples. "What has Bacchetta to do with Naples?" "That I leave to your interpretation." And I awoke immediately.

According to Cardanus's interpretation, it means that a hard life awaited him. The palaces would be the books that he would publish. The woman stands for power, the boy for his indecision concerning what he should or should not do. Bacchetta means birch, and that means he would get a birching.[128] In his autobiography, he interprets the dream as saying that he would later live in Rome.[129]

[128] *Synesiorum somniorum*, 5: 721.

[129] In Hefele (*Des Girolamo Cardano . . . Lebensbeschreibung*, 117) the text is slightly different: "Another dream indicated that I would later live in Rome. In 1558, on January 8, when I lived in Milan without any public position, I saw in a dream that I was in a city filled with many magnificent palaces. Among other things I noticed a house with golden ornaments, very similar to one I saw in reality when I had come to Rome later on. It seemed to be a holiday, and I was alone with a servant and a mule; both of them had stayed back behind me, however, hidden by a house. People came my way, and I was curious and asked all of them about the name of the city, but nobody gave me an answer, until finally an old woman said the city was called 'Bacchetta,' which in Latin means *virga* (rod, staff, wand), which is usually used to beat boys, or *ferula* (stick, rod), as one used to say in older times. . . . Distressed, I continued my way and wondered who might be able to tell me the true meaning of the word, because I told myself that this was no foreign word, and that I had never heard of a city of this name in Italy. And immediately I confronted the old woman with it, whereupon she only added: 'There are five palaces in this city.' 'As far as I see,' I said, 'there are more than twenty.' But she repeated: 'There are not more than five.' And then I was

This is no simple dream. It is even very complicated. You will have noticed that it has different layers. It is divided into different parts. In the first part Cardanus thinks in the dream that he is actually in one dream, and wishes to be in another one. Then the dream changes. So there is a hiatus between the first and the second part. The subject of the first part is that of the woman with the dowry of 6,000 pounds. Obviously this subject is different from that of the second dream. There again the motif reappears that he actually knows it to be a dream. He half awakes from this dream and now says something about it. This is another part of the dream, in which again a change of consciousness has occurred. Naturally such a dream is never "right," never well composed. There are all kinds of disruptive moments in it, which prevent a clear structuring of the problem. Such dreams are therefore very often difficult to interpret in practice, even in the case of a contemporary person whom we know better than Cardanus. So I don't expect very much from an interpretation of this dream. It is too difficult.

To begin with, we can see in any case that his concern for his son plays a role in the first dream. Money, too, plays a not inconsiderable role for Cardanus. It is surely quite nice that his son married a woman with a dowry, but quite probably not as welcome for the father. He experiences the question, "Would you marry a woman who has 6,000 pounds?" as a mocking question because of his son. This shows that he does indeed care a lot about the son's marriage. At that moment the son had just married. So the sorrow that the daughter-in-law did not bring any dowry was very recent. Well, of that he is aware. You can find many dreams in which one dreams of something that is conscious, and then one thinks one dreams it because one has experienced it. The mere fact that he dreams of a woman without much of a dowry proves that he was particularly stung by the fact that his son had married without a dowry. But now the question of whether he would marry such a woman is put to another person, who denied it. Thus there is someone in him who would indeed marry her, because supposedly the other one, who puts the question, would marry her. So we may assume that there

---

not to find again either my servant or the mule, and woke up. What can I still add? I do not know anything for sure, only the meaning of the word 'Bacchetta' is entirely clear, and that Rome had to be meant by it. Someone also applied the word to Naples. I had this dream when my situation was highly complicated; perhaps it was formed naturally, or it was the result of divine providence" (G).

is at least a doubt in Cardanus regarding this question. Immediately there follows, "In the dream I wished that it were only a dream." What is the reason that is regularly present when such a passage appears in a dream?

Participant: That one cannot accept what the dream says.

Professor Jung: Then a certain condition will exist, when one starts reasoning about the dream. What condition?

Participant: If there is a problem that comes near consciousness.

Professor Jung: Yes, either if an affect appears in the dream, which although not at all close to consciousness is nevertheless quite strong, so that it causes palpitations and labored breathing in the dreamer and wakes him up; then one knows that one is dreaming. Or when some problem is touched upon that in a way is already very conscious, one slips into waking up. Obviously, he was very much concerned at that time about that problem of the dowry, and was partially wakened by it. Now of course this doesn't tell us anything about the symbolism of this conflict. We only know that it occupied, angered, or hurt him. He would have preferred it to be different. The question of whether it were better to have a woman with or without a dowry is so natural that a reasonable person doesn't even think to look for something behind it. If someone asks, "I wonder what that could mean?" it sounds far-fetched. We have to assume, however, that something is indeed hidden behind it.

Participant: There are two reasons for a marriage: either simply because of the dowry, or out of an anima projection, from really being in love. This happened in the son. It is a love match, and the question for Cardanus is whether he should refrain from looking into the anima problem. Because right after that the mule and the old woman come along.

Professor Jung: But it's not the anima problem of the son, it is his own. So what does the woman with a dowry mean when seen as an anima? One can't marry the anima in reality. It is fairly certain from what follows, however, that this is indeed about the anima. So let us assume the anima to be a female being whom one could marry. One time she has a dowry of 6,000 pounds, the other time none. What's the matter with her, *with* a dowry and *without* a dowry?

Participant: In folktales we very often find the motif of the real bride, a poor kitchen maid, and the rich, false bride. So couldn't we say that in the one case this figure is more of a persona than actually an anima? Because this anima is also something that is very useful to him in the outer world. She does not pose a social problem, because it is very advantageous socially to marry the one with the 6,000 pounds. But then it will be distorted, because the anima is facing the outside, not the inside.

Professor Jung: Here comes a difficult problem. How does the anima express itself in the intimate soul life of a man? In this respect women have misconceptions. The anima has to do with the kinds of desire. She represents certain desires and expectations. Therefore she is directed toward somebody, projected onto a woman, who should live up to certain expectations, one-sided expectations, a whole system of expectations. This is what one more or less pictures in an anima figure. You see, the anima is a system of relationships in a man. One can say that it is the system of erotic relationships, whereas the animus in a woman is precisely not that, but a spiritual problem, a system of understanding. In the case of the anima it is a desire, an expectation or a way of expecting.

So, when Cardanus expects, or wishes, or is prepared to marry a woman without a dowry, this means that he has an anima that cares, so to speak, only about the kind of relationship, and not about the 6,000 pounds, that is, what one might gain in addition through the relationship. So in a way this is about the problem of the anima as an end in itself, or as a means to an end, meaning: I love you in order to get you to give me your dowry, or, I love you because your father has so much money in his bank account, or, so that I will inherit this bank account. That's the one case. Or: I love you for yourself, or for the sake of love; because I love, I love you; because this is sufficient for me. If I follow my love, my love will be fulfilled. These are two totally different attitudes: either to take the anima as eros, as an end in itself, at first completely regardless of a projection onto the woman, that is, to have an expectation for expectation's sake, or else the expectation also serves some purpose of power, for example, possession. When he has 6,000 pounds, it immediately follows that the sky's the limit! In the latter case, if the man marries because of the dowry, it will be to buy the world, to gain power. He doesn't follow love for love's sake. As Dante put it, "Musing, I am following the path of love." There you can find the description of how Dante follows his anima, that is, the expectation of his love, *for the sake* of love, not to gain riches but as an end in itself. So for him who follows the anima as an end in herself, she will be his Beatrice, she will become a bridge for him, a passage, because she is a relational function, a relation with what love as such is. But if he loves her because of her dowry, because of what she could make available to him, he will actually eliminate eros and transform it backhandedly into power. Then he will desire power. This is the basic problem, the exposition to the next dream segment. After all, Cardanus is a great man. We can't approach his dreams with the psychology of little school kids. That's why it's difficult.

Participant: When someone carries the inner image of an anima who owns nothing, who is dispossessed, that would lead to a claim of totality, and that would be the end of the story.

Professor Jung: As soon as that is projected, it is no longer an end in itself. But take the contrary case, for example, Spitteler's *Prometheus and Epimetheus*. It's about mistress "Soul," the soul for the soul's sake, not for worldly gain. Whereas this story with his son is problematic for Cardanus. One side in him says yes, the other says no. One side says: I'll be damned! Why didn't he marry a girl with money? The other says: better not. Because it concerns his own problem: should he follow his soul, or should he sell it to get the money? This is the problem of "Prometheus and Epimetheus." There a relationship with the soul exists. The gem comes to him, and he cannot appreciate it because he has become shallow, because he has not seen the magnificence of the gem, because he uses it "in order to," and not as an end in itself.

Well, that is the exposition, and since this thought in the dream is part of a problem he is already conscious of anyway, he wakes up. He is embarrassed by it, because it is a fateful problem, although nobody knows it. It takes someone like Spitteler, writing *Prometheus and Epimetheus*, for us to realize what it is all about.

Participant: St. Francis, who marries Lady Poverty, is also an example. He accepts the soul without dowry.

Professor Jung: St. Francis—that's a very good example in its purest form. Only he has become a bit too saintly. That's why it was possible for Boniface to get him into the Church. It took several tricks to get him in. Brother Sun and Sister Moon, Brother Wolf and Brother Fire—here you can see the soul as such; that is soul. Among all the saints, therefore, he is the one who has the most soul.

But if somebody chooses the anima as such, things will not be easy for him; he will always fare like Spitteler's Prometheus, that is, he will always be confronted with the most difficult task, because he never makes a pact with that which is, nor desires what everyone desires— the 6,000 pounds. Well, so Cardanus is on the laborious ascent. And the anima is his guide, who always leads him to the strenuous climb— namely, with a mule, while in reality he used to travel with two palfreys. What is the advantage of the palfrey over the mule?

Participant: A horse is faster than a mule.

Professor Jung: Yes, and also much more dignified. A palfrey is a typical mount for a lady. Therefore, ladies in the Middle Ages rode palfreys. So Cardanus does not have the palfreys, doesn't have his noble, comfortable horses, but has to make do with a mule and a manservant. Well, what does the mule represent, which noble characteristics does it have?

Participant: It is mulish.

Professor Jung: But that's not noble.

Participant: It is infertile.

Professor Jung: That's not noble either.

Participant: It stands in relation to the ass that carried Christ.

Professor Jung: That's not the mule's doing.

Participant: It can go into uncharted territory.

Professor Jung: The horse can do that too, but the mule is an extremely reliable mount, adapted to mountainous routes, extremely frugal and tremendously persevering. But it is an abstemious animal, and also of a strangely obstinate character. Whoever has once had to deal with mules can tell a thing or two about that. I was once doctor for *Saum* squads,[130] a group consisting of human and animal mules!

[130] Cf. 154n52, this chapter.

The one and a half hours in Cardanus's dream could refer to one and a half years. He is en route to his destination.

G. At a Later Meeting of the Seminar

Professor Jung: Last time we dealt with Cardanus's dream of the woman with a dowry of 6,000 pounds. The dream was unpleasant for him, because the dowry of the daughter-in-law did not exist. Cardanus was very much interested in money. We get a somewhat unfavorable impression from his dream. But that is because he says what he thinks in an unusually honest way. Other people, too, would appear in such an unfavorable light if they told all their thoughts. That's why we don't tell them.

So he wished the dream would stop and change. And there he is on his way with his servant, riding a mule. We already said that this is not the usual form of traveling. Usually one used palfreys. But the mule plays a very great role in his dreams. It appears frequently. It is a regular motif. So this has to mean something. Well, we've already said a few things about the mule: it's a very able animal, eager to work, well adapted for mountain travel, of distinctive female gender but infertile because of the mixture of two widely separate stocks. So where does this point us? What element in Cardanus's psychology is this?

Participant: Last time we figured that because of his negative attitude toward the unconscious, it seems to him to be something mulish and sterile.

Professor Jung: In this sense the mule represents the instinctual unconscious, the unconscious in animal form. As is generally known, animal nature is subject to many changes. Changes in this figure depend on the attitude of consciousness. If we are afraid of the unconscious, for instance, it will appear in a frightening form. If I cannot recognize it because I'm afraid of it, it will appear as a dangerous animal, or a robber, or a murderer. But if I have a friendly attitude toward the unconscious, it will appear in the form of more favorable figures. So when the unconscious is insinuating and inviting, what form will it take, provided I am inclined to let it in?

Participant: A sympathetic form.

Professor Jung: Yes, for example, the form of the beautiful maiden. This is what is attractive for a man. The classical anima figure, therefore, has all kinds of attractions. She is a type that is attuned to the man. In this case, therefore, we have to say that the mule takes the place, as it were, of an anima.

Participant: You emphasized that the mule is so good at climbing.

Professor Jung: Yes, the anima is someone to be reckoned with. She is an instinctual force. She is a guide. I remember a dream in which the anima appears as a mountain guide. Well, the anima is also present in a man's ambition. If a man is very ambitious and greedy for money, such as Cardanus, the anima will naturally take the form of ambition, and therefore an ambitious person is called "a climber"[131] in English. That's what Cardanus is. He always boasts of his acquaintance with sovereigns and cardinals. So, the mule, which can climb very well, represents the anima who serves him, so to speak, in the form of a laborer. The whole force of the unconscious is used for a purpose. He sits down on it, as it were, and lets himself be carried by it. And whatever consciousness presents to the anima she will naturally accept, provided that what develops serves the anima's interest, what she actually wants. Thus, for instance, when a man lets ten thousand women beguile him, or when a woman is taken in by every animus; when someone has only vague thoughts, but expresses them in clever words, she will be taken in by him, and all the more so if he also has curls and worn-out heels! Then the unconscious will take possession of consciousness. But to which end?

Participant: She wants to acquaint the man with his relational function.

Professor Jung: I'm afraid it's too late for that. What devilish stories will be brewing then? What happens when a man or a woman is possessed by an animus or an anima?

Participant: There will be isolation from the outer world.

Professor Jung: That too, perhaps, but before that all kinds of things happen.

Participant: They are taken in.

Professor Jung: Meaning what?

Participant: Precisely what they least wanted will happen.

---

[131] This expression in English in the original, obviously referring to a "social climber."

Participant: They are slaves to a countless number of persons and objects.

Professor Jung: Take a specific case. What happens in reality?

Participant: He chases after Helen, like Faust.

Professor Jung: And what else?

Participant: He enters the underworld.

Participant: He is after power.

Professor Jung: Yes, quite correct. And how does Faust meet his fate in Part II? All of this is already implicit in Gretchen.

Participant: "To earth, this weary earth, ye bring us."[132]

Professor Jung: Yes, that's it. These are the forces of the unconscious. "To earth, this weary earth, ye bring us, / To guilt ye let us heedless go, / Then leave repentance fierce to wring us: / A moment's guilt, an age of woe!" That's what the anima does.

A woman possessed by the animus will become entangled with countless men and will always get the short end of the stick, until all men steer clear of her. She will become someone to fear. She circulates everywhere, and gets through nowhere. In the case of a man possessed by the anima it usually starts with mere sensuality; he is taken in by every silly goose, if only she makes eyes at him. Or he is the type who has sold his soul completely. He gets entangled everywhere in the world. That is possession. The person gets entangled in the world. The unconscious wants him to get entangled in the world. The unconscious has the unconditional tendency to push humans into the world but, strangely enough, also to isolate them. He does not really come into it, but comes as a victim, backward. Everywhere he gets kicked out. So, at first into it, and then not into it after all. Everywhere into it in this way, connected everywhere and nowhere. Removed from everywhere. Such persons will grow utterly lonely. I have seen cases of women possessed by the animus, who then told me long stories of relationships that all went sour. And in the end they stand there empty-handed, completely isolated, and surrounded by nothing but countless devils. Such a woman once said: "I've always seen what it was all about. I am

---

[132] From a poem by Goethe, in *Wilhelm Meisters Lehrjahr* II.xiii: "Who never ate his bread in sorrow, / Who never spent the darksome hours / Weeping and watching for the morrow, / He knows ye not, ye gloomy Powers. / To earth, this weary earth, ye bring us, / To guilt ye let us heedless go, / Then leave repentance fierce to wring us: / A moment's guilt, an age of woe!" (in the translation by Thomas Carlyle, 1824): "Wer nie sein Brod mit Thränen ass, / Wer nicht die kummervollen Nächte / Auf seinem Bette weinend sass, / Der kennt euch nicht, ihr himmlischen Mächte."

always right. See, you understood me. I am always right." Then they are beyond help. The same is true for men. They ruin their relationships by running blindly after one urge, and thus become isolated. Therefore one must be conscious of one's goals, because the unconscious does not know about the world. The unconscious hasn't got a pocket watch. It does not know human life. It treats everybody as if he were a god and not a man, as if he had ten thousand women, and it treats a woman as if she were a university or a judge of everything. The unconscious knows only divine possibilities, inhuman possibilities. And the fact that the mule is actually the anima in the case of Cardanus shows that his unconscious is sterile. It is simply used as a pack animal. It also lets itself be used as a pack animal with pleasure. And that is what's dangerous. Then follows the illusion: one can do anything one wants to. One can arrange one's life the way one likes, but with the inevitable consequences: one falls victim to a possession. The lad going with Cardanus has had it already. This is the master with his servant, the man with his shadow. They go up there and come into a very beautiful city. Cardanus asks for the name of the city and learns from an old woman, who is not described in more detail, that it has a strange name. Now this is the great unknown person. This is the anima again who, strangely enough, has already taken human form again. Why does she have a human form here? What could that indicate?

Participant: When consciousness comes near the anima, she will become more human. Could this be possible in one and the same dream?

Professor Jung: Something has happened in this dream that could explain this.

Participant: He asks for the name of the city.

Professor Jung: And still before that? It's nearly invisible: he has ventured on this journey. He goes with the mule. This suffices to cause an advance from the other side. The mule comes from reality, in which he treats his unconscious like a mule. In a dream the symbols are all there and alive, but not in reality. Somebody who uses his unconscious only to give himself certain airs, to play a special role, treats his unconscious like a machine that should carry him to a certain destination. If he then dreams that he is sitting on this machine, this car, bicycle, or lift, however, then that image will be the living symbol, also including the other meaning—namely, the unconscious one. When consciousness is erased, the unconscious is not forced to be only that. It goes like this:

Case 1: in the waking state   Attitude A   Consciousness
                               Attitude A_1 plus Unconscious

The effect of attitude A is that a goal emerges. Then the representative of the unconscious, the anima, takes the form of A_1, which corresponds to this A.

Case 2: in the sleeping state   Consciousness erased
                                Unconscious A_1 / B_1 / C_1 etc.

Now, in the unconscious (seen as [Attitude] A_1 by the conscious state) the whole unconscious stands behind the anima, and is, as it were, veiled by this symbol. For it [in Case 1, the attitude A_1] brings about a force from above, which crosses over and represses the unconscious with what stands behind this figure. Now in Cardanus's dream this is not the case, for the direction is reversed (as in Case 2). The unconscious flows into consciousness. Therefore, the figure of A_1 is followed by B_1, and it is no longer just a mule, but a beautiful horse. Then come C_1, centaurs, D_1, a beautiful maiden, and so on. And then comes the entire sequence of anima figures. Everything is now populated. All this surges up into consciousness, because it isn't inhibited from the side of consciousness. Consciousness pushes everything that doesn't suit it to one side. Consciousness doesn't want the unconscious to be a noble horse, but simply an animal that can be worked to death; not a noble horse with its own whims, and not a beautiful maiden—because in that case one's ambition would be blocked. Therefore, the mule is already a woman in this dream. Because if it were no woman, nothing would prevent him from speaking of a *mulus*.

Participant: By day the animus is often an animal figure in folktales. At night he is a prince.

Professor Jung: Exactly. At night everything changes, because the inhibition by consciousness shuts down. Think of Nietzsche's beautiful passage: "It is night. . . . And my soul is a gushing fountain."[133] For

---

[133] *Thus Spoke Zarathustra*, second part, *The Night Song* [*Das Nachtlied*] / Nacht ist es: nun reden lauter alle springenden Brunnen. Und auch meine seele ist ein springender Brunnen. *Also sprach Zarathrustra: Ein Buch für alle und keinen* (Stuttgart: Kröner Verlag, 1930), 113. (It is night: now all fountains speak more loudly. And my soul too is a [gushing] fountain.) (*Thus Spoke Zarathustra: A Book for All and None*, trans. Adrian del Caro [Cambridge: Cambridge University Press, 2006], 81.)

that's when one hears it. One hears the language of the birds when they're not yet singing. One hears what is behind it. Well, you see, what emerges is that the *mulus* is a *mula*, and Cardanus gets involved with her and goes off with her. In the dream he cannot pursue the same goals as in consciousness, and now all the figures he had ordered around during the day are talking. They all start acting now, but due to the unconscious forces behind them.

Suppose, for example, that you are employed somewhere, and that you have a boss whom you have sized up exactly. You make him into a terrible tyrant. Maybe he really is one. Well, he's a father figure, and in the unconscious the father figure is, of course, much more than simply this tyrant. And so it may happen that this gentleman, your lord and master, appears at night, and you fling your arms around his neck. In reality you can't stand him. In the dream he flirts with you in the most amazing way, due to the fact that in the dream he is not only himself but also much more.

In A_1 all the other meanings are also added. Thus the mule already appears at the next peripateia, when Cardanus is impressed by something he did not know, that is, a completely new city. Then he realized that there is something behind it. And at that moment the mule turns into a human figure and tells him that this city is called Bacchetta, which means birch. The woman also adds that this city has only five palaces. He is certain, however, that there have to be more than twenty, and also that one of them is magnificent and even gilded. Well, what does that mean? Above all seen under the aspect of Cardanus's psychology? Why must the city have more than twenty palaces, and not five?

Participant: Five is human limitation.

Participant: Five isn't enough for him. When he arrives, there will be more than just five palaces in it.

Participant: I wonder if the number five indicates that the city suggests a certain order, a certain law, not only a quantity but also a secret meaning.

Professor Jung: You are quite right there. We'll come back to this.

Participant: It's as if he bargained. If he gets involved in the first place, he wants twenty palaces, not five.

Professor Jung: It really is bargaining, you are absolutely right. You see, he simply can't accept that the woman speaks only of five. There should be twenty or more.

Participant: Man has five fingers on one limb, and twenty altogether. He wants more.

Participant: Usually there are many palaces in a big Italian city.

Professor Jung: The city is big and beautiful. In his view it can't possibly have only five.

Participant: The quality would be five, which is a kind of order. The other thing is quantity, not order.

Professor Jung: Why five, of all numbers? So we have to assume that the unconscious does mean five. Now we know that numbers were used very symbolically in the Middle Ages. We have to ask, therefore, if five has a meaning.

Participant: Five is the female number, associated with Venus.

Professor Jung: For Cardanus, five is most definitely a male number. Odd numbers are male. You see, the original symbolism of numbers is based on vivid images. As is generally known, all the numbers between one and ten are sacred numbers, and for ancient philosophers ten is the most sacred and most important number. That was not so to begin with. The original symbolic numbers ended with nine. They are all sacred, one number more so for certain peoples, another one for others. For Christians, for instance, the trinity is especially sacred, and also seven. For others it is quaternity, for instance for North American Indians. The six is Jewish, the Star of David, etc. And the five is a special number, insofar as it has a special form. You must not think of Arabic numbers here, but Roman ones.

Participant: It is half of the Roman ten.

Professor Jung: Where does the five stem from?

Participant: It represents the hand.

Professor Jung: Yes, and ten is the double hand. That was the way of counting. One had two hands, two feet; five and twenty are very primary, original numbers. So when the woman says five, she says: one hand. And he says: two hands, two feet, and even more. But the five has yet another concrete meaning.

Participant: It represents man, with head and arms and legs.

Professor Jung: Yes, of course, the human figure. One is a man; two is a couple or two friends. Three is Daddy, Mummy, and the son. Four is around the table. Five is the whole person. He has five points; he makes a pentagon. He stands there making a pentagon. This is the original illustration of five. Six is a multiple of two and three. These are two principles. The first numbers always represent principles: *monas, dyas, trias*. This is already a process and represents a higher wholeness. The two is also called the first real number, for this number is purely female, whereas the three, as a male number, is a perfect number. And so then five is the whole human being—namely, the natural human being. So these basic ideas are absolutely a given for Cardanus. He lived in an era when such ideas were customary. And what does it mean when the woman says five, and he says twenty and more? How was this meant? Well, he would expect twenty and even more. That's actually his wish.

Participant: What is meant are material riches. It gives expression to a conscious prejudice.

Professor Jung: It's a matter of prestige.

Participant: The woman says five, and then he thinks he'd have the whole person. So he adds even more hands and feet, without realizing that many hands and feet do not yet constitute a person.

Professor Jung: Now we must have still another meaning of five.

Participant: The five senses.

Professor Jung: It's the four corners with the center, that is, not the pentagram, but fourness with unity, the quaternity with the *quinta essentia*. And, of course, this is something that plays a great role for Cardanus. He wrote an essay about the meaning of numbers in which he says, for one thing, that the One is good, but that the Few is already bad. Now there is a representation that differs from the pentagram—namely, the representation of quaternity in the form of

Five represents the unity of four, the *quinta essentia*. This is something we absolutely must bear in mind, because this pattern is the opposite of fiveness. Fiveness simply represents natural man,[134] in this way:

What is the classical difference between fiveness and fourness?

Participant: Fiveness has no center.

Professor Jung: And what is the case then?

---

[134] Cf. Jung's brief discussion of the naked, spread form of humanity in the medieval *melothesia*, in *Visions: Notes of the Seminar 1930–1934*, vol. 2 (Lecture III, November 13, 1932), 819–21.

Participant: Because a person's unconsciousness is not centered, it lacks consciousness that would create order.

Participant: It's governed by the head, because the head is above.

Professor Jung: Yes, and all the corners are the same. You can rotate it any way you like. Usually, however, it is depicted with the head above. This is simply the natural anatomical form, whereas the other one is an abstraction. But it is also a portrayal of man, because man consists of four elements and possesses a highest soul, which is the *quinta essentia* of the four elements.

Participant: For Aristotle there is a transition from natural man to spiritual man, the fifth element, the ether as *quinta essentia*.[135]

Professor Jung: Yes, the first state of man is chaos, the *massa confusa*, a seething mass, where there is nothing on top and nothing at the bottom, where there is no differentiation. Chaos must be divided, therefore, into the four elements. That's the course of development. In alchemy, for example, the elements must be separated from chaos; four irreducible elements must crystallize out of the synthesis of these four most extreme differences, resulting in a cross: utmost differences, which contain all pairs of opposites, whose elements cannot be reduced to each other. Then the One must be made out of these utmost differences. This is the epitome of the alchemical process. This is a different fiveness. And when the anima says five, we may doubt whether she means the chaotic, natural man, or alludes, in an enigmatic way, to the *quinta essentia*.

Participant: Since the city is also an alchemical symbol, which later has a secret order, couldn't it rather be the *quinta essentia*?

Participant: Perhaps it could be both?

Professor Jung: Quite right, I would think so. Because when he sees a beautiful city and supposes that it must have many palaces, he is thinking, "This means good business." He's a doctor, is he not, always striving to become a personal physician for princes and noblemen. Now the anima tells him: there are only five palaces. He replies that this isn't worth it. So why the ascent? But it could be the steep path to that other city. When the city is called "the birch," he will be chastised.

Participant: For him it means being chastised.

---

[135] The ether is the fifth classical element in ancient Greek philosophy and science. Aristotle included it as a fifth element (the quintessence) on the principle that nature abhorred a vacuum.

Professor Jung: Yes, of course, for him it is a punishment. That is what's so dubious about this whole story. On the one hand his ambition, the material side, constantly plays the leading role, while on the other hand the woman says, it's the birch.

Participant: Before that, he led the unconscious, the mule, with the whip.

Professor Jung: The city isn't called Bacchetta for nothing; as you rightly say, one needs a whip to lash on pack animals. When someone has mistreated an animal, he will be punished by being turned into that animal after death. So, in a way, one is promised the birch. So this city is not some vain pleasure or simply food for his ambition.

It's also strange how the twenty occurs to him. It is five multiplied by four. In any case, it's essential that it be a multiple, because five is definitely not enough for him. Therefore it must grow by all means. So this is his claim, his ambition, his expectation, to bring off a big deal there.

Participant: I was surprised that he has the idea of a particular palace. It seems to me that here, too, he introduces the idea of centering, so this would mean that the twenty are also arranged around this center.

Professor Jung: Well, yes, if we start with the hand we have five. If we add everything, including the toes, there are twenty. So he multiplies by four, and says in addition that one palace is particularly beautiful and gilded. That expresses an overvaluation. At the same time, however, he repeats a symbol that the woman had already mentioned, only made bigger by his claims to prestige. It's as if somebody comes up with the idea of a mandala he could draw, but when he finds that the result is much too meager for what he really wants to express, he will add a whole human figure to embellish it as much as possible. Then one starts to multiply. That's the way of common exaggerations. One could simply state it, but then one states it by way of a multiplication, without ever getting out of the symbolism. And for this a palace is excellent; it's a gilded palace, and now it starts getting quite wondrous. Not even in the Renaissance were there gilded palaces. What palace could that be?

Participant: The Heavenly Jerusalem.

Professor Jung: Yes, something like that. The city with the fortress of God. And now he discovers that the young man had let the mule disappear. The young man does hear him, but there is a house between them. And the mule is no longer there.

Participant: It has turned into the anima.

Professor Jung: Yes, but why so completely? What happened?

Participant: In the dream he did reach the destination.

Professor Jung: Exactly. He has reached the central place, so to speak. He has realized what the anima wanted to convey in an enigmatic way. As a result, in any case the figure of the mule has disappeared in the dream. So many archetypal images have come up that this form, the "mule," has been erased.

Participant: Doesn't it also mean at the same time that here there is no longer any going back?

Professor Jung: Yes, that's right. When he loses his mount, he can't go back any longer.

Participant: It also seems right to me that it's a pack animal onto which the anima is projected. As soon as the center has been found, the pack animal vanishes.

Professor Jung: Of course, then he is burdened with the situation, confronted with it, and that is when he thinks that he awakes and now tells it to someone whom he knows in the dream, but not in reality. He wanted to ask what city this might be, and the other tells him that it's Naples. What does that mean?

Participant: Naples, the new city.

Professor Jung: Yes, *neapolis*.[136] And he asks, "But what has Naples to do with Bacchetta?" The other replies, "That I leave to your interpretation." Now what has this *neapolis* got to do with the birch?

Participant: Perhaps Naples being situated at the foot of the Vesuvius. The city is in danger of being buried.

Professor Jung: That's no clue.

Participant: Inasmuch as Naples is a birch, it also has this name. Five palaces, that is his cross, so that he'll come to his birch in this city.

Professor Jung: How can it be proven that this new city really has to do with the cross?

Participant: The Heavenly Jerusalem and the lower city. Christ comes into this city along the thorny path.

Professor Jung: That's right. Regeneration is always associated with the idea of pain. Pain is really the crux, being crucified. Think of the passage in Zosimos I read to you. Being crucified is a torture. But how is the form of the cross linked to the upper city?

---

[136] Greek, Νέα Πόλις, new city.

Participant: Precisely by this "four times five." When you connect the four corners, you will get a cross:

⊠

In the mandalas there are always four gates and one center.

Professor Jung: The Heavenly Jerusalem has twelve gates. And then there is still another Biblical mandala.

Participant: Paradise with the four rivers.

Participant: The cross itself is also a rod.

Professor Jung: Yes, the tree of life. The cross is made from the wood of the tree of life. There are medieval illustrations in which Christ is crucified on the tree of life, with its fruits and its leaves. You see, the evidence is everywhere. This heavenly city is built on the principle of fourness, as are those on earth. What do you know about ancient town planning?

Participant: Roman cities are quadrangles. They have two main roads that intersect, and gates at four places.

Professor Jung: This is the Roman camp, and that's how Roman streets were laid out. Whenever the terrain allowed it, there was one main road and one that intersected it; this was the basic pattern for the arrangement of streets in general. What was done when the city was founded?

Participant: One walked around the *temenos*.[137]

Professor Jung: How was that done?

Participant: By circumambulations.[138]

Professor Jung: Yes, and with what?

Participant: With a plow.

Professor Jung: Yes, it was used to plow the *sulcus primigenius*.[139] This was a mandala, and what was done in the middle of this plowed-up area?

Participant: Fruits and sacrifices were buried.

Professor Jung: At first a hole, the *fundus*, was made, and then sacrifices to the chthonic gods were put into it; in other words, the center was accentuated. If you ever come to a house in a Roman highway fortress, you will still find a hole at the center. I don't know if this is the

[137] Greek: a protected piece of land set apart as a sacred domain, a sacred (L. *sacer*: set off and protected) precinct or temple enclosure, dedicated to a God.

[138] See chapter 11, 100n12.

[139] A magical furrow around the center of the temple *temenos*.

original *fundus*, but in any case it holds that position. In China there is a whole science about how to build a house. The same was true for the building of a temple in Assyria.

The equinox [heading] at the vernal equinox was also taken into account in the construction, so as to make sure that the orientation was absolutely correct.[140] Well, at the end of the dream there comes this very important remark,[141] made by the interlocutor in the dream, as if to provoke Cardanus. Now what does it mean when a modern dream features such a remark at the end?

Participant: That one has got to think about it.

Professor Jung: Yes, one has always got to think about it. When the teacher asks a trick question, one will think it over. One knows that it's about something important. It has been phrased that way for a specific purpose. What effect does this have on Cardanus?

Participant: He doesn't easily forget the dream.

Professor Jung: Yes, and he also says that no other dream has amazed him as much as this one.

I have still another dream I'd like to mention:[142]

12. Cardanus dreamed of a snake of extraordinary size. And he was very afraid that the snake would kill him. Although it seemed to him that the snake was quiet, he was still so frightened that he awoke.

The snake doesn't harm him. It was simply there and looked at him.

Participant: It's the awakening of the Kundalini. It doesn't move yet.

Professor Jung: It could also refer to something like that. But in this case an important link emerges from the associations, a warning against

---

[140] Jung seems to allude to the older Roman method of surveying field boundaries and building sites described by Pliny in the *Natural History*, Book III. See Joseph Rykwert's classic study, *The Idea of a Town: The Anthropology of Urban Form in Rome, Italy, and the Ancient World* (Cambridge, MA: MIT Press, 1988), 48–49. Using one's own shadow cast south at midday, one scores a line in the earth, bisects it, then intersects its midpoint navel or *umbilicus* with another line, the *decumanus*, oriented on the equinoctial sunrise. The resulting "wind-rose," although produced in a crude fashion, underlay the more sophisticated procedures of Roman agrimensors or surveyors. "No other civilization . . . had practiced, as the Romans did during the late republic and the empire, the imposition of a constant, uniform pattern on the towns, on the countryside, and also on their military establishments, with almost obsessional persistence" (62).

[141] "That I leave to your interpretation" (see dream text).

[142] In Hefele, *Des Girolamo Cardano . . . Lebensbeschreibung*, 99, where it is reported in indirect speech (G).

carelessness during a certain treatment. At that time he was doctoring the terminally ill, seven-year-old, only son of Count Camillo Borromeo. The case was hopeless; at first he had written out a prescription, but then changed it at the last minute and had it confirmed by colleagues. So he was able to escape just in time. And so he said: Without the dream's warning I would not have been able to escape death. He would even owe his lasting fame to this dream. This is interesting insofar as the heraldic animal of the Borromei is that well-known serpent, a long, coiled snake. I don't know if it's the one with the child in its mouth. But in any case I know that the Borromei have such a serpent in their coat of arms. So that snake could really be linked to this. For this is a dream we can't possibly understand completely without taking into account what happened later. It could be a dream that warned him against the serpent of the Borromei. They were very powerful. In Milan at that time, it was of course a tricky thing to be a doctor in such a place. And a couple of times it did him no good. So he made off just in time.[143] You see, dreams also have this aspect. We surmise something about the dream that may even be correct but that has no direct and particular bearing on it. Under certain circumstances, however, it can be absolutely essential. I have already seen many such dreams, where I myself had the feeling that they would point to something about to happen. This kind of interpretation—which he himself constantly aims at, and in which he very rarely succeeds—is indeed justified, but unfortunately not technically feasible.

Participant: But it can also be interpreted in the sense that he is split off from the unconscious, so that the mighty snake appears.

Professor Jung: Such an interpretation only makes sense if we have Cardanus in treatment. But in his life this Borromeo snake had a very practical meaning.

---

[143] Jung alludes to these narrow escapes in his "Paracelsus the Physician" (1941), CW 15, para. 36: "If the indications elicited from the patient's horoscope were unfavorable, the doctor had an opportunity to make himself scarce—a very welcome one in those robust times, as we also know from the career of the great Dr. Cardan."

CHAPTER 14

Discussion of Three Dreams of Dr. John Hubbard,[1] alias Peter Blobbs

(The Censer, the Swinging Ax, and the Man at the End of the Corridor)[2]

Paper by Carol Baumann[3]

1. The first dream reported by Hubbard goes as follows:[4]

It was the eve of the Coronation. I found myself in a vast and lofty cathedral, so lofty that I could see no roof, and so vast that all the outlines were vague, and left but little impression on my mind. I was one of a crowd assembled to witness the strange ceremony known as "The Night of the Flaming Censer." During the night preceding the Coronation of their King, peasants and yeomen have the immemorial right to occupy the cathedral in which the ceremony takes place

---

[1] Dr. Arthur John Hubbard first published *The Fate of Empires: Being an Inquiry into the Stability of Civilisation* (London: Longmans, Green, 1913). The dreams discussed are found in *Authentic Dreams of Peter Blobbs, M.D. Dunelm, L.R.C.P. London, M.R.C.S. Eno., L.S.A. London, and of Certain of His Relatives, Told by Himself with the Assistance of Mrs Blobbs* (London: Longmans, Green, 1916). The relatives include his mother, wife, daughter, and one of his sisters (G). Hubbard (1856–1935) retired early from the practice of medicine in 1910 ("his heart was not in it," opined a relative), and studied and traveled (to Iceland and the Balkans). He identified prophetic dreams as "proleptic dreams."

[2] Meeting of December 10, 1940 (G).

[3] The paper could not be obtained (G).

[4] This and the following dream are quoted here from the original text by Hubbard. The text includes ten dreams; those dealt with here are numbers 1, 2, and 5, respectively. For online access to the text, consult http://www.oddbooks.co.uk/oddbooks/dreams-of-peter-blobbs.html.

on the following day. I found myself surrounded by whispering groups of country-folk, attired in curious old-world dress. [. . .] But the object that most attracted my attention, and that was the center of interest to all eyes, was a huge silver-gilt censer, suspended from the gloom of the roof of the nave. It hung halfway between the west window and the high Gothic arches supporting the tower of the cruciform building, and must have weighed many tons. Perhaps ten feet high, and as big round as an ox, its surface was made up of an interlacing tracery, leaving holes which, in its upper part, were two or three inches across. From some of these the smoke of the burning incense gently curled in minute spirals.

As evening drew on, I observed that the bystanders were regarding it with increasing attention, and, as the sun was setting, I saw, to my amazement, that the huge censer was no longer at rest. With a movement that was almost imperceptible at first, the ponderous mass slowly gathered way, swinging to and fro with the stately movement of the bob of a gigantic pendulum.

It is difficult to describe the slowness with which its impetus was increased; but the arc through which it swept was greater with every beat, and, as the hours passed, it swung with a steadily increasing speed and momentum. Flames began to issue from the openings in its tracery, and, as the night wore on, it moved with awful speed, and a violence impossible to describe. Its maximum was reached at midnight. Filling the cathedral with the smoke of its incense, the glowing monster swung to and fro, in a semicircle which extended from end to end of the nave, hissing, roaring, and followed by a stream of sparks and flame. As the hours of the new day waxed, so its movements waned. Its path became shorter and shorter, and with a gradation as slow as that by which it had increased, the great censer slowly sank to rest, and, as the sun rose, it hung motionless, red-hot and unapproachable.

2. THE PATH OF THE SWINGING AX

The day had dawned; the Coronation of the King was at hand. Again I found myself in the vast cathedral, but now the scene had changed.

Since the morning, wooden stages had been erected, and, instead of the peasants, the cathedral was filling with princes and lords and gaily dressed ladies. [. . .] Toward the west window, an oblong space extending nearly across the nave was kept vacant. Its long diameter began under one of the great arches forming the south side of the nave, and reached as far as three-quarters of the way toward those on the north. The sides of this, the long diameter of the oblong space, were enclosed by a high and heavy, unscaleable iron railing.

The north end, which, of course, was in the nave, was open and unprotected; but the south end, that under the arch, was furnished with iron gates of the same heavy construction as the railing. [⁵Near the open northern end of the axis stood a table, covered with red velvet. On it lay all the royal insignia. In the same area, right in the axis of the nave, there hung an eerie object: a gigantic double-headed ax hanging down from the roof to one foot above the ground.] Somehow— dreamwise—I became aware that this gigantic ax had been preserved by these strange people as a national possession from time immemorial. It looked to me as though it were made of bronze, and its shape was exactly that of the Labrys of the prehistoric Cretan civilization.⁶ It hung motionless, as though guarding the regalia.

People were still pressing into the cathedral, filling the nave, except for a lane along the middle of it, and crowding the stages in the aisles. The chancel was raised high above the level of the nave, and I could see but little of what was going on there. I never saw the altar, for all was hidden by the clouds of incense that filled the chancel. Every now and then, however, when the clouds were partly swept aside, I saw white-robed ecclesiastics, and, at intervals, the monotonous droning of an interminable litany came faintly down the nave.

Then the great event of the day began. The iron gates at the south end of the oblong space were flung open, and the upright figure of the King about-to-be appeared in the gateway. There he paused. As though

---

⁵ The passage following the square brackets is missing in the online version of the book, and has been retranslated into English from the German.

⁶ The labrys is a double-headed ritual ax, found in ancient Minoan depictions of the Mother Goddess. The word "labrys" is Minoan in origin, from the same root as the Latin "labrum," or lip.

inspired by his presence, the great ax quivered, and began to swing to and fro, from east to west, from west to east, much as the great censer had done in the night, but of course with a shorter sweep. Then I saw that, with every sweep, the ax moved nearer to the King. The King stepped forwards toward the ax, advancing at right angles to the line of its swing. The iron gates, not to be opened again, clanked to behind him, and the real ceremonies of the coronation had begun. In my dream I knew that once, some five hundred years ago, the King then chosen lost his nerve and feared to face the ax. The ax moved ever toward him, horrible and unrelenting, and the King shrank before it, pressing himself in terror against the iron gates. Just as the ax reached him, he screamed aloud to the horror-stricken multitude. What he said was well known, but was never communicated to me, a foreigner. The night after this horrible event, the great censer was set swinging again, and by the following day a braver king had been found.

No such calamity marred the ceremony that I witnessed. As the ax drew nearer to the King, so the King drew nearer to the ax. Every time that the ax swept before him, the King advanced a short pace toward it. Now, in the tense silence of the cathedral, they were close together: the strain became unendurable. Once more the ax swept past the King, the wind of its passage stirring the hem of his gold-embroidered robe; and then, with one long stride, he crossed its path, and by the time that the ax returned, the King had reached the table. There he paused again, while the ax swung harmlessly behind him. I cannot remember that there was any noise of cheering; there were no shouts, no signs of welcome—the tension of the appalling scene appeared to have paralyzed the spectators.

In a silence only broken by the droning of the litany, the King, now cut off from all other men, stood motionless before his people. Then, slowly, he raised the crown in both hands, and—for now no other had the right to do so—he set it upon his own head. One by one he took up the other emblems, and then, in all the splendor of royalty, he passed out into the nave and commenced his solitary progress through the cathedral. Slowly, slowly he ascended the steps that led up to the chancel and was lost to sight in the cloud of incense. I never saw him again.

3. The Dream of the Man at the End of the Passage

I dreamed that I was standing at a railway bookstall, idly turning over the leaves of a list of illustrated publications. The advertisements referred to a compilation of stories taken from history, apparently intended for children. The specimens of illustrations showed me King Alfred burning the cakes, William Tell shooting the apple from his son's head, and other historical incidents equally well known to intelligent infants. One of them, however, I could not recognize. It represented a naked, emaciated man, holding the handle of a door at the end of a long and gorgeous passage. "Good gracious I," I thought, "what is this? What on earth is the story connected with this?" I paused for a moment. "How stupid I am!" I thought. "Of course it was so-and-so and such-and-such." Then, as is the way of dreams, I became one of the witnesses of the tragedy illustrated in the publisher's circular.

The circular and bookstall vanished, and I found myself engaged on a journey. For a week or more I travelled by train with a little black bag, which was examined at many frontiers. At length I found myself in the region of adventure. Two countries were at war: I never learned their names; in dreams such names are superfluous, and I must distinguish them as the Greater Land and the Lesser Land.

Through all the scenes that I am about to describe, I was with the people of the Greater Land. They were a remarkable mixture of old and new. Their dress was that of five hundred years ago, but their weapons were up to date. The origin of some of their ceremonies was lost in the dim mists of a prehistoric past, but their methods of warfare were those of today.

The war between these two countries had persisted for many months before I arrived upon the scene, and it is not too much to say that I witnessed the closing act of a long-drawn tragedy.

The Greater Land, at the beginning of the war, was a monarchy, and their King had belonged to a dynasty of immemorial descent. The inhabitants of the Lesser Land were far less numerous, but were, individually, of a higher type. The war brought to the surface one of the officers of the Lesser Land, who became the hero of my dream.

A long succession of actions had been fought, in which the armies of the Lesser Land, though vastly outnumbered, had been frequently victorious, owing to the skill and intrepidity of this officer. He became their commander in chief, and had won, by his resourcefulness and unfailing cheerfulness, not only the respect, but also the devoted love of his fellow countrymen. The war had been waged with bitterness: it was a war of extermination, and the victories of this hero, whose name, like those of the countries engaged, I never learnt, had been marked by a strange peculiarity. In every battle one or more of the Royal House of the Greater Land had fallen. At length the King himself had lost his life, and royalty had vanished from among them.

Meanwhile, these victories had cost the Lesser Land dearly: their resources had become exhausted, and the struggle became more and more unequal. The tide of war had turned. The numbers of the Greater Land at length wore down and finally destroyed the thinned battalions of the Lesser. Their hero maintained the struggle to the last, but shortly before my arrival, he, too, was captured, and, in this war, the fate of all prisoners was death.

He was brought in triumph to their capital, and placed in a small guardroom in the vacant palace of the Royal Family. By order of the government he was detained there and treated with every contumely.

The people among whom I found myself were indeed an extraordinary race. Fierce and unscrupulous, they were, nevertheless, capable of a vivid hero-worship, and able to appreciate the greatness of the prisoner whom fate had placed in their hands. I shared the general surprise at the fiendish treatment meted out to him by the government. Starved to emaciation, he was daily beaten, and brutally ill treated by his three guards. Then came the denouement. One day his guards entered his room, and, with their accustomed violence, stripped him naked. I ought to have said that his room opened upon a long and magnificent passage, at the end of which was a large door leading to the interior of the palace. The doomed man was then commanded by his guards to go, all naked as he was, to the door at the end of the passage, to turn the handle, and to advance into the room beyond. Then the first of his guards addressed him. Turning to the lost man, "In that room," he said, "you will find the sword." Then the second spoke. "In that room," he said, "you will find the sword that is for you."

Then the third spoke. "In that room," he said, "you will feel the weight of the sword that is for you."

The broken and hopeless man went slowly down the long passage. Taking the handle of the door in his hand, he paused for a moment—and I recognized the scene that had been depicted in the publisher's circular. Slowly he turned the handle, passed into the inner room, and closed the door behind him. Arrived, as he believed, in the chamber of execution, he paused again; then, raising his downcast eyes, he ventured to survey the scene before him. To his astonishment he discovered that the room was empty: no judge or executioner was there: he was absolutely alone.

I saw that he had found himself in a vast, dim chamber, so dim that it was difficult to distinguish the details of what was before him. Presently he made out that it was a royal apartment, magnificently appointed. A rich, warm carpet was beneath his bare feet, dark tapestries covered the walls, and light was admitted faintly through stained glass in the roof. Gradually he recognized that this was no place of execution; and, thereafter, one surprise crowded upon another before his astonished gaze. In the middle of the room was a table draped in purple; and there, indeed, lay the sword. But it was no sword of execution. Upon a silken cushion, in a golden scabbard, rested the great sword of state; and on other cushions on either side, were the crown and scepter. Then, as his eyes became accustomed to the dim light, the naked man saw, disposed in various parts of the room, all the raiment of a King. As is the way of dreams, he grasped without an effort the meaning of the discipline through which he had passed, and of the scene that lay before him. He had slain their King indeed, but had been purged of the horrible crime. Stripped and sent naked down the passage, he had left his old life and his former self behind him. And now he divined that he, the slayer of their King, had been chosen to fill the vacant throne.

One by one he assumed the robes of royalty. He lifted the heavy sword and girded it on; he set the Crown upon his head, and, taking the Orb and the Scepter in either hand, he passed out through the door by which—a doomed man—he had so lately entered. Once more he slowly passed down the passage, robed in all the habiliments of a King, and bearing the insignia of royalty. No longer was the passage empty. There, on each side, stood the chancellors and the great officers of state, all waiting to make due obeisance to the King of the Greater Land as he left his palace to show himself before his people, and to receive the acclamation of the waiting multitudes.

Professor Jung: To begin with, I would like to answer the question that Ms. Baumann asked me. Of course my remark[7] did not refer to the geometrical figure of the cross, which is universal. It can be found everywhere. But the specific meaning of *crux*, meaning "excruciation," is uniquely Western. The moment of the painful *transitus* is something completely atypical for the East. For the East, this is a natural development out of the earth, and does not have this peculiar sacrificial symbolism,[8] so to speak. That is something characteristic of the West. Insofar as the cross is a symbol of the ordeal, or represents an execution, it is typically Western in this sense.

As far as the dream is concerned, Ms. Baumann has made an important contribution by unearthing the identity of the source.[9] So he is also a member of our trade, he is a doctor. That's no coincidence. He is a doctor because he has to deal with suffering humankind. He gets in touch with suffering people, and his whole life consists of experiences with sufferers, which establishes a very close relationship with them. That is why many old doctors quite naturally develop some philosophy and are known for having their own views. This has always been so, also in the Middle Ages. These dreams of Dr. Hubbard are the fruit—as we can feel—of a life marked by human experience, not only the dream of the king, but also the other dreams. What immediately catches our eye in this dream?

Participant: The scale, the dimension.

Professor Jung: I was thinking of the structure.

---

[7] This refers to an incidental remark during the presentation.

[8] "Which refers to the Sacrifice of the Mass"—bracketed in the transcript.

[9] Jung dealt with this material initially during his first English seminar, at Sennen Cove, near Land's End, Cornwall, in the summer of 1920 (with "about twelve participants": see Gerhard Wehr, *Jung: A Biography* [Boston: Shambhala, 1987], 218). From Jung's comment here, it seems that until the later 1930s he knew only the writer's pseudonymous identity, "Peter Blobbs." To date, no record of this seminar has been found. William McGuire says of the seminar, "It was arranged by Constance Long, and its members included M. Esther Harding and H. Godwin Baynes—the three of them British physicians and early adherents of analytical psychology," adding that two further seminars, in 1923 at Polzeath, Cornwall, and in 1925 at Swanage, Dorset, both larger affairs, were the first recorded seminars of Jung. See *Dream Analysis: Notes of the Seminar Given in 1928–1930 by C. G. Jung* (London: Routledge, 1984), introduction, ix. See also Jung's brief summary of the swinging censer dream, and McGuire's note, in *Introduction to Jungian Psychology: Notes of the Seminar on Analytical Psychology Given in 1925 by C. G. Jung*, ed. McGuire and rev. ed. Sonu Shamdasani (Princeton, NJ: Princeton University Press, 2012), 67–68. On that summary, see footnote 11 below.

Participant: It is clear and distinct.

Professor Jung: What is this dream about?

Participant: It could almost be a story.

Professor Jung: But what kind of story?

Participant: It's about heroism, about the achievements of the hero.

Professor Jung: Yes, that is certainly the characteristic feature. And then something else immediately catches one's eye. What actually happens in these dreams? Didn't you notice anything regarding the question of opposites in these dreams? The swings of the ax and the censer already are enormous contrasts. To what can we refer this in the dreamer's life? When were these dreams dreamed? Well, on the eve of the great world war, on the eve of our present time. What do these opposites represent? In times when the whole difficulty of our time came to the fore?

Participant: A hubris of consciousness on the one side, and the unconscious on the other.

Professor Jung: That already leads us to an interpretation that is rather difficult to make. That's not easy at all. Theoretically speaking, these dreams are very difficult. No, what I mean is the following: at a time when there is an enormous conflict and the plot thickens, a certain tension arises in us, a prewar tension. The opposites are clearly visible all over the place.

Participant: The contrast between the people and the king.

Professor Jung: Yes, social contrasts, for example. This was in the air at that time. What can this bring about in the individual? What does it set in motion in the individual?

Participant: Either he identifies or he distances himself.

Professor Jung: When there is tension, people choose sides. But let us suppose somebody stands in between. What happens then?

Participant: An inner conflict begins.

Professor Jung: What will happen to you if you come under attack from both sides?

Participant: One has a conflict.

Professor Jung: All that is outside is within, as Goethe and Salomon Trismosin[10] say. When we're in such a situation, we are split into opposites ourselves. What would you call these opposites when they have an upper layer and a lower layer?

[10] Salomon Trismosin, the German sixteenth-century alchemist, author of the philosophical, illuminated *Splendor Solis* (1532–35) and probably the teacher of Paracelsus.

Participant: Culture and nature.

Professor Jung: What is primitive and deeply rooted on the one side, and what is civilized and well behaved on the other. Or, reasonableness is above, and what is unreasonable is beneath it, or, instinctuality and chaos are underneath, and the rational side is above. These are typical opposites that can lead to the greatest conflicts in the individual. All this gets mirrored in the individual. One cannot live undisturbed in such times; after a short while one is afflicted. When you're living in Europe these days, there's no way you can escape this influence, much as you may struggle against it. Even when you live far away in your corner, you yourself will mirror what has come to life over there. Well, these dreams come from that time full of tension, when nothing had yet erupted, nothing had happened. That was when they were dreamed, and that's why they contain these opposites. Then follow allusions to great, cataclysmic events.[11]

Now let's have a closer look at this dream of the king, or rather of the two countries at war with each other. Well, it's quite possible to have different opinions on what the larger and smaller countries represent. Here we can't refer them to something external, but must understand them as expressing a psychological state in which the dreamer was put under the influence of the outer situation at the time. Of necessity, therefore, the larger country must correspond to a larger part of the psyche. So that's the state we are dealing with, and the question now is: what do we call the larger part, and what the smaller one? Which part is greater?

Participant: The unconscious.

Professor Jung: Well, we don't know about the extension of the unconscious. But what would support that assumption?

Participant: The foretime of the ancestors. It lasted longer than the period since the development of consciousness.

Professor Jung: Yes. Since when can we reckon with greater consciousness?

Participant: Since the last five hundred years.

---

[11] This analysis is supplemented by Jung's earlier comment on the dream from his 1925 seminar: "This is an extremely fine demonstration of the movement of the unconscious. As day fades the unconscious is activated, and by midnight the censer is in full blaze, but lighting up the past. As the dynamic principle increases in power, and the further back we go, the more we are overcome by the unconscious." Shamdasani, *Introduction to Jungian Psychology: Notes of the Seminar on Analytical Psychology Given in 1925 by C. G. Jung*, 67.

Professor Jung: That's a pessimistic view.

Participant: Since the invention of writing.

Professor Jung: Yes, I always take the invention of writing as the criterion for when responsible consciousness came into existence. That's a particular period in the development of consciousness. It is decidedly the beginning of reflecting consciousness, not of consciousness itself, mind you. We must completely abandon the idea of finding out when that began. That goes way back to God knows when. But we may say that the beginning of writing shows the moment when reflection began. No other consciousness can justifiably be called human. There is an element in reflection, a divine element, so to speak, that elevates at least part of the human being out of the general "natural soup." When can we date that beginning?

Participant: In the Age of Taurus, 4500 BC.

Professor Jung: The oldest written monuments date back to 4200–4100 BC. The first texts in cuneiform writing and hieroglyphs are from about the same period. Since then, for about six thousand years, that is, we can speak of human consciousness. One may well think that this isn't such an enormous period of time. It is a relatively short span in the whole history of mankind. So we may say that we have come quite a considerable distance. But in view of what is perhaps still possible, or in view of the immense extension of the unconscious, it is probably very little. So if someone should say that our consciousness has not gotten anywhere yet, he may be right. In any case, I see infinite possibilities for human consciousness. We always think we have reached a certain level, but we are nowhere near the summit yet. So I would say that the unconscious constitutes the greater part. But what about the dreamer? For him, it's the other way around. For an Englishman and a doctor in prewar times, consciousness is greater. Once again we ask ourselves, where does the dreamer stand? Is he in the collective or in the individual?

Participant: Neither nor.

Professor Jung: So he is outside. So this belongs to his psychic perimeter.

Participant: And to the time. Both will be there in the unconscious.

Professor Jung: Yes, both of them are unconscious.

Participant: This often happens in the event of war.

Professor Jung: Yes, the dreamer travels into a country at war. What does it mean that he must cross many borders?

Participant: There are many obstacles.

Professor Jung: Many obstacles are in the way. He travels with a small suitcase.

Participant: He has no idea about the length and the difficulties of the journey.

Participant: The doctor keeps instruments in it.

Professor Jung: It's not unlikely that it's a medical kit.

Participant: He takes his personal belongings with him.

Professor Jung: Exactly. It's a small suitcase. One goes to the train station, one has to deal with pieces of baggage that are bound to tumble down, one is late. These dreams correspond to a state in which one is burdened with all kinds of complexes. Bags are impediments, obstacles, baggage. One drags along all kinds of complications. Now he, too, has got his pack of complications in his suitcase. These are his personal affairs that he carries with him, and he takes them rather lightly. This stands in contrast to neurotic dreams, in which someone is troubled by terrible baggage woes, the dreams of those who are still much too afflicted with their personal complexes. They are still attached to them. These are really impediments, whereas in our dream the dreamer has more or less mastered the common little problems. And I'd guess too that, having managed to carry all his complications in a little travel bag, he's a rather prudent man. Then it can begin. Then he can venture on the great journey into the collective unconscious, where a terrible war rages. Now what does this war mean?

Participant: The dichotomy.

Professor Jung: What kind of state reigns?

Participant: An active one.

Professor Jung: War has already begun. All hell has broken loose already. So the opposites jump at each other. As already mentioned, this can be entirely unconscious. I would assume that it is also unconscious in this case. Well, how is an unconscious conflict, of which the person is completely unaware, represented in dreams?

Participant: It is fought by animals.

Professor Jung: Yes, animals that devour each other.

Participant: This is the early Middle Ages.

Professor Jung: Think of Romanesque churches and the churches in Lombardy, where one animal eats up the other. Those people were not conscious of inner conflict. That's the way in dreams, too. I would suppose that the conflict occurring in this dream is a war between a greater and a lesser part of the unconscious. How are these two parts characterized? One has greater numbers, but is inferior in quality. The other is of superior quality, a higher type of man. Quality versus quantity. Now we come to the development of the hero. There is no indication that the representatives of quality would have a king. But then during the fight, one officer of great military prowess emerges. On the other hand, there is a king who dies in battle. How would you explain that?

Participant: The guiding idea is on the other side.

Participant: It's like a new dichotomy; those who have the numbers also have leadership.

Professor Jung: But how is it portrayed in the dream? What does the dream say about it? What about the side of the quantity people? They still have prehistoric customs, wear the dress of five hundred years ago, whereas their weapons are state of the art. A rigid traditionalism must reign where people are both barbaric and civilized in a kaleidoscopic way. We may assume, therefore, that this is an expression of traditionalism. Ms. von Franz has stated correctly that the king expresses the fact that the many without quality are held together by the One, the king, while the relatively few quality people on the other side lack a king because they possess quality. The individual has the moral responsibility. They can actually lead themselves and do not need a king. The king, the visible head, is necessary where quality does not suffice. Where quality suffices, there is no need for a king. It's simply a quite natural, psychical fact that unity is greatly needed with a huge crowd, while that stress on unity is superfluous where no such mass exists. Now we have to deal with the fact that a kind of unity emerges in fights involving those who do not unite, while this unity is killed on the other side where unity does exist.

Participant: It is the individual's task to discover unity.

Professor Jung: What quality does the king have?

Participant: A collective one.

Professor Jung: Yes, of course. He is the more or less coincidental center of the general lack of quality. In the other case, however, when the opponent comes from the other side and becomes king—who becomes king in that case?

Participant: The one who can really assert himself.

Participant: An optimum of individuality.

Professor Jung: He comes from the other side, and so has quality too. What wins out, therefore, is the quality principle. The quality principle has to confront quantity. It is of course the ideal condition when the head, the unity of those without quality, has what the others don't have. It's not simply that he is the center. It's like sugar and salt: salt in the one corner, sugar in the other. That's how opposites meet. What does this strange exchange happening here remind you of? You saw it. Ms. Baumann demonstrated it to you.

Participant: The Tai-gi-tu, the transformation of opposites.

Professor Jung: A white fish with a black eye, and a black fish with a white eye. Together they represent the movement of the world. One moment the one is above, the next moment the other. One always devours the other, that is, *yin*, the dark, female principle, devours *yang*, so that what is light, male, bright, and white, vanishes completely, so to speak. The *yin* has completely swallowed *yang*. In the hexagrams of the *I Ching* this is represented by six broken lines (Hexagram 2, Field).

In the Tai-gi-tu, the *yang* is a tiny dot at this stage, no longer visible from the outside, but at the center where *yin* predominates. The *Book of Changes* says about this situation (Hexagram 36, Hiding Brightness)

that the *yang* is nearest to the heart or head of darkness at that moment, and that it can take possession of darkness. If that's the case, darkness will collapse and we will have a full *yang*. This is shown by the fact that if you have a strong *yin* in the *I Ching*, a broken line, this strong *yin* will be stretched tight as seen from the outside, because it started as something divided, the two halves are drawn to each other. They have a tendency to close up; therefore we get a *yang* afterward in the changed line, whereas a weak *yin* is composed of two *yang* elements and one *yin* element. It is therefore weak and does not pull together. So here we don't have a change, but again a *yin*, because it doesn't come together. Conversely, if we have a nine, that is, a solid *yang* line with great tension because it holds together, it has the tendency to expand, then to snap, and to become a *yin* line in the next change. That's how prognoses are arrived at in the *I Ching*.[12]

This dream is about something very similar, that is, just as the *yin* is dark and female and much more besides, contrary to the *yang*, so are those without quality. Everything in the quantity types actually stands in contrast to the quality types. What is valuable in quantity is worthless in quality, and the other way round. And because these two should not be separated from each other, the two elements of the unconscious should, like *yang* and *yin*, cooperate in order to achieve something in common. This is a fierce fight between opposites, and it has to be fought. So my assumption would be that Dr. Hubbard travels with his personal baggage into the unconscious, arrives there, and discovers the real facts—namely, that the unconscious consists of two completely different principles. A process of unification is about to happen, in which the quantity types—let's call them the black principle—have conquered the white principle. And the white, shrunk to a little dot, has been taken prisoner by the black. In this state, the truly immense transformation occurs: all of a sudden, what is least, last, and apparently doomed reappears at the summit of things, overcomes anything black, and changes it into a realm of light.

Participant: I'd like to ask what it means that such strong political and historical overtones are in play here, and why it's not natural principles that stand opposed to each other?

Professor Jung: That's due to the fact that we don't have any concrete image for this in religion and philosophy. A Westerner, however, whose whole nomenclature and terminology, whose whole vocabulary of con-

[12] Cf. *I Ching, The Book of Changes*, at that time as edited with commentary by Jung's friend, the sinologist Richard Wilhelm. Jung later supplied a foreword to the Cary Baynes translation of Wilhelm (2nd ed., 1961). The strong yin has the value six, and the weak yin eight.

cepts is so completely different, has to express it in the language at his disposal: kingdom, democracy, etc.

AT A LATER MEETING OF THE SEMINAR

Professor Jung: Last time we saw that this dream is about the regulation of opposites in the unconscious, which cannot be attributed to the dreamer himself. We have to assume that our dear fellow Dr. Hubbard, living when he did, was not aware that the unconscious is a fact of life, but had a more or less naive attitude toward these things, and a merely intuitive notion of the importance of such dreams. In any case, he would have been hard-pressed to tell us why these dreams are especially important. The most probable assumption, therefore, is that in essence these dream events unfolded unconsciously. It's a regulation of opposites, not in consciousness, but between two unconscious principles. Our best analogy would be the principles of Chinese philosophy, that is, a positive and a negative principle, *yang* and *yin*. Naturally, however, such a dream doesn't usually occur without the participation of the subject, for the dream occurs within him and affects him, after all. In general, therefore, a certain involvement of the subject is found in such dreams, which is also the case in this dream. The danger then arises that the ego gets involved in the unconscious mechanism, and what is the natural consequence?

Participant: An identification with the hero.

Professor Jung: Yes, with what consequences for consciousness?

Participant: An inflation.

Professor Jung: Surely, by all means an inflation. In any case the hero is an *Übermensch*, and when the ego identifies with him, an inordinate aggrandizement of the ego will ensue. It gets completely swallowed up by him and consequently becomes unreal. How does this manifest itself?

Participant: In megalomania.

Professor Jung: Yes, how else?

Participant: In schizophrenia.

Professor Jung: Yes, if it goes completely wrong. That is a special case . . . but what else?

Participant: Physical complaints, because one is not living on the ground.

Professor Jung: It is a physiological phenomenon, such that the relation between psyche and body is so seriously disturbed that phenomena in the sympathetic nervous system develop. What I mean, however, are not physiological phenomena, but psychic ones, symptoms of inflation. Please don't get lost in the interplay of the unconscious opposites, because you'll instantly go gaga. What other symptom is there?

Participant: Lack of human contact.

Professor Jung: Surely, by all means, yes. Because when I am the Savior, you can kiss my ass.

Participant: The ego is not separated from the emotions.

Professor Jung: The very fact that you use so many words proves that you are not answering my question. Well, what else does one have besides megalomania?

Participant: Feelings of insecurity.

Participant: Inferiority feelings.

Professor Jung: Yes, instead of megalomania one has "micromania." Inferiority feelings are typical characteristics of inflation. There are these tiny, tame, and inconspicuous little mice, and they tyrannize the world. They suffer accordingly, and everybody must suffer from this inflation along with them. For one can also have a negative inflation, so that one nearly bursts with inferiority feelings. One has to steer clear of these people, as if they were the Pope himself. They have inferiority feelings, and the whole world has to bow down, because otherwise the poor creature is hurt, just imagine! Inferiority feelings are just as exacting as megalomania.

As far as identification with the role of the hero is concerned or, even more, with the divine role, one doesn't need to have schizophrenia to feel like a hero. One can let it simmer on one's private stove, until one day it comes to light that one is the Messiah. One has terrible feelings of inferiority and consoles oneself at home with the idea that one day it will become apparent what an incredible guy one is. For the very small and the very big stand in relation to each other. It's all the same.

So when these opposites do not touch consciousness, there will be possession. When someone is infected with the hero's role, he'll be possessed by it. Dr. Hubbard is not possessed, so there is hardly any evidence that he is identified with this hero figure. That he likes it, that he thinks deep down in his heart: I am the hero—well, I'd like to see someone who could escape such influence. A little of that exits in all of us, of course.

Ms. Baumann has already cued me to the fact that the next dream concerns the problem that he should not identify, because he dreams that he produces and recites a poem, and comments that at first he did not quite understand it himself. In this hymn he praises the sun, rising and setting in all its glory, but the voice of omniscience says, things are not so. It is you, not the sun, who is moving. So a distinction is made between him and the sun. He is taught that the sun is standing still and that *he* is moving, that by no means is he like the sun. This dream indeed differentiates him from the sun. Now, we know that the hero is always the sun. You can find the solar attributes of the hero in countless myths.

Well, this case, in which something is happening in the unconscious, and something very decisive to boot, a conflict between opposites and a unification of opposites, without the participation of consciousness—this case is a special case, a bit out of the ordinary. But there are numerous cases like this one, not only in dreams, for we also have literary documents from movements in intellectual history in which opposites were perceived through introspection, where the processes of transformation were intuitively perceived by consciousness. Alchemy, for example, is such a field. There we find stories, so-called allegories or parables, that contain this motif of inner transformation, in which the dreamer himself does not actually participate. There is also a very good example in the writings of Count Bernhard of Treviso, called Trevisanus. I have brought with me an old German translation by Tanck. The Latin text is more complete, but the translation will do. The idea is that he goes into a city in India where a powerful and learned man, obviously a prince, has offered a prize for the winner in a philosophical disputation. He goes there and wins the prize. After the disputation he is tired and says,

Exhausted by mental effort, I went in search of beautiful fields and meadows to recuperate, and accidentally came across a crystal-clear little fountain [spring], which was walled in by a magnificent stone to protect it—above it the stump of an oak tree; everything else was enclosed by a wall, so that no animals could approach and no birds could bathe in it. . . . Then an old, highly dignified man of priestly appearance approached. I greeted him reverently and asked why this fountain was so . . . enclosed and protected on all sides. And he answered in a friendly manner, saying: "You must know, my friend, that this fountain possesses an extremely peculiar and terrible power—more than any other fountain in the world. It belongs solely to the king of this country; the fountain knows him best, and he the fountain. When the king passes by, it always attracts him, but it itself is not attracted by the king. In this bath he remains for 282 days, during which he is rejuvenated to such an extent that he can no longer be defeated even by the strongest man."[13]

So Trevisanus went for a walk and came to this fountain. The king goes into the *fontina*[14] and stays there for 282 days. In that bath he is dissolved into his atoms. The fountain puts him back together, and he steps out of it rejuvenated. He is dissolved in the fountain in order to be transformed into an immortal human being.

What is described here, that is, what Trevisanus sees, is a process that happens again and again. When dawn broke, this fantasy occurred to him, as if he had peered into something within. The king is the father of the father, the father of the mother. Both are *prima materia*. It is a completely paradoxical story. Just as an Egyptian king is called the father of his mother, or the bull of his mother, so this king, too, stands in a reciprocal relationship to his mother fountain, in which he revitalizes himself. Every now and then this process repeats itself. Simply by virtue of having seen it, the philosopher is involved in any case, whether present or not.

A similar story can be found in the visions of Zosimos.[15] There Zosimos sees an altar that has fifteen steps. A priest completes the descent down those fifteen steps into darkness, and then climbs up again. There is a spring in which he is spiritualized. The priest tells him that someone came early in the morning, pierced him with the sword, and

[13] J. J. Manget, *Bibliotheca Chemica Curiosa*, vol. 2 (Geneva, 1702), 388–91 (G).
[14] Latin: little fountain.
[15] The following vision also is dealt with in CW 13, paras. 85ff.

expertly dismembered him. It is a quartering, in which all extremities are chopped off. The fifth part is the head, and it is the *quinta essentia.*[16] Then the body is transformed and "has turned into a spirit." And while the priest was still explaining this to him, Zosimos saw that the priest's eyes became like blood and that he spat out all of his flesh. He turned into a homunculus who had lost a part of himself, a mutilated little man. With his own teeth he mauled himself and collapsed into himself. The text is in poor repair and therefore not entirely clear. But the idea is simply as follows: first of all, the transformation process consists in this priest's being boiled or burned in the fire, so that he is transformed. He is also the actor, performing it on himself; he eats himself up and then spits himself out. This idea is expressed in more detail in the ouroboros, the snake that eats itself up beginning with the tail, transforms itself, and then gives birth to itself again. So the stereotypical phrase runs, "the ouroboros that marries, impregnates, and kills itself, and rises again out of itself," and this in the form of a bird, for instance, the Phoenix: his ashes turn into a snake, and the snake turns into a bird again. This is one version of the king myth; the motif of opposites devouring each other is plentiful in alchemy.

So these dreams are very important in theory, but in practice they are important only if we succeed in explaining such a dream to someone— and in most cases this is very difficult, because we all have the prejudice that dreams deal only with our personal psychology. We are the center of the world, you know. That's why we are so hard put, particularly in the case of intelligent people, to make this clear. I don't know if I would have succeeded in explaining to Dr. Hubbard what his dream actually meant. These matters immediately come into conflict with one's worldview. For the true Catholic, for example, such dreams don't exist at all; they simply cannot exist. The conflict between the opposites doesn't take place on earth; it is a metaphysical phenomenon. It is the dichotomy between Christ and the devil. It does not take place within myself. He will readily accept it when I tell him that the devil is quantity and the good is quality. But with that move, the whole problem has been translated into metaphysics, and he may suppose that it is a revelation, a dream sent by God, informing him about the mystery. If he is not

[16] Latin: literally, the fifth essence or substance = quintessence.

a Catholic, the person in question—be he a Jew, pagan, Muslim, or a Protestant—will be very inclined to assume that the dream, if it makes sense at all, will mean something personal. But psychology is by no means only personal. A very large part of it is not personal. The unconscious has its own laws, and so things can happen autonomously. Naturally, we are very much influenced by it. It's like a cosmic interference. We are helped or harmed as if by a cosmic or meteorological catastrophe.

Participant: So when thunderstorms appear in dreams, can we also then say that it's impersonal?

Professor Jung: If it's a real thunderstorm, we may draw the conclusion that it refers to emotions of an archetypal nature, not personal, which reach far into the instinctual sphere, in which, as we know, we are not personal. So, for instance, we are not personal in the way our liver or kidneys function. You can't prove your identity with the help of your personal urine, that's impossible.

Participant: But there may exist a connection with conflicts.

Professor Jung: It can stir up personal conflicts, but usually in a way that has the conflicts behave like chickens—when it's dark, they go into the henhouse—or like cats that leave the house before the storm. There are personal interferences.

Participant: Do you think that the dreams had no influence on the life of Dr. Hubbard?

Professor Jung: Why of course, and very much so! But not in a personal way. You can't file a claim for damages because of a collision between the moon and the sun.

Participant: What is the collective problem? There still comes the last dream, in which the king is found dead. It happens during the fight. A group of soldiers wants to make ready to flee; the fight has been lost. Then they learn that the king is missing. They ride along with a peasant who claims to have seen the king. They find him dead, take flight in order to rescue survivors, and leave the dead king lying there. Strangely enough, the peasant becomes the leader after the king's death.

Professor Jung: All this belongs to the same motif, that it is always the king of the quantity people who gets killed; and this will probably go on in just that way. It is the execution or annihilation of the principle.

Participant: I wondered why this dream is so abstract. One has no idea which principle it is.

Professor Jung: Because it is the Self.

Participant: Historically speaking, it's a specific king.

Professor Jung: If Dr. Hubbard had dreamed that the English had lost their king, it wouldn't have been much off the mark.

Now let us turn to one last point, the principal meaning of the king as the unifier of heaven and earth. This is, if you will, a cross symbolism, but the word *cross* has too specific a meaning. Linked with this symbol also, however, is the idea of the *transitus*,[17] of a very painful bearing of loads, a burdensome crossing over. This is the ordeal of portage, like the carrying of the bull in the Mithras cult. These are *transitus* symbols. All this is expressed by this or similar figures. It is the idea of the gem and perfection. We find similar symbols everywhere here, owing to the fact that the hero's role always represents an unbreakable coherence. It is an archetype, always embedded in something convoluted, in overlapping ideas. You will never be able to disentangle an archetype. It is always interwoven in a carpet of related ideas, which lead ever further toward other archetypal formations, which constantly overlap and together knit the wondrous carpet of life.

Participant: The symbol of the double-headed ax appears. Why not a different one?

Professor Jung: It is a bit unusual. But we must bear in mind that this is a learned man. The double-headed ax is a magical object that plays a great role especially in Cretan and Mycenaean cultures.

Participant: There it is matriarchal.

Professor Jung: Of course, these symbols are matriarchal symbols, but the double-headed ax also played a role later on, for example, as an executioner's ax, and also as a weapon in general. Thus I would not dare to read something special into it.

Participant: And the symbolism of the cross?

Professor Jung: We can't discuss this; it would lead too far. We'd have to view it from the king's standpoint, but that would lead much too far.

Participant: I find it strange that the whole first dream occurs in a cathedral full of incense. The whole problem of the opposites takes place in a specific place, in a dogmatic construct. The question is whether he is able to grasp the problem of time.

---

[17] Latin: passage, crossing, transition.

Professor Jung: But it's a very peculiar cathedral; this is the sanctified chamber in which the unification of opposites takes place.

Participant: There is incense, used in exorcism; there is no room for the devil in it.

Professor Jung: The devil appears nowhere in the whole account; at most, the censer itself might be devilish. In any case, we must not go beyond the dream. I don't want to make too much of it. We don't know the man, as things stand. We would have to have more material.

At a Later Meeting of the Seminar

Participant: Didn't you give a completely different portrayal of the dream last time than Ms. Baumann?

Professor Jung: Of course I introduced certain variations. The only point is that I'm not of the opinion that the swinging between pairs of opposites is connected to consciousness, so to speak. In my view, the conflict essentially takes place in the unconscious. That was the main point of the difference. And as far as the functions[18] are concerned, that is a hypothesis. One may raise the question of whether the types play a role, but I was tactful enough not to state that the quality people were the introverts, and the others the extraverts. So why don't you just let me be tactful!

As far as becoming conscious of the opposites is concerned, we don't know how that actually happens. We can only deduce it from certain symbols. So, for example, if someone suffers from a psychical stomach-ache, so that it somehow rumbles in his psychic belly, that can mean anything. When we ask him what's the matter, he answers, "I have no idea." To which I say, "Let's hope you have a dream." Then comes the following dream: The person in question goes for a walk (this is an actual dream, not my invention—the dreamer is a natural scientist), he comes to Mount Vesuvius. Rushes grow around the lake, but the water is very calm and deep between the roots of the rushes. All of a

[18] This refers to the general psychological types of introversion and extraversion, as well as the function-types; cf. C. G. Jung, CW 6, paras. 631ff. (G).

sudden he notices a movement in the water. A fat little minicrocodile comes swimming along, very fat and very well fed, and now there comes another being bouncing round the other corner, a little nixie. She is extremely fat, a very plump nixie. And at that moment he knows intuitively, "Ah, there are those who always eat each other, and that's why they are so fat; this means that there are many little crocodiles and nixies that eat each other up and thus get fat." Then he wakes up in great confusion, as if he had discovered a great secret. So the dream gives the following answer to the question: the nixies eat up the crocodiles, and the crocodiles the nixies. Both are water animals. The one is the crocodile, a saurian, a highly unconscious being, and so is the nixie, a soulless being, as we know, half animal and half human. One mythical creature eats an ordinary animal, but neither of them is entirely ordinary but reduced in size and small; they are so little that eating each other up can take place in a small zone inside. It is inconspicuous; nobody has discovered it. The dreamer himself has never seen such a thing. The whole thing is microscopic. One has to pay close attention to notice it. That is also the reason why the enormous giant, who carries the world, is a Tom Thumb, because he is an unconscious quantity. Nobody had any idea that a fight is going on in the calm waters between little nixies and crocodiles; that is the unconscious play of opposites.

From then on I knew, Aha, a drama has started in the unconscious. This mutual devouring has been going on for a long time already, as in the case of the lions that got into a store and were eating for weeks, and because the store was so big that no one noticed it. That's what happened in this case, and one could base a prognosis on it: something is bound to happen after a while, the conflict will grow, gradually become conscious, and seize the ego. Naturally, this dream is quite different from that of Dr. Hubbard. The doctor's conflict has already risen high, but is not yet conscious. It is still expressed mythologically. Do you know the parallel to those little crocodiles and nixies? It is the ouroboros, the winged and unwinged snakes that always fight against each other, or the winged and unwinged lion.[19] So these are the opposites that fight each other in the unconscious.

[19] Cf. the illustrations in C. G. Jung, *Psychology and Alchemy*, CW 13, e.g., illustrations 46 and 47 (G).

Participant: There is a parallel: the story of the singing, springing lark.[20] The lion prince disappears. His bride goes in search of him. Finally she finds him far, far away, overseas; there a lion fights with a serpent. The latter turns out to be another lover of the lion prince, the daughter of a sorcerer.

Participant: Perhaps the fact that there is no anima figure in the dream is proof that the relation between consciousness and the unconscious is missing?

Professor Jung: You are quite right. Wherever there is an anima figure, we may assume that a relational function is constellated. In a man, the anima is always a relational function. It is typical that no anima figure appears in Dr. Hubbard. From this we may conclude that the relation is missing, and it is indeed missing. In other places, where relations exist, anima figures can usually be found too. You see, that's the relation with the unconscious, and there is also a classical example.

Participant: Dante and Beatrice.

Participant: Helen in *Faust*.

Professor Jung: Yes, it already begins with the Greeks. The whole process is such a mystery.

Participant: Athene is the anima of God the Father.

Participant: Spitteler.

Professor Jung: Yes, and how! The Mistress Soul. And I know of still another example, *The Shepherd of Hermas*.

---

[20] A Brothers Grimm folktale, no. 88 ("The Lilting, Leaping Lark") (G). Grimm's Tales for Young and Old, trans. Ralph Manheim (London: Gollancz, 1977), 301.

- Bibliography -

Angulo, Jaime de. *Jaime in Taos: The Taos Papers of Jaime de Angulo*. Compiled with a biographical introduction by Gui de Angulo. San Francisco: City Lights Books, 1985.

Apuleius. *The Metamorphoses of Lucius Apuleius of Madaura; or, The Golden Ass*. Translated by Richard Adlington [1566]. Cambridge, MA: Harvard University Press, 1915. *The Transformations of Lucius, Otherwise Known as the Golden Ass*. Translated by Robert Graves. Harmondsworth: Penguin, 1950.

Aristotle. *Aristotle's Poetics: A Translation and Commentary for Students of Literature*. Translated by Leon Golden. Commentary by O. B. Hardison. Englewood Cliffs, NJ: Prentice-Hall, 1968.

Aurigemma, Luigi. *Jungian Perspectives*. Translated by Craig Stephenson. Scranton: University of Scranton Press, 2008 [1989].

Bash, Kenover W. "Gestalt, Symbol, und Archetypus." *Schweizerische Zeitschrift fur Psychologie* 5 (1946): 127–38.

Bergson, H. "Le rêve." (a) Bulletin de *l'Institut générale. psychologique* (1901, Ire année), 103–22; (b) *Revye. Scientifique* 4e s. XV (June 8, 1901), 703–13. Also in *L'Energie spirituelle*. Reprint; Paris: Presses Universitaires de France, 1940 (1919).

Bernays, Jakob. *Grundzüge der verlorenen Abhandlung des Aristoteles über Wirkung der Tragödie*. Hildesheim and New York: Goerg Olms Verlag, 1970 (1858). Reprinted by Bernays as *Zwei Abhandlungen über die Aristotelische Theorie des Dramas*, 1880.

Bishop, Paul. *The Dionysian Self: Jung's Reception of Friedrich Nietzsche*. Berlin and New York: De Gruyter, 1995.

———. *Reading Goethe at Midlife: Ancient Wisdom, German Classicism, and Jung*. New Orleans: Spring Journal Books, 2011.

Bluhm, Amy. "An Introduction to Carol Sawyer Baumann (1897–1958)." *Jung History* 1 (Winter 2005–6): 16–19.

Bowker, John. *The Oxford Dictionary of World Religions*. New York: Oxford University Press, 1997.

Bregman, A. J. *Synesius of Cyrene, Philosopher-Bishop*. Berkeley: University of California Press, 1982.

Cambray, Joseph. "The Place of the 17th Century in Jung's Encounter with China" (on Leibniz and supervenience). *Journal of Analytical Psychology* 50, no. 2 (2005).

———. *Synchronicity: Nature and Psyche in an Interconnected Universe*. College Station: Texas A&M University Press, 2009.

Cardano, Girolamo. *Des Girolamo Cardano von Mailand eigene Lebensbeschreibung*. Translated from Latin by Herman Hefele. Jena: Eugen Diederichs Verlag, 1914; 2nd ed. Munich, 1969.

———. *De propria vita: The Book of My Life*. Translated by Jean Stoner. Toronto: J. M. Dent and Sons, 1931.http://dictionary.sensagent.com/Hermann_Hefele/de-de/

Cicero. *De Re Publica*. Edited and translated by James Zetzel. Cambridge: Cambridge University Press, 1995.

————. *Somniorum Synesiorum, omnis generis insomnia explicantes libri IV.* Basel: Sebastianum Henriepetri, 1562, 1585. As in: Cardano. *Opera Omnia V.* Lyon: C. Spon, 1663. Repr. Johnson Reprint Corp., introd. August Buck, 1967.

————. *Tusculan Disputations.* Edited and translated by A. E. Douglas. Warminster: Aris and Phillips, 1985.

Colonna, Francesco. *Hypnerotomachia Poliphili...* (1499). *Le songe de Poliphile ou hypnerotomachie de frère F. C.* (1883). *Hypnerotomachia Poliphili, the Strife of Love in a Dream.* Translated by Jocelyn Godwin. London: Thames and Hudson, 1999.

Craik, Elizabeth, "Tragedy as Treatment: Medical Analogies in Aristotle's *Poetics.*" In *Dionysalexandros: Essays on Aeschylus and His Fellow Tragedians,* edited by Douglas Cairns and Vayos Liapis, 283–99. Swansea: Classical Press of Wales, 2007.

Davis, Michael. *Aristotle's Poetics: The Poetry of Philosophy.* Lanham, MD: Rowman and Littlefield, 1992.

Delage, Yves. *Le Rêve: Étude psychologique, philosophique et littéraire.* Nantes: Imprimerie du Commerce, 1920.

Deussen, P. *Die Geheimlehre des Veda.* Leipzig: Brockhaus, 1907.

Driesch, Hans. *The Science and Philosophy of the Organism.* 2nd ed. London: A. and C. Black, 1929 (resp. vol. 2 of the 1st ed., 1908; both in the author's English).

Dronke, Peter. *Women Writers of the Middle Ages: A Critical Study of Texts from Perpetua to Marguerte of Porete.* Cambridge: Cambridge University Press, 1984.

Dunne, J. W. *An Experiment with Time.* Newburyport: Hampton Roads Publishing, 2001 (1927).

Durkheim, Émile. "Origine de la pensée religieuse." *Revue Philosophique* (January 1909).

Erskine, J. Adam, and Eve Erskine. *Though He Knew Better.* Indianapolis: Bobbs-Merrill, 1927. Reprinted in 2003.

Facos, Michele. *Symbolist Art in Context.* Berkeley: University of California Press, 2009.

Fierz-David, Linda. *The Dream of Poliphilo: The Soul in Love.* Bollingen Series 25. New York: Pantheon, 1950. Reprint; Dallas: Spring, 1987.

————. *Women's Dionysian Initiation: The Villa of Mysteries in Pompeii.* Translated by Gladys Phelan. Dallas: Spring, 1988. Reprinted with additional chapters by Nor Hall, in *Dreaming in Red: The Women's Dionysian Initiation Chamber in Pompeii.* Putnam, CT: Spring, 2005

Flaubert, Gustave. *The Temptation of St. Anthony.* New York: Random House, 2002 (Paris, 1874).

Flammarion, Camille. *L'inconnu et les problèmes psychiques.* Paris: E. Flammarion, 1900.

Foucault, Marcel. "L'évolution de rêve pendant le sommeil." *Revue Philosophique* 57 (1904): 459–81.

————. *Le rêve: Études et observations.* Paris: F. Alcan, 1906.

Franz, Marie-Louise von. *Number and Time: Reflections Leading toward a Unification of Depth Psychology and Physics.* Translated by Andrea Dykes. Evanston, IL: Northwestern University Press, 1974.

————. *Die Passio Perpetuae.* In C. G. Jung, *Aion, Untersuchungen zur Symbolgeschichte,* part 2. Zurich, 1951. *The Passion of Perpetua.* Translated by Elizabeth Welsh, 1949. Dallas: Spring, 1980. *Die Passion der Perpetua: Eine Frau zwischen zwei Gottesbildern.* Einsiedeln: Daimon Verlag, 1982.

Freud, Sigmund. *The Interpretation of Dreams.* Translated by A. A. Brill. New York: Random House, 1950.

Golden, Leon, and O. B. Hardison Jr. *Aristotle's Poetics: A Translation and Commentary for Students of Literature*. Englewood Cliffs, NJ: Prentice-Hall, 1968.

Globus, Gordon. *Dream Life, Wake Life: The Human Condition through Dreaming*. Albany: State University of New York Press, 1987.

Goethe, Johann Wolfgang von. *Faust, Part I*. Translated by David Constantine. London: Penguin, 2005. *Faust, Part II*. Translated by David Constantine. London: Penguin, 2009.

———. *Faust*. Herausgegeben u. kommentiert von Erich Trunz. Munich: C. H. Beck Verlag, 1989.

———. *Wilhelm Meister's Apprenticeship*. Translated by Thomas Carlyle. Edinburgh: Oliver and Boyd, 1824.

———. *Wilhelm Meister's Lehrjahr* (1795–56). *Goethe's Wilhelm Meister's Travels: Translation of the First Edition by Thomas Carlyle*. Columbia, SC: Camden House, 1991.

Goldenwieser, Alexander. *Early Civilization: An Introduction to Anthropology*. New York: Knopf, 1922.

Grafton, Anthony. *Cardano's Cosmos: The Worlds and Works of a Renaissance Astrologer*. Cambridge, MA: Harvard University Press, 1999.

Grimm, Brothers. *Grimm's Tales for Young and Old*. Translated by Ralph Manheim. London: Gollancz, 1977.

Grutzmacher, Georg. *Synesios von Kyrene: ein Charachterbild aus dem Untergang des Hellenentums*. Leipzig: Deichert'sche Verlags buchhandlung, 1913.

Gurney, Edmund, F.W.H. Myers, and Frank Podmore. *Phantasms of the Living*. 2 vols. London: Truebner, and Society for Psychical Research, 1886 (1918; reprint 2010).

Halliwell, Stephen. "Aristotelian Mimesis Reevaluated." In *Aristotle: Critical Assessments*. Vol. 4, *Politics, Rhetoric, Aesthetics*, edited by Lloyd Gerson. London: Routledge, 1999.

Hannah, Barbara. *Encounters with the Soul: Active Imagination as Developed by C. G. Jung*. Boston: Sigo, 1981. Reprint; Wilmette, IL: Chiron, 2001.

Hartmann, Eduard von. *Philosophie des Unbewußten*. Berlin, 1869 (11th ed., 1904).

Haule, John. *Jung in the 21st Century*. Vol. 1, *Evolution and Archetype*. Vol. 2, *Synchronicity and Science*. London: Routledge, 2011.

Heerwagen, F. "Statistische Untersuchungen über Träume und Schlaf." *Philosophische Studien* 5 (1888): 301–20.

Henderson, Joseph. *Thresholds of Initiation*. Middletown, CT: Wesleyan University Press, 1967.

Hermae Pastor [Shepherd of Hermas]. *Graece add. vers. Lat. Recens*. Edited by O. de Gebhardt and A. Harnack [Patrum apostolicorum opera, fasc. III]. Leipzig, 1877.

Hildegard, Saint. *The Letters of Hildegard of Bingen*. Vol. 1, edited and translated by Joseph L. Baird and Radd K. Ehrman. New York: Oxford University Press, 1994.

Hillman, James. "Responses" [to David Griffin]. In *Archetypal Process: Self and Divine in Whitehead, Jung, and Hillman*, edited by David Ray Griffin. Evanston, IL: Northwestern University Press, 1989.

Hubbard, Arthur John. *Authentic Dreams of Peter Blobbs, M.D. Dunelm, L.R.C.P. London, M.R.C.S. Eno, L.S.A. London, and of Certain of His Relatives, Told by Himself with the Assistance of Mrs Blobbs*. London: Longmans, Green, 1916.

———. *The Fate of Empires: Being an Inquiry into the Stability of Civilisation*. London: Longmans, Green, 1913.

I Ching, The Book of Changes, 2nd ed. Edited by Richard Wilhelm. Translated by Cary F. Baynes. Foreword by C. G. Jung. Princeton, NJ: Princeton University Press, 1961.

Janet, Pierre. *L'automatisme psychologique*. Paris: F. Alcan, 1899.

Jung, C. G. *Aion: Researches into the Phenomenology of the Self*. 2nd ed. Translated by R.F.C. Hull. CW 9.ii. Princeton, NJ: Princeton University Press, 1959.

———. *Analytical Psychology: Notes of the Seminar Given in 1925 by C. G. Jung*. Edited by William McGuire. Princeton, NJ: Princeton University Press, 1989.

———. "Archetypes of the Collective Unconscious," 1934/1954. In *The Archetypes and the Collective Unconscious*. 2nd ed. Translated by R.F.C. Hull. CW 9/i. Princeton, NJ: Princeton University Press, 1969.

———. "Child Development and Education," 1923. In *The Development of Personality*. CW 17. Translated by R.F.C. Hull. Princeton, NJ: Princeton University Press, 1954.

———. "Comments on a Doctoral Thesis" [1952]. In *C. G. Jung Speaking: Interviews and Encounters*, edited by William McGuire and R.F.C. Hull, 207, 211. Princeton, NJ: Princeton University Press, 1977.

———. *Dream Analysis: Notes of the Seminar Given in 1928–1930 by C. G. Jung*. Edited by William McGuire. London: Routledge and Kegan Paul; Princeton, NJ: Princeton University Press, 1984.

———. *Introduction to Jungian Psychology: Notes of the Seminar on Analytical Psychology Given in 1925*. Edited by William McGuire. Revised and with a new introduction by Sonu Shamdasani. Princeton, NJ: Princeton University Press, 2012 (1989).

———. *Liber Novus* [The Red Book]. Edited by Sonu Shamdasani. Translated by Mark Kyburz, John Peck, and Sonu Shamdasani. New York: W. W. Norton, 2009.

———. *Memories, Dreams, Reflections*. Recorded and edited by Aniela Jaffé. Translated by Richard and Clara Winston. New York: Pantheon, 1963.

———. "The Phenomenology of Spirit in Fairytales" (1945, 1948). CW 9.i. Princeton, NJ: Princeton University Press, 2nd ed., 1968.

———. "The Practical Use of Dream Analysis," 1934. In *The Practice of Psychotherapy*, 2nd ed. Translated by R.F.C. Hull. CW 16. Princeton, NJ: Princeton University Press, 1966.

———. *Psychologische Typen*. Zurich: Rascher, 1921. CW 6. Translated by H. G. Baynes (1923). *Psychological Types*. A revision by R.F.C. Hull of the translation by H. G. Baynes. Princeton, NJ: Princeton University Press, 1971.

———. "A Radio Talk in Munich," 1930. In *The Symbolic Life: Miscellaneous Writings*. CW 18. Translated by R.F.C. Hull. Princeton, NJ: Princeton University Press, 1976.

———. *Seminar Kinderträume: Zur Methodik der Träuminterpretation—Psychologische Interpretation von Kinderträumen*. Edited by Lorenz Jung and Maria Meyer-Grass. Düsseldorf: Walter-Verlag, 1987; Zurich: Patmos Verlag, 2001.

———. *The Structure and Dynamics of the Psyche* ("On the Nature of the Psyche," 1954). CW 8, 2nd ed. Translated by R.F.C. Hull. Princeton, NJ: Princeton University Press, 1969.

———. "A Study in the Process of Individuation" (1933, 1950), 2nd ed. Translated by R.F.C. Hull. CW 9.i. Princeton, NJ: Princeton University Press, 1968.

———. "The Symbolism of the Mandala." In *Psychology and Alchemy* [1943; 1935–36], 2nd ed. Translated by R.F.C. Hull. CW 12. Princeton, NJ: Princeton University Press, 1968.

————. "Theoretical Reflections on the Nature of the Psychical." CW 8, 2nd ed. Princeton, NJ: Princeton University Press, 1969.

————. *Two Essays on Analytical Psychology* ("On the Psychology of the Unconscious," "The Relations between the Ego and the Unconscious") (1916–43). CW 7. Princeton, NJ: Princeton University Press, 1996 (1953).

————. *Visions: Notes of the Seminar Given in 1930–1934*, vol. 2. Edited by Claire Douglas. Princeton, NJ: Princeton University Press, 1997.

————. "The Visions of Zosimos," 1937. In *Alchemical Studies*. Translated by R.F.C. Hull. CW 13. Princeton, NJ: Princeton University Press, 1967.

————. *Wandlungen und Symbole der Libido*. Zurich: Rascher, 1925. *Symbols of Transformation*, 2nd ed. Translated by R.F.C. Hull. CW 5. Princeton, NJ: Princeton University Press, 1967 (1956).

————. "Zur Empirie des Individuationsprozess." GW Bd. 9/I. Düsseldorf: Patmos/Walter Verlag, 2006 (1995).

————. "Zwei Schriften über Analytische Psychologie." GW Bd. 7. Düsseldorf: Patmos/Walter Verlag, 2006 (1995).

Lapique, L. "Principe pour une théorie de fonctionnement nevreux élémentaire." *Revue Générale Scientifique* 21, no. 3 (1910): 103–17.

Le Blant, Edmond. *Artémidore*. Paris: Editions Klincksieck, 1899.

Leeds-Hurwitz, Wendy. *Rolling in Ditches with Shamans: Jaime de Angulo and the Professionalization of American Anthropology*. Lincoln: University of Nebraska Press, 2004.

Lersch, Philipp. *Der Traum in der deutschen Romantik*. Munich: Hueber Verlag, 1923.

Lévy-Bruhl, Lucien. *La mythologie primitive*. Paris: 1935. *Primitive Mythology*. Translated by Brian Elliott. Saint Lucia: University of Queensland Press, 1983.

Lincoln, Jackson Steward. *The Dream in Primitive Cultures*. Introduction by C. G. Seligman. London: Cresset Press, 1935.

Littmann, Mark. *The Heavens on Fire: The Great Leonid Meteor Storms*. Cambridge: Cambridge University Press, 1998.

Macrobius, Ambrosius Aurelius Theodosius. *Commentary on the Dream of Scipio by Macrobius*. Translated and introduction by William Harris Stahl. New York: Columbia University Press, 1990 (1952).

————. *In Somnium Scipionis*. In *Macrobe, Varron et Pomponius Méla*. Translated by D. Nisard. Edited by M. Nisard. Paris: Dubochet, Le Chevalier, and Garnier, 1883 (1850).

Mangetus, J. J. *Bibliotheca Chemica Curiosa*. Vol. 2. Geneva, 1702.

Marais, Eugène. *Die Siel van die Mier*. Pretoria, 1925. *The Soul of the White Ant*. Translated by Winifred de Kok. London: Penguin, 1973 (1937).

Maury, A. "De certains faits observés dans les rêves et dans l'état intermédiaire entre le sommeil et la veille." *Annales médico-psychologiques* 3 (1857).

————. *Le sommeil et les rêves*, 4th ed. Paris, 1878.

Mead, G.R.S. *A Mithraic Ritual*. London and Benares: The Theosophical Publishing Society (*Echoes from the Gnosis* 6 [1907]: 22).

Miller, David. "Fairy Tale or Myth?" *Spring* (1976).

Miller, Patricia Cox. *Dreams in Late Antiquity: Studies in the Imagination of a Culture*. Princeton, NJ: Princeton University Press, 1974.

Mourre, C. "La volonté dans le rêve." *Revue Philosophique de la France et de l'Étranger* (May 1903).

Nagy, Marilyn. *Philosophical Issues in the Thought of C. G. Jung.* Albany: State University of New York Press, 1991.

Neihardt, J. G. *Black Elk Speaks: Being the Life Story of a Holy Man of the Oglala Sioux.* Lincoln: University of Nebraska Press, 1988.

Nietzsche, Friedrich. *Also sprach Zarathustra: Ein Buch für alle und keinen.* Stuttgart: Kröner Verlag, 1930.

———. *The Gay Science: With a Prelude in German Rhymes and an Appendix of Songs.* Translated by Josefine Nauckhoff (poems translated by Adrian del Caro). Edited by Bernard Williams. Cambridge: Cambridge University Press, 2001.

———. *Thus Spoke Zarathustra: A Book for All and None.* Edited by Adrian del Caro and Robert B. Pippin. Translated by Adrian del Caro. Cambridge: Cambridge University Press, 2006.

Peck, John. "Etwas geschah: Orphaned Event and Its Adoptions." *Spring* 84 (Fall 2010).

———. "The Visio Dorothei: Studies in the Dreams and Visions of St. Pachomius and Dorotheus, Son of Quintus." Thesis, C. G. Jung Institute, Zurich, 1992.

Peucer, Caspar. *De somniis.* Chapter in *Commentarius de praecipuis divinationum generibus.* Wittenberg, 1553.

Pliny the Elder. *The Natural History* [Book III]. Edited and translated by John Bostock and H. T. Riley. London: Taylor and Francis, 1855.

Plutarch's Lives: The Translation Called Dryden's [The Life of Kimon]. Edited by Arthur Hugh Clough. Translated by John Dryden et al. 5 vols. New York: Little, Brown, 1878.

Portmann, Adolf. "Recollections of Jung's Biology Professor." *Spring* (1976): 151.

Radestock, Paul W. *Genie und Wahnsinn: Eine psychologiscche Untersuchung.* Breslau: Trewendt, 1884.

———. *Habit and Its Importance in Education: An Essay in Pedagogical Psychology.* Translated by F. Caspari. Introduction by G. Stanley Hall. Boston: Heath, 1897 (1886).

———. *Schlaf und Traum: Eine physiologische-psychologische Untersuchung.* Leipzig: Breitkopf and Härtel, 1879.

Reizenstein, R. *Poimandres: Studien zur griechisch-ägyptischen und frühchristlichen Literatur.* Leipzig: B. B. Teubner, 1904.

Renan, Ernest. *Dialogues et fragments philosophiques.* Paris: Calmann-Lévy, 1876.

Richard, Jérôme, l'Abbé. *Théorie des songes.* Paris: Les frères Estienne, 1766.

Rivari, Enrico. *La Mente di Girolamo Cardano.* Bologna: Zanichelli, 1906.

Rowland, Alan. *Dreams and Drama: Psychoanalytic Criticism, Creativity, and the Artist.* Middletown, CT: Wesleyan University Press, 2003.

Rykwert, Joseph. *The Idea of a Town: The Anthropology of Urban Form in Rome, Italy, and the Ancient World.* Cambridge, MA: MIT Press, 1988.

Saint Anthony. Life of: *The Book of Paradise, Being the Histories and Sayings of the Monks and Ascetics of the Egyptian Desert by Palladius, Hieronymus, and Others.* Edited by E. A. Wallis Budge. London: W. Drugulin, 1904.

———. As in: *The Sayings of the Desert Fathers: The Alphabetical Collection, and Lives of the Desert Fathers.* Translated by Benedicta Ward. Kalamazoo, MI: Cistercian Publications, 1975 and 1981.

Salisbury, Joyce. *Perpetua's Passion: The Death and Memory of a Young Roman Woman.* New York: Routledge, 1997.

Schaff, Philip, ed. *The Ante-Nicene Fathers: Hippolytus, Cyprian, Caius, Novation.* Peabody, MA: Hendrickson Publishing, 1994 (1885).

Schubert, Gotthilf Heinrich von. *Altes und Neues aus dem Gebiet der innern Seelenkunde.* 7 vols. 2nd ed. Leipzig: Reclam, 1851–59.

Shamdasani, Sonu. C. G. *Jung: A Biography in Books.* New York: Norton in association with the Martin Bodmer Foundation, 2012.

———. *Jung and the Making of Modern Psychology: The Dream of a Science.* Cambridge: Cambridge University Press, 2003.

Smith, Theodate. "The Psychology of Day Dreams." *American Journal of Psychology* 15 (1904): 465–88.

Spence, Lewis. *Encyclopedia of Occultism and Parapsychology.* Whitefish, MT: Kessinger Reprints, 2003.

Splittgerber, Franz. *Schlaf und Tod, nebst den damit zusammenhängenden Erscheinungen des Seelenlebens. Eine psychologisch-apologetische Erörterung des Schlaf- und Traumlebens, des Ahnungsvermögens und des höheren Aufleuchtens der Seele im Sterben.* Halle: Julius Fricke, 1866.

Synesius. *De insomniis* [Peri enupnion logos]. In *Patrologia Graecae*, edited by J. P. Migne. 66: 1281–320.

———. *De Somniis.* In *Iamblichus, de Mysteriis Aegyptiorum . . . etc.* Translated by Marsilio Ficino. Venice: Manutius, 1497.

———. *Synésios de Cyrène IV: Opuscules I: Le traité sur les songes.* Translated by Noël Aujoulat. Paris: Les Belles Lettres, 2004.

Thorndike, Lynn. *The Place of Magic in the Intellectual History of Europe.* New York: Columbia University Press, 1905.

Tresan, David, MD. "Jungian Metapsychology and Neurobiological Theory." *Journal of Analytical Psychology* 41, no. 3 (1996).

Vaschide, N. "Recherches expérimentales sur les rêves." *Comptes Rendus de l'Académie des Sciences* (July 1899): 183–86.

———. *Le sommeil et les rêves.* Paris, 1911.

———, and P. Meunier. "Projection du rêve dans l'état de veille." *Revue de Psychiatrie* (February 1901).

Volkmann, Richard. *Synesius von Cyrene: Eine biographische Charakteristik aus dem letzten Zeiten des Untergehenden Hellenismus.* Berlin: Ebeling & Plahn, 1869.

Wehr, Gerhard. *Jung: A Biography.* Boston: Shambhala, 1987.

Wickland, Carl A. *Thirty Years among the Dead.* Los Angeles: National Psychological Institute (1924). Los Angeles: Newcastle Publishing, 1974, 1990.

Winthuis, J. *Das Zweigeschlechterwesen bei den Zentralaustraliern und anderen Völkern.* Leipzig: Hirschfeld, 1928.

Zitman, Willem. *Egypt: Image of Heaven.* Translated by Peter Rijpkema. Amsterdam: Frontier Publishing, 2006.

∽ Index ∽

The Collected Works of C. G. Jung

Editors: Sir Herbert Read, Michael Fordham, and Gerhard Adler; executive editor, William McGuire. Translated by R.F.C. Hull, except where noted.

(continued)

(continued)

A Review of the Complex Theory (1934)
The Significance of Constitution and Heredity and Psychology (1929)
Psychological Factors Determining Human Behavior (1937)
Instinct and the Unconscious (1919)
The Structure of the Psyche (1927/1931)
On the Nature of the Psyche (1947/1954)
General Aspects of Dream Psychology (1916/1948)
On the Nature of Dreams (1945/1948)
The Psychological Foundations of Belief in Spirits (1920/1948)
Spirit and Life (1926)
Basic Postulates of Analytical Psychology (1931)
Analytical Psychology and *Weltanschauung* (1928/1931)
The Real and the Surreal (1933)
The Stages of Life (1930 – 31)
The Soul and Death (1934)
Synchronicity: An Acausal Connecting Principle (1952)
Appendix: On Synchronicity (1951)

9. PART I. THE ARCHETYPES AND THE COLLECTIVE
   UNCONSCIOUS (1959; 2d ed., 1968)
   Archetypes of the Collective Unconscious (1934/1954)
   The Concept of the Collective Unconscious (1936)
   Concerning the Archetypes, with Special Reference to the Anima
      Concept (1936/1954)
   Psychological Aspects of the Mother Archetype (1938/1954)
   Concerning Rebirth (1940/1950)
   The Psychology of the Child Archetype (1940)
   The Psychological Aspects of the Kore (1941)
   The Phenomenology of the Spirit in Fairytales (1945/1948)
   On the Psychology of the Trickster-Figure (1954)
   Conscious, Unconscious, and Individuation (1939)
   A Study in the Process of Individuation (1934/1950)
   Concerning Mandala Symbolism (1950)
   Appendix: Mandalas (1955)

9. PART II. AION ([1951] 1959; 2d ed., 1968)
      RESEARCHES INTO THE PHENOMENOLOGY OF THE SELF
   The Ego
   The Shadow
   The Syzygy: Anima and Animus
   The Self
   Christ, a Symbol of the Self

(continued)

19. COMPLETE BIBLIOGRAPHY OF C. G. JUNG'S WRITINGS (1976; 2d ed., 1992)

20. GENERAL INDEX OF THE COLLECTED WORKS (1979)

THE ZOFINGIA LECTURES (1983)
Supplementary Volume A to the Collected Works.
Edited by William McGuire, translated by
Jan van Heurck, introduction by
Marie-Louise von Franz

PSYCHOLOGY OF THE UNCONSCIOUS ([1912] 1992)
A STUDY OF THE TRANSFORMATIONS AND SYMBOLISMS OF
THE LIBIDO. A CONTRIBUTION TO THE HISTORY OF THE
EVOLUTION OF THOUGHT
Supplementary Volume B to the Collected Works.
Translated by Beatrice M. Hinkle,
introduction by William McGuire

Notes to C. G. Jung's Seminars

DREAM ANALYSIS ([1928–30] 1984)
Edited by William McGuire

NIETZSCHE'S *ZARATHUSTRA* ([1934–39] 1988)
Edited by James L. Jarrett (2 vols.)

ANALYTICAL PSYCHOLOGY ([1925] 1989)
Edited by William McGuire

THE PSYCHOLOGY OF KUNDALINI YOGA ([1932] 1996)
Edited by Sonu Shamdasani

INTERPRETATION OF VISIONS ([1930–34] 1997)
Edited by Claire Douglas

CHILDREN'S DREAMS ([1936–40] 2008)
Edited by Lorenz Jung and Maria Meyer-Grass, translated by Ernst Falzeder
with the collaboration of Tony Woolfson

DREAM INTERPRETATION ANCIENT AND MODERN ([1936–41] 2014).
Edited by John Peck, Lorenz Jung, and Maria Meyer-Grass, translated by
Ernst Falzeder with the collaboration of Tony Woolfson.